The Answer/
La Respuesta

The Answer/ La Respuesta

Including a Selection of Poems

Sor Juana Inés de la Cruz

Critical Edition and Translation by
Electa Arenal and Amanda Powell

The Feminist Press
at the City University of New York

Published by the Feminist Press at the City University of New York
The Graduate Center, 365 Fifth Avenue, Suite 5406
New York, NY 10016
www.feministpress.org
First edition 1994

08 07 06 05 04   9 8 7 6

Library of Congress Cataloging-in-Publication Data

Juana Inés de la Cruz, Sister, 1651-1695.
   [Respuesta a sor Filotea de la Cruz. English & Spanish]
   The answer = La respuesta / Sor Juana Inés de la Cruz : critical
edition and translation by Electa Arenal and Amanda Powell.
   p.   cm.
   Includes bibliographical references and index.
   ISBN 1-55861-076-6 : $35.00. – ISBN 1-55861-077-4 (pbk.) : $12.95
   1. Juana Inés de la Cruz, Sister, 1651-1695 – Biography.
2. Authors, Mexican – 17th century – Biography. 3. Nuns – Mexico –
Biography. 4. Women – Social conditions. I. Arenal, Electa.
II. Powell, Amanda. III. Title. IV. Title: Respuesta.
PQ7296.J6R413   1994
861 – dc20
[B]   93-41115
                                                           CIP

This publication is made possible, in part, by public funds from the
New York State Council on the Arts and the National Endowment
for the Humanities. The Feminist Press is also grateful to Ellen Bass,
Sallie Bingham, Mariam K. Chamberlain, Helene D. Goldfarb,
Joanne Markell, Caroline Urvater, and Genevieve Vaughan.

Cover art: *Retrato de Sor Juana Inés de la Cruz* by Miguel Cabrera,
1750, oil on canvas. Courtesy of Instituto Nacional de Antropología e
Historia (CNCA), Mexico.
Cover design by Lucinda Geist
Text design by Paula Martinac

Typeset by The Type Set, New York City
Printed in the United States on acid-free paper by McNaughton &
Gunn, Inc., Saline, Michigan

Contents

Preface

Few documents of the seventeenth century embrace matters of learning, intellectual freedom, and power with such erudition and eloquence as does the *Respuesta a Sor Filotea de la Cruz* (1691) by Sor Juana Inés de la Cruz.[1] No other treats these concepts so clearly through the lens of gender. A fundamental work in Western feminism, the *Respuesta* (or *Answer to Sor Filotea de la Cruz*) stands as a link between Christine de Pizan's *The Book of the City of Ladies* (1403–04) and Mary Wollstonecraft's *A Vindication of the Rights of Woman* (1792). De Pizan's fifteenth-century French *City of Ladies* initiated a long tradition of women's "answers" to their male literary attackers; Wollstonecraft's eighteenth-century treatise in English envisioned women's free and equal participation in a world based on reason. Bridging medieval allegory and early modern rationalism, Sor Juana's seventeenth-century essay in Spanish defended women's right to develop and use their minds. The document became known early in the twentieth century as a declaration of the intellectual emancipation of women of the Americas.[2] Sor Juana's intellectually and literarily active life challenged the social, cultural, and religious mores that kept women physically and mentally confined. At issue for Sor Juana in 1691, when she wrote the *Answer,* was whether she would be made to conform to the rules she had embraced upon taking the veil. For more than two decades, as an illustrious exception, she had led a studious and creative existence akin to that of only a

---

[1]The author's dates are 1648 (or, by her account, 1651) to 1695. "Sor" means "sister"; she is known by her convent name.

[2]Dorothy Schons was the first to coin this oft-repeated characterization. See Schons, "The First Feminist in the New World" (1925). In 1974, with public pomp in Mexico, Sor Juana was awared the title of "First Feminist of America."

few of the most privileged minds of her epoch. In 1691, the church hierarchy wished to impose on her its narrow concept of womanhood, especially religious womanhood. If not her life, certainly her way of life was at stake.

The translation that follows is the first English version of the *Respuesta* to focus, as Sor Juana does in the original, on gender. A major objective is to do justice, by means of our introduction, annotations, and the translation itself, to its complexity of thought. The *Respuesta* is not an easy text; Sor Juana's ambiguities are essential to her intent. In all her poetry and prose – and never more so than in the *Respuesta* – Sor Juana plays with the many resources of language beyond denotation. Furthermore, her intricacies nearly always have political meanings. That is, she situates her wordplay and its subversions within institutional as well as intellectual structures of power. Like all religious writers of the period (especially women), Sor Juana repeatedly professes her lack of talent and of learning – her intellectual powerlessness. While so doing she in fact displays an erudite negotiation of the central discourses of power of her culture: theology, law, and the forms of classical rhetoric. Always conscious of her gender, she interrogates these forms as she manipulates them, questioning the uses to which such power is put. An outsider by birth, being both female and "illegitimate," she was drawn inside her culture's central intellectual concerns – primarily theological – by her "studious inclination." At the same time, she remained acutely aware of the culture's exclusions.

Feminism animates the *Respuesta*. But is that term anachronistic when applied to Sor Juana's seventeenth-century colonial Mexico? This edition investigates the question by drawing on feminist considerations by a number of scholars, representing varied theoretical and methodological perspectives. Simultaneously, we make use of other historical, theological, biblical, and literary scholarship in the translation itself as well as in the notes and introductory material. The institutional context within which Sor Juana lived, thought, and wrote is itself a difficult "translation" for us; a secular culture does not "read" religious thought and practice with ease or contextual sympathy. Furthermore, Sor Juana wrote from a context of writing women that has been, until recently, buried. In sixteenth- and seventeenth-century convents, peninsular and colonial women from a wide range of class backgrounds wrote prose and verse in many forms. These include the *narraciones de espíritu* (spiritual narrations) and *vidas* (Lives) that were scrutinized for signs of grace or temptation, plays for performance in the convent, poems, and letters.[3] Knowledge of these religious and literary activities, present to Sor Juana, has enriched the translation and our accompanying discussion. While "feminism" has its current meanings within a context of twentieth-century women's movements for equality and liberation, a "woman question" debate raged in Europe through the medieval and early modern period. Sor Juana consciously entered this controversy. Because she wrote as a woman aware of her gender status and because she intended her arguments to be applied on behalf of other women *as women,* she is certainly a precursor to worldviews and activities we call feminist.

Other translations of the *Respuesta a Sor Filotea de la Cruz* exist in English; this one differs by more fully drawing in and upon the spiritual, cultural, social, and female context in which the author lived and wrote her *Answer,* and to which she refers in the text. Sor Juana's politics (especially her positioning of herself in relation to her religious superior, Bishop Manuel Fernández de Santa Cruz) and her philosophical and theological reasoning (peculiarly her own, because she writes as a woman always attuned to gender) enter the language of the *Respuesta*—its vocabulary, grammer, and connotative meanings. A translation must be aware enough to render, as Sor Juana did, her problematic stance as an outsider and to capture the resources that she rallied in order to bring the outside in. To preserve Sor Juana's meaningful ambiguities intact, her translator must know the contexts on which they play and must keep that play between text and contexts in the translated version. To do otherwise mistranslates the author's multiplicities into a fixity.

There may be dangers, however, in lifting a major figure from one culture to long-overdue prominence in another. One hazard for a writer thus brought to view, especially if she is a woman, may be the acquisition of a symbolic aura that blinds us to her greatness as an artist. In her day, Sor Juana awed her contemporaries with her poetic and intellectual gifts, although at times their praise appeared in patronizing language. Even her continuing status as a kind of icon (her image graces the thousand-peso coin in Mexico) has not saved much of her work from neglect. Contemporary attention to her feminism, especially as expressed in the famous prose self-defense translated here, may underscore central aspects of her work only to marginalize others. Historically and linguistically, Sor Juana stands at a great remove from

---

[3]See Arenal and Schlau, *Untold Sisters.*

modern English-speaking readers. In highlighting her outstanding prose work, it is important that we not forget her prodigious creativity as a poet.

Our edition begins with an introduction aimed to help the general reader approach this major figure of Hispanic letters and to illuminate for all readers essential aspects of Sor Juana's feminist importance, particularly as reflected in the *Answer*. We include an index and a substantial selected bibliography to facilitate further study. In the bibliography some present-day editions of Sor Juana's writings are listed first, followed by the earliest printings in Spain. Then we list some of the most widely distributed translations of her work, studies in Spanish particularly influential in our readings of Sor Juana, Sor Juana criticism in English, and other works we have consulted.

Information on Sor Juana's life and works is presented in the first section of the two-part introductory essay. The second section, *"La Respuesta/The Answer:* A Reading," serves as a guide through the rewarding complexities of this document. The text itself follows, in both Spanish and English, with accompanying notes. The annotations clarify particular points and refer both to Sor Juana's sources and to other scholars' reflections on the work. Finally, a sampling of poems in Spanish and in English translation offers a sense of the poet's literary power and the woman-centered vision that inspired it.

Acknowledgments

Contributions from several sources assisted this project, including a Scholar's Incentive Award from the College of Staten Island/ City University of New York, travel grants from the Center for Feminist Research/University of Bergen (Norway), and a publication subvention grant from the National Endowment for the Humanities. A Massachusetts Artists Foundation Fellowship Award and the Centrum Artists-in-Residence program in Port Townsend, Washington, provided essential support for the translation.

An edition of this sort is made possible by the work of dozens of scholars who have come before us. Many colleagues and friends helped directly in its preparation – more of them than we can list. We thank them all. To Florence Howe, who first envisioned this as a Sourcebook, and to Susannah Driver, our editor, who assured its realization, our deepest gratitude. Charles Purrenhage accomplished the complicated tasks of copyediting with ease and elegance.

Barbara Roseman read through many times with acuity and insight. Stacey Schlau, who at times lent both a hand and a shoulder, helped in the initial shaping of the introduction. Ruth El Saffar and Frederick Luciani wrote detailed recommendations, which won further support and gave helpful guidance. Mary Giles and Kathleen A. Myers have given visionary succor and bibliographic counsel. Barbara Bowen, Robert Chiles, Sister Teresa Lamy, and Kathryn Kruger-Hickman read and responded with enthusiasm and corrections. Kristin Natvig Aas, Rebecca Lippman, and Helen Kierulf Svane provided research assistance, and Matthew Lyons helped put the chronology and bibliography all the way through to their final form.

For helpful suggestions and information along the way we thank

Helene Farber de Aguilar, María Isabel Barbeito Carneiro, Magda Bogin, Kari Elisabeth Børresen, Thomas Cohen, Ragnhild Finnestad, Jean Franco, Naomi Goodman, Joan Hartman, Anne Michelini, Elías Rivers, Georgina Sabat de Rivers, Nina Scott, Vita C. Shapiro, Steven Shankman, Maya Thee, Martha Thunes, and Marcia Welles.

Members of the Los Angeles writing group—Sally Cragin, Dianne Dugaw, Rachel Fretz, and Jayne Lewis—especially abetted any grace and vigor found in the translated *Answer*. Generous observations by Elizabeth Davis and Richard Saez, and the astute eagerness of Norma Comrada and the Eugene, Oregon, translators' gathering, have greatly helped the Englishing of selected poems. Students in the undergraduate/graduate seminar on Sor Juana at the University of Oregon (summer 1992) put the draft manuscript to an edifying test-run.

Lively personal and familial gratitude go to these *sine qui non*: the Powells, Freda Wright, Lynn Fogus, Lita Newdick, Bartholomew, and H.P. Most deeply, no part of this book could be what it is without the wit, passion, and scholarly perspective of Dianne M. Dugaw.

For intellectual, emotional, spiritual, and practical support every step of the intercontinental way, thanks to Martha T. Zingo.

Collaborative work requires imagination, forbearance, and affection; thanks to ourselves for seeing it through.

Acknowledgments

Abbreviations

BAC	*Sagrada Biblia*, Biblioteca de Autores Cristianos
BLQ	*Book of Latin Quotations*
CCE	*Concise Columbia Encyclopedia*
DCLL	*Dictionary of Christian Lore and Legend*
DRA	*Diccionario de la lengua española*, Real Academia Española
LCD	*Lempriere's Classical Dictionary*
NCE	*New Catholic Encylopedia*
OC	Sor Juana Inés de la Cruz, *Obras completas* (Méndez Plancarte and Salceda; references are in this format: volume. page: lines [i.e., OC 4.37: 292–93])
OED	*Oxford English Dictionary*
SJ	Sor Juana Inés de la Cruz

Chronology

Life	Years	Principal Works	Contemporary Women in the Arts, Sciences, and Religion
Baptized December 2, Chimalhuacán, Mexico	1648		1606–87 Sor Marcela de San Félix. Poet, playwright, Spain
According to first biographer, born November 12, Nepantla, Mexico	1651		1607–78 Anna Maria von Schurman. Philosopher, scientist, Netherlands
Learns to read at an "Amiga" school, Amecameca	1654		
	1658	Composes a *loa* to the Holy Sacrament	1608–75 Bathsua Makin. Educator, England. *An Essay to Revive the Ancient Education of Gentlewomen*
Moves to Mexico City	1661		
Arrival of viceregal couple, Marquise and Marquis de Mancera	1664		1612–72 Anne Bradstreet. Poet, North America.
SJ enters the viceregal court as lady-in-waiting			
	1665	Poem on the death of Philip IV, King of Spain	1619–64 Barbara Strozzi. Composer, singer, Italy
Enters the convent of the Discalced Carmelites, leaves after three months	1666		1620–1704 Isabella Leonarda. Composer, convent leader, Italy
Viceroy organizes oral examination to test SJ's knowledge	1668		

Takes the veil at the convent of San Jerónimo. Signs last will and testament, February 4	1669		1621–69 Lady Jane Cavendish. Poet, playwright, England
Appointment of Fr. Payo Enrique de Rivera as viceroy	1674	Three sonnets on the death of "Laura" (the Vicereine)	1623–73 Margaret Cavendish, Duchess of Newcastle. Poet, writer of scientific treatises, England
	1676–1691	Fifteen sets of villancicos commissioned	1626–63 Lady Elizabeth Cavendish. Poet, playwright, England
	1677	First publication: *Villancicos de San Pedro Nolasco*	1626–96 Madame de Sevigné, Marie de Rabutin Chautal. Wrote over 1500 letters, later published, France
Arrival of viceregal couple, Marquise and Marquis de la Laguna	1680		
	1680 /81	*Neptuno Alegórico*	1631–79 Anne Conway, Viscountess of Conway. Philosopher, writer, England. *The Principles of the Most Ancient and Modern Philosophy*
	1681 /82	Letter to Reverend Antonio Núñez, SJ's confessor	
	1685?	*Primero sueño*, not published until 1692.	1634–93 Marie Madelaine de La Fayette. Writer, France. *La Princess de Cleves*

Life	Years	Principal Works	Contemporary Women in the Arts, Sciences, and Religion
Arrival of viceroy, Count de Monclova	1686		1635–1719 Françoise d'Aubigne, Madame de Maintenon. Established schools, France
	1688	Sonnet to "Lysis" ("Lysi" in Spanish – the Vicereine)	
			1640–83 Marie-Catherine Hortense Desjarelin, Madame de Villadieu. First novelist to sign her name, France
Arrival of viceregal couple, Countess and Count de Galve	1689	First edition of volume 1 of SJ's works, *Inundación Castálida* (Madrid, Spain)	
	1690	*El Divíno Narciso*, sacramental play, first separate printing, written in 1688?	1640–89 Aphra Behn. Playwright, first professional writer in England
		Carta Atenagórica printed and dedicated by Sor Filotea de la Cruz	1656–1719 María de San José. Religious writer, nun, Mexico
	1691	*La Respuesta* written *Villancicos de Santa Catarina de Alejandría*, SJ's last set of villancicos, sung in the Cathedral of Oaxaca, November 25	1656–1704 Luisa Roldán. Artist, sculptor, Spain
			1658–1708 Lady Damaris Mashaim. Philosopher, theological writer, England
	1692	First edition of volume 2 of SJ's works, *Obras* (Seville)	

SJ's general confession	1693	1661–1720 Anne Finch, Countess of Winchelsea. Poet, England
Signs in blood a declaration of faith, repenting and giving up secular studies	1694	
Dies during an epidemic, April 17	1695	1665–1736 Karen Brahe. Writer, established library, Denmark
First edition of volume 3 of SJ's works, *Fama y Obras pósthumas* . . . Includes *La Respuesta*, published for the first time (Madrid)	1700	1666–1729 Elisabeth-Claude Jacquet de la Guerre. Composer, harpsichordist, France

Introduction

I. Sor Juana's Life and Work

Juana Ramírez / Sor Juana Inés de la Cruz (1648/51–1695): A Life Without and Within

Sor Juana Inés de la Cruz, author of the *Respuesta a Sor Filotea de la Cruz* (as the *Answer* is titled in Spanish), is a major figure of Hispanic literature, but still little known to readers of other languages.[1] Her poetry, plays, and prose move within and reshape the themes and styles of Renaissance and Baroque Spain and its far-flung empire. Indeed, she is considered the last great author of Spain's Golden Age (Siglo de Oro), during which an extraordinary number of outstanding writers and artists were active.[2] The emergent, differentiated, and multicultural New Spain—Mexico's telling name during the colonial period—was fertile soil for Sor Juana's imagination. In turn, her influence helped create a Mexican identity, contributing to the consciousness and sensibility of later scholars and writers.

Sor Juana's prodigious talent, furthered by intense efforts that began in early childhood, produced a serious intellectual while she was still in her teens. She taught herself the forms of classical rhetoric and the language of law, theology, and literature. At every turn, from her courtly and learned yet marginalized standpoint, she contradicted—or deconstructed—artistic, intellectual, and religious views that would refuse her and others like her the right to express themselves.

---

[1]Her name is pronounced HWA-na ee-NES day-la-KREWS.

[2]The term "Siglo de Oro" is applied to a period extending roughly from the mid-sixteenth century through the last decades of the seventeenth century.

1

The stratagems Sor Juana found useful for artistic and intellectual survival were so subtle that, given the continuity and pervasiveness of patriarchal values up to the present, the magnitude of her reinterpretations has often been missed or distorted even in our time. Sor Juana's power reaches us today both in her revolutionary reversal of the gender identifications typical of her culture and in the beauty of her expression. With most aspects of the literary tradition of the Renaissance and Baroque at her command, she crafted exquisite poems. The ease with which she versified, the verve and versatility of her style, and the irony with which she applied her wit gave her an enormous literary mobility.

Similarly, her status as a rara avis (strange bird), while setting her apart from others of her sex and class in the public regard, made possible the physical and psychic space in which she thought and wrote. Respect for exceptionality was in part a reflection of the profound seventeenth-century interest in unusual natural phenomena that viewed artistic talent and intellectual drive in females as fascinating abnormalities. Sor Juana learned to exploit the fact that she was catalogued as a prodigy; she both defended and derided the hyperbolic terms of praise her exceptionality attracted (see the poem "¡Válgate Apolo por hombre!" [May Apollo help you, as you're a man!]). Known to this day as the "Tenth Muse,"[3] in her own time Sor Juana was also called the "Mexican Phoenix." Such epithets of exceptionality, though common enough, kept Sor Juana on a pedestal, provisionally protected yet isolated amid the ceremony and turbulence of Mexico City. Praised and envied, criticized and acclaimed, for twenty-six years she wrote for the court and for the church as one of the most celebrated writers in the Hispanic New World.

Early Years: Country and Court. Juana Ramírez y Asbaje was born – in 1648 or 1651 – in Nepantla, some two days' travel from Mexico City by mule and canal boat, on lands her grandfather leased from the church.[4] There, perhaps more than her contemporaries, Juana was exposed early in life to all levels of culture. She experienced music, art, and magic, native and imported. She

---

[3]"Tenth Muse" was a common term for women poets, whom men could not conceive of as other than unearthly. Sappho herself was referred to thus, as were poets of the seventeenth century, including Anne Bradstreet of England and the Massachusetts Bay Colony.

[4]Different sources give Juana's name in various combinations and orders of her mother's (maternal grandfather's) and father's last names: Juana Inés de Asbaje y Ramírez de Santillana.

heard the liturgy in Latin, cultured conversation in Spanish, and colloquial communication, including Indian, African, and *ranchero* (rural) dialects. Juana's grandfather, Pedro Ramírez de Santillana, was a learned man, although his daughter Isabel Ramírez, Juana's mother, was not educated. His large library fed the young Juana's appetite for reading. By the time her elders wished to still her curiosity, she had become so knowledgeable that they could neither put a stop to her restless quest nor convince her it was inappropriate. From book learning she drew authority and legitimacy for differing in her studious propensities, views, and aims from other Catholics, women, and Mexicans. Society's stigmas against *marisabias* (Mary-sages [female know-it-alls]) could not destroy her intellectual bent. The charm of Juana's own account (given in the *Answer*) of how she could read soon after she learned to walk, how she took to rhyming as others take to their native tongue, and how she became competent in Latin shortly after taking up its study has in the imagination of readers outweighed her insistence that her prodigious learning reflected tenacious effort even more than a sharp memory.

Tenaciousness may have been one of her mother's legacies. Isabel Ramírez was a strong and smart woman. Illiteracy did not impede her from managing one of her father's two sizable farmsteads for more than thirty years. She had six children, three with Pedro Manuel de Asbaje, Juana Inés's father, and three with Diego Ruiz Lozano; to neither man, she stated in official documents, had she been married.

Before the age of fourteen, Juana wrote her first poem. Knowing that women were not allowed to attend the university in Mexico City (*Respueta / Answer,* par. 8) she made the best of an isolated, self-directed schooling: she devoured books initially in Panoayán, where the family farm was located, then at court in Mexico City, and finally in the voluminous library she amassed in the convent. A convent was the only place in her society where a woman could decently live alone and devote herself to learning. Her collection of books and manuscripts, by the time she gave it away for charity near the end of her life, was one of the largest in the New Spain of her era.

According to Diego Calleja, a Spanish Jesuit priest who wrote her earliest biography, the young Juana while at court submitted to a public examination of her already notorious intellectual gifts by forty of the most knowledgeable men of the realm.[5] She de-

---

[5]Calleja's biography appears as the substantive part of the required permission for publication (the *nihil obstat*) of the third and final volume of her works – that is, the assurance that nothing in its pages went against church teachings.

fended herself, reported Calleja, "like a royal galleon attacked by small canoes."[6] Sor Juana's poetry sometimes expresses mistrust and mockery of her many admirers and defenders for seeing her in their own image and for turning her into a circus rarity: "What would the mountebanks[7] not give, / to be able to seize me, / and carry me round like a monster, through / byroads and lonely places" (¡*Qué dieran los saltimbancos,* / *a poder, por agarrarme* / *y llevarme, como Monstruo, por esos andurriales!* OC 1.147:177–80).

Were she to be compared with anyone, her preference – implicit in the numerous parallels she draws in her poems – would be the learned and legendary St. Catherine of Alexandria, who had also been subjected to an examination and who had furnished ultimate proof that neither intelligence nor the soul were owned by one gender above the other. Some of Sor Juana's last compositions were songs of praise to the saint (see Selected Poems, below).

Entrance into the Convent. Juana gave her age as sixteen when, after five years as lady-in-waiting at the viceregal court of New Spain, she entered the convent in 1668 to be able to pursue a reflective, literary life. Sor Juana Inés, as she became known, claimed that her parents were married and that her birthdate was November 12, 1651. The church establishment officially required legitimacy for nuns; youth supported her reputation as a rarity. A baptismal record for one "Inés, daughter of the church," however, dated December 2, 1648, is generally accepted as hers; it lists an aunt and uncle as godparents. This earlier date establishes her age as nineteen when she entered the cloister. Modern awareness of the revised birthdate hardly tempers the myth of young Juana's precocity; she can be considered no less "a marvel of intelligence."[8]

Sor Juana's confessor, Antonio Núñez de Miranda, was not one

---

[6]A few decades earlier the Catalonian Juliana Morel, another child prodigy, who would become a nun and translator of St. Augustine into French, had been examined publicly in Lyon and Avignon. Reports of other precocious European women indicate that Sor Juana's status may not have been as unique as claimed. Public examinations by "experts" also reflected the Baroque fascination with prodigiously learned (young) women and with the commingling or blurring of gender categories. It was a hagiographic topos as well: St. Catherine of Alexandria had undergone perhaps the most famous of such legendary tests (see the discussion of *villancicos* in Selected Poems, below).

[7]*Saltimbanco* (or *saltabanco*) may be translated variously as mountebank, charlatan, trickster, puppeteer.

[8]Doña Leonor, the supposedly autobiographical protagonist of Sor Juana's *Los empeños de una casa* (*The Trials of a Household*), says that she was known in this way ("celebrada por milagro de discreción") OC4. 37:292–93.

4

who would graciously admit defeat before her prowess. A powerful, intelligent, and extremely ascetic man, Núñez was also confessor to the viceroy and vicereine and to many other members of the nobility. For him, as for those vanquished by St. Catherine, gender determined duty as well as destiny; the use of reason was an exclusively masculine privilege. In a world where females were associated with the Devil and the flesh, intelligent and beautiful women especially were blamed for all manner of ills; to lessen the threat to men's uncontrollable passions, they should be sent to a nunnery to embrace holy plainness and ignorance. If Núñez considered the young Juana's position in the limelight at court dangerous and untenable, her continued study and writing after entering the convent, especially on worldly subjects, he judged nothing short of scandalous. Indeed, "[H]ad [I] known [she] was to write verses [I] would not have placed [her] in the convent but arranged [her] marriage," he was reported to have said.[9]

Núñez, not being a relative, had no legal right to dispose of her thus. At first Sor Juana bore the humiliation of his remarks, she tells us. But as she achieved recognition and patronage from a new viceregal governor and his wife, who were closely connected to the Spanish king, Sor Juana gained confidence in herself. Eventually, she responded angrily to Núñez and relieved him of his duties to her as confessor.

Now her ex-confessor, Núñez nevertheless continued to hold sway in Mexican society. Sor Juana's ultimate clerical superior in Mexico, Archbishop Francisco Aguiar y Seijas, was a legendary misogynist.[10] Her friend and admirer Manuel Fernández de Santa Cruz, the bishop of Puebla, donned the name "Sor Filotea" when he finally threw in his lot with those who demanded conformity. These three ecclesiastics wanted Sor Juana to stop thinking and writing with the latitude she had exercised. She was warned to be more like other women in the convents of Spanish America, who were supposed to serve as both subjects and agents of a regime undertaking massive imperialist endeavors. That is, nuns were to be subjects of the Spanish church and crown; to serve as agents of the church's mission to Christianize heathens; to guard

---

[9]Quoted by Sor Juana in a letter to Núñez. See Paz, *Sor Juana,* p. 500.

[10]See Paz, *Sor Juana,* pp. 408–9. Paz cites a nineteenth-century history of the church in Mexico and a biography of the archbishop written by the latter's confessor: these are, respectively, Francisco Sosa, *El episcopado mexicano* (Mexico City: H. Iriarte y S. Hernández, 1877–1879); José de Lezamis, *Breve relación de la vida y muerte del Ilmo. y Revmo. Señor Doctor Don Francisco Aguiar y Seijas* (Mexico, 1699).

orthodoxy; and to ensure social obeisance. Beyond their spiritual roles, nuns—*criollas*[11] like Sor Juana and even a few *mestizas*[12]—were also influential in economic, social, and educational spheres. They contributed to the arts, crafts, music, and cuisine of the larger community. They dealt in real estate, lent money, and employed servants and slaves, without whom most of their activities would have been impossible. Many nuns wrote. The very nature of a female community allowed them to develop voices that were separate from those of the priests and confessors who officially controlled their lives. Sor Juana, though, was most unlike other women in her intellectual ecumenism and religious rationality as well as her celebrity. She was envied and considered arrogant.

For centuries scholars refused to believe the reasons Sor Juana gave in the *Answer* for taking the veil. They speculated airily on some unfortunate love affair. Yet, early and extensive readings in Christianity, the experiences of many of the women in her family (including her own mother), and not least her consuming interest in satiating her intellectual appetite easily explain her "absolute unwillingness to enter into marriage" (*Answer,* par. 9). She first tried the strictly ruled and aristocratic Carmelite convent, but she became ill and had to leave. Within a few months, after recovering, she entered the more relaxed Hieronymite[13] convent of Santa Paula, where she found some of the tranquillity she desired for study—the real love of her life.

The cloistered Sor Juana spent the rest of her days (from 1668 until 1695), in quarters whose comfort and amplitude made them seem more salon than cell. Attended by several servants and for ten years by a mulatta slave her mother had given her,[14] Sor Juana entertained numerous visiting aristocrats, ecclesiastics, and scholars, conducted wide but now lost correspondence with many others, and held monastic office as mistress of novices and keeper of the convent's financial records. Although the dates of her terms in office are unknown, news of that service survived along with such details as her extraordinary brilliance as a conversationalist. Several contemporaries claimed that listening to her surpassed reading her work. Much of her poetry was destined to be

---

[11]Native-born of Spanish ancestry.

[12]Of mixed white (peninsular Spanish or *criollo*) and Native American ancestry.

[13]Followers of St. Jerome.

[14]The forty-nine professed nuns (those who had taken solemn vows) were supported by about a hundred and fifty other women, including some slaves. The nuns lived in independent, two-storied quarters, shared at times by younger relatives.

6

[margin note: Sor Juana becomes a nun]

heard. State and church officials commissioned all manner of compositions for the observances of holy days, feast days, birthdays, and funerals. Sor Juana earned not only favor but a livelihood—for each nun had a "household" to support—by fulfilling such literary orders.

It is hard to imagine exactly what a day in the life of Sor Juana may have included. The daily patterns for all nuns were set by the rules of the order. Upon becoming brides of Christ they vowed chastity, poverty, and obedience; but just as in Rome, where luxury surrounded the higher echelons of church officialdom, austerity was the exception in religious houses established by royalty. Actual practice at the wealthy convent of Santa Paula was far from ascetic. Laxity, as it was called, characterized observance in most convents of Mexico and Peru. Nevertheless, the normal day was punctuated by prayer time: it began at midnight with matins; lauds followed at 5:00 or 6:00 A.M.; then came prime, terce, sext, and none, the "little hours" spaced during the day; vespers were said at approximately 6:00 P.M.; and finally compline at 9:00 or 10:00 at night. There would be recreation periods, a time, often, for needlework. Periodically, nuns would go on retreat to remove themselves from the hustle and bustle of normal monastic existence. Sor Juana, as she mentions in the *Answer*, would retreat from time to time, to study and write.

Regular intervals were set for community work, prayer, confession, and Communion. Many holy feast days interrupted routines, calling for special masses, meals, and festivities. Pomp and circumstance accompanied the taking of final vows. Music—singing and playing instruments—and theatrical performances provided inspiration, religious instruction, and entertainment at all such events. Sor Juana was probably among the most visited of the nuns at her cloister. In addition to family members she received dignitaries from around the world. She would often be called to the *locutorio* (grate) to meet her guests, among whom on occasion were representatives of the *cabildo* (city council) with writing commissions.

In unstructured moments, some nuns chatted and gossiped; others subjected themselves to penances. Capable and creative, Sor Juana took the advantageous circumstances of her life and an ability to "condense [*conmutar*] time," as she phrased it, and put them to what she considered better use. Conservative elements within the church in Mexico preferred penances.

Conflict Intensifies. Troubles, as we have seen, had started almost from the beginning of Sor Juana's time in the convent. For more than a decade after taking the veil, she kept still in the face of the reports that her confessor was voicing disapproval of her scholarly and literary activities, even when he claimed they constituted "a public scandal." She outdid herself in public visibility, however, when in 1680, after showing initial reticence, she accepted the responsibility of devising one of two architectural-theatrical triumphal arches that were to welcome the new viceregal couple (the other was entrusted to her friend Carlos de Sigüenza y Góngora).[15] The ambitiously mythological artwork, inscriptions, narrative poems, and prose explanations of her "Allegorical Neptune" both established her reputation throughout contemporary society and, because of the extraordinarily public nature of the occasion, deepened the rift with Núñez.

At last, in 1681 or 1682, Sor Juana decided to take steps to ease her plight and relieve her pent-up animosity – the result, she said, of holding back her reactions to his animosity. She would exercise her right to engage a new confessor. The letter she wrote to Núñez, distancing herself from him, bristles with ironic and prideful sarcasm. "Not being unaware of the veneration and high esteem in which Y[our] R[everence] (and justly so) is held by all, so that all listen to you as if to a divine oracle and appreciate your words as if they were dictated by the Holy Ghost," she writes, "nor unaware that the greater your authority, the more my good name is injured," Sor Juana sees no alternative but to change confessors. "Am I perchance a heretic?" she asks, concluding with further rhetorical questions: "What obligation is there that my salvation be effected through Y.R.? Can it not be through another? Is God's mercy restricted and limited to one man, even though he be as wise, as learned, and as saintly as Y.R.?"[16] On her own path toward salvation, with a more sympathetic confessor, Sor Juana spent the next decade studying and writing her most enduring works. The viceregal couple continued to visit almost every day, on their way to or from vespers, until they returned to Spain in 1687.

Love Poems to Lovers of Poetry. With patronage such as the viceroy and vicereine provided, Sor Juana was free to persevere in her manner of being a nun. This was not so unusual from the

---

[15]The ancient Roman religious tradition of constructing arches of wood and painted canvas, elaborately decorated with mythological themes, was revived during the Renaissance. See Sabat de Rivers, ed., *Inundación castálida,* pp. 63–71.

[16]In Paz, *Sor Juana,* pp. 495–96, 500, 502. (trans. modified by Powell).

standpoint of a long, scholarly, and even at times worldly women's monastic tradition, but it was certainly uncommon in her place and time. No doubt the churchmen were further scandalized by her "unchaste" writings, by what her poems indicated about an imagined if not a lived experience. Only verses that transposed courtly love into a divine framework of religious ardor, and clearly mystical writing infused with eroticism, were deemed orthodox by the censors. Sor Juana's courtly yet personal poetry followed the Renaissance conventions of troubadour love lyrics and Petrarchan sonneteering to express deeply felt earthly friendship, kinship, and sexual attraction.

Little can be known directly about Sor Juana's intimate loves, though speculation abounds. Finding that she wrote with an acute understanding of lovers and their emotional travails, readers have been convinced that she knew whereof she spoke. Did she have suitors at court? Did she suffer first-hand the sort of abuse and loss some descry in her poems? Was she in love with a man or men? With a woman or women? Biographical documentation is lacking. Her poetry attests first that she knew well the expectations of literary practice on these topics, and second, that the deepest personal ties she expressed were those to two recognizable figures: Leonor Carreto and María Luisa Manrique de Lara y Gonzaga, two vicereines (wives of the viceroys) of New Spain.

The social distance between Sor Juana and these two noblewomen, whom she wrote of lovingly and also served, was not unlike that of the Provençal troubadours (men and women) and their lords and ladies. That very distance allowed her to be explicit in expressing her affection, providing a public barrier to the realization of such sentiments. These were widely perceived as relationships that could not be consummated. What other forms, besides the written, her expressions of feeling may have taken remains unknown. No one denies that Sor Juana displayed in her writing depths of emotion and erotic desire associated for us with intimate relationships.[17]

Notably, her most ardent love poems were dedicated to the two vicereines mentioned above. Well-educated and sophisticated readers, it was they who most energetically encouraged her scholarly and literary pursuits. When the first of the two aristocrats,

---

[17]Ester Gimbernat de González (in "Speaking through the Voices of Love") discusses three love sonnets by Sor Juana (nos. 177, 178, and 183) addressed to women. While Gimbernat identifies the (conventionalized) speaker in all three as male, evidence internal to the poems supports this determination only in no. 178 – the speaker's gender is not explicit in the other two.

the vicereine Leonor Carreto, Marquise de Mancera, died in 1674, Sor Juana had been in the convent for six years. But for almost the same number of years immediately before her entrance in the convent, Juana had been in Leonor's service – a favorite companion at court. Sor Juana used the literary "Laura" as the marquise's name in poems:

Death like yours, my Laura, since you have died,
to feelings that still long for you in vain,
to eyes you now deny even the sight
of lovely light that in the past you gave.

Death to my hapless lyre from which you drew
these echoes that, lamenting, speak your name,
and let these awkward characters be known
as black tears shed by my grief-stricken pen.

Let compassion move stern Death herself
who (strictly accurate) brooked no excuse,
and let Love lament his bitter fate;

who boldly hoping at one time to woo you
wanted to have eyes simply to see you,
that now do nothing more nor less than mourn you.

(OC 1.300–301, trans. Amanda Powell)

Mueran contigo, Laura, pues moriste,
los afectos que en vano te desean,
los ojos a quien privas de que vean
hermosa luz que un tiempo concediste.

Muera mi lira infausta en que influíste
ecos, que lamentables te vocean,
y hasta estos rasgos mal formados sean
lágrimas negras de mi pluma triste.

Muévase a compasión la misma Muerte
que, precisa, no pudo perdonarte;
y lamente el Amor su amarga suerte,

pues si antes, ambicioso de gozarte,
deseó tener ojos para verte,
ya le sirvieran sólo de llorarte.

This elegiac sonnet gives rein to Sor Juana's grief, implying a literary as well as affectionate relationship. It is one of three sonnets that issued from her sorrow over the loss of the woman who, her first biographer, Calleja, claimed, "could not live an instant without her Juana Inés."

Similar terms were used to describe her next long relationship of devoted friendship. To Vicereine María Luisa Manrique de Lara y Gonzaga, Marquise de la Laguna, Countess de Paredes, who became "Phyllis" in the poems, Sor Juana wrote:

> . . . as air is drawn to what is hollow,
> and fire to feed on matter,
> as boulders tumble to the earth,
> and intentions to their goal;
>
> indeed, as every natural thing,
> —all united by the desire
> to endure, which ties them tight
> in bonds of closest love . . .
>
> But to what end do I go on?
> Just so, my Phyllis, do I love you;
> with your considerable worth,
> this is merely an endearment.
>
> Your being a woman, your being gone:
> neither hinders my love for you,
> for who knows better that our souls
> notice neither geography nor sex.
>
> (OC 1.56–57:97–112, trans. Amanda Powell)

> como a lo cóncavo el aire,
> como a la materia el fuego,
> como a su centro las peñas,
> como a su fin los intentos;
>
> bien como todas las cosas
> naturales, que el deseo
> de conservarse, las une
> amante en lazos estrechos . . .
>
> Pero ¿para qué es cansarse?
> Como a ti, Filis, te quiero;
> que en lo que mereces, éste
> es solo encarecimiento.
>
> Ser mujer, ni estar ausente,
> no es de amarte impedimento;
> pues sabes tú, que las almas
> distancia ignoran y sexo.

María Luisa, Marquise de la Laguna, was a frequent visitor at the convent during the seven years she spent in Mexico, and she was an avid supporter of Sor Juana. It was she who took Sor Juana's poems to Spain and arranged for her first book to be published. With the exceptionally successful appearance of *Castalian Inundation* in 1689, the poet's celebrity grew in educated circles throughout Spain and its colonies (including the Philippines).[18] To the chagrin of many of her superiors, spurred by her own great gifts and by María Luisa's instrumental patronage, Sor Juana flourished as a literary figure of the Spanish-speaking world.

Gradually, however, other factors began to weigh more heavily than viceregal support and fame. As the seventeenth century reached its last decade, Sor Juana's situation and that of New Spain veered drastically. Economic, social, and political crises engulfed the realm. Nature itself seemed bent on intensifying the troubles. A solar eclipse spread fear among the population, crops not devastated by rain in the countryside were eaten by weevils, and floods inundated Mexico City. Speculation and hoarding worsened the scarcity of fruit, vegetables, maize, bread, firewood, and coal. Rising prices touched off spontaneous protests. The viceregal palace and municipal building were set on fire. Punitive responses triggered panic, further rioting, penitent religious processions, and executions. Sor Juana's most significant supporters had returned to Spain or had fallen out of favor. The pressures mounted—perhaps in her own mind as well as from without. Her writing, on religious and mundane subjects alike, came under more direct fire.

The Bishop, the Answer, *and—Silence.* If it was irreverent for a nun to write love poems, it was worse for her to meddle in theology. For Sor Juana's biography and for the study of her writing, the significance of the "Letter Worthy of Athena," this nun's one incursion into theological argumentation—the only one in prose, written down and printed, that is—resides as much in its having heightened the envy and antagonism of the ecclesiastic establishment as in its admirable reasoning and style.

Piqued by Antonio Vieira's claim to have improved on the arguments of the fathers and doctors of the church[19] (viz., Sts. Augustine, Thomas, and John Chrysostom) concerning Jesus Christ's highest favor to humanity, Sor Juana in 1690 had ventured to refute the famous preacher's "Maundy Thursday Sermon" (written forty years earlier!). The refutation was heard in a conversation

---

[18]In Sor Juana's lifetime, three more editions (entitled simply *Poems*) followed in 1690, 1691, and 1692; by 1725, a total of nine had appeared. See Sabat de Rivers, ed., *Inundación castálida*, pp. 26–27, 72–73.

[19]Vieira (b. Lisbon, Portugal, 1608, d. Salvador, Brazil, 1697) was a prominent Jesuit, considered to be one of the great prose stylists of his day.

with guests at the convent, among them Bishop Manuel Fernández de Santa Cruz, who was on a visit to Mexico City. At his behest, she wrote down her critical disquisition disputing Vieira's argument as to the highest example of Christ's love. Three times she mentions her trust that the text will be seen only by the bishop's eyes; she invites his correction and claims that, not having had the time to polish it, she remits it to him *en embrión, como suele la osa parir sus informes cachorrillos* ("in an embryonic state, just as the bear gives birth to her unformed cubs," OC 4.434:904).

Her double-edged claims of humility did not obscure the virtuosity of her argumentation, or her skill at logic. Was the bishop conspiring to silence her when he requested a written copy? He had long been an admiring friend, but he was also an official of convent governance, known for inspiring nuns with fanatical piety. He, too, must have been distressed by this, in his eyes, arrogant and wayward daughter. For years Archbishop Aguiar y Seijas and Fr. Núñez had sought to command from Sor Juana behavior more befitting a nun. Now, they were poised for their chance. Wittingly or unwittingly, the bishop of Puebla joined forces with them.

With the viceroy and vicereine gone, ecclesiastics may have found it easier to instigate or fuel the storm of controversy that broke out over the "Letter Worthy of Athena," as the bishop of Puebla titled her critique when he delivered it to the press, appending a letter signed "Sor Filotea" as a preface. Ambivalent and ambiguous enough to have confused many generations of readers, the bishop's letter was for Sor Juana a purportedly friendly — and therefore wily and more painful — attack. It prompted her to explain and defend herself as she never had before — to write the *Answer to Sor Filotea de la Cruz,* the only avowedly self-descriptive piece of prose she produced. For her, the printed letter from the bishop of Puebla disguised as Sor Filotea, with its pretense of saintly guidance (St. Francis de Sales had used the same pseudonym to write to nuns), served as a public admonition and delivered a threat of persecution. It is reasonable to assume that the letter produced in Sor Juana a combination of anger, resentment, shock, hurt, contempt, and fear, and that these emotions precipitated a decision to silence herself that had already been forming within her. In any case, in the three months it took to write the unusual reply to "Sor Filotea," Sor Juana created a text we now consider essential to a full understanding and appreciation of her genius.

From Spain the former vicereine, María Luisa, followed the events that would ultimately lead the poet to silence herself in the face of discouragement and inquisitional mentalities. The aristocratic Spaniard did all she could to come to the rescue. When the manuscript of Sor Juana's theological critique was circulated in Spain, many people took the nun's side or at least defended her right to argue. In Mexico, where Vieira was greatly favored by the Jesuits, Sor Juana was refuted with virulence, although she also had a few defenders. In Spain, the former vicereine marshaled seven respected theologians to praise the *Crisis* [Critique], as Sor Juana's refutation of Vieira was now called. Disregarding the bishop of Puebla's hyperbolic title ("Letter Worthy of Athena"), the marquise had it reprinted along with defenses and numerous poems of praise for Sor Juana, "Phoenix of America." The laudatory pages comprised the initial third of the second volume of Sor Juana's *Obras* [Works], a book that the author herself had cooperated in preparing so that some of her finest writing would see print. Behind the "Knight of the Order of Santiago" to whom Juana Inés was asked to dedicate the volume stood the tireless efforts of the ex-vicereine, who expedited publication in Seville, where she and her husband had considerable influence. But the paeans to Sor Juana's talent and glory that prefaced this 1692 volume probably backfired, causing Sor Juana even more problems with her superiors in Mexico.

That same year, in 1692, Sor Juana sold her library and musical and scientific instruments, contributing the proceeds to charity. She wrote her last set of *villancicos* (carols), those to St. Catherine. Little more would come from her pen. Two years later, in 1694, she renewed her vows, signed a statement of self-condemnation, and turned to penance and self-sacrifice.

Was Sor Juana's retreat from writing, study, and society a religious conversion? Was she under compulsion? How much the pressure came from without, how much from within is rigorously debated by scholars. It is notable that, at the end, Sor Juana took the ascetic path Núñez had earlier prescribed. In fact, in 1693 he became her confessor once again. Sor Juana's life ended two months after his, in 1695, when she fell victim to an epidemic while caring for her sisters.[20] The last of her three volumes of work was not published until five years later, in Madrid, in the first year of the new century.

---

[20]The exact nature of the "plague" is not known.

A Poet-Scholar: Sor Juana's Writing

Humorously quoting Ovid, Sor Juana described herself as a born poet – when she was spanked, her cries issued forth in verse – and claimed that she first spoke in rhyme and then had to learn to speak in prose. Part of her modern appeal resides in the amazing skill and grace with which she uses language. Her very survival as an exception, a courtly churchwoman, and her productivity and excellence as a writer, required adept handling of Mexico's multiple linguistic codes, its ways of seeing and putting things – cultured and popular, legal and literary. Like her "father" St. Jerome, she read books, the world, and, to a lesser extent, people in classical as well as Christian terms. She absorbed, but as a female reader also resisted, the words of the ancients – the classical writers of Greece and Rome – and of the Bible and the church fathers as well. In writing she interpreted and revivified their style and thought, applying them to what was most relevant for her. She knew and emulated or mimicked such Spanish authors as Cervantes, Quevedo, Góngora, Lope de Vega, and Calderón de la Barca.[21]

Living in a world of real and verbal mirrorings, conscious of the specular role assumed involuntarily by women, Sor Juana crafted poetic mirrors and lenses that continue to reveal the submerged realities of her times. Her work reflects how actively the masculine culture assigned women secondary, invisible, silently reflective roles in society. Indeed, the poet frequently manipulated images of reflection and its associated phenomena. She painted portraits in words: to express love of María Luisa Manrique de Lara, to ridicule the preposterous exaggerations used to describe women in poetry, to disparage the expectation that women never age. Men put up mirrors, she showed, to view what they wanted to see. Hers bore a different image.

Sensitive to the reproduction of hierarchies in emblematic and rhetorical renditions of the various social and divine estates (such renditions circulated widely at the time), Sor Juana replaced fig-

---

[21]In one of Sor Juana's poems the Virgin appears as a Don Quijote, saving people in distress. Some of her sonnets have been compared to those of Góngora: the title and style of *Primero sueño* [First Dream] are inspired by that poet. Lope de Vega's conceptual games, his tender lyrics, and incorporation of music and dance into theater all find their counterparts in Sor Juana's works. The enormous influence of Calderón de la Barca can be summarized in her variations of two of his titles: he wrote "Los empeños de un ocaso," she "Los empeños de una casa"; he "El divino Orfeo," she "El divino Narciso."

ures at strategic points along the traditional echelons.[22] She included the Virgin Mary, for example, in references to the Trinity, placing her at the pinnacle of the sacred and even the poetic pyramid; she traced a holy female lineage that went through Mary back to Isis; she sanctified Mother Nature and Discourse — language — itself. The widely accepted custom among Mexicans of expressing ardent reverence for their patron, the Virgin of Guadalupe (unacknowledged descendant of a Nahua mother goddess), provided a cover for Sor Juana's at times almost heretical and pantheistic redeifications.

Colloquial and cultured, Sor Juana's verse skillfully spoke to audiences throughout her vastly diverse society. The Catholic church therefore sought out her empathetic voice, her capacity to bring religious thought and legend to life and to make it playfully meaningful, commissioning her to write texts (*villancicos*) for holy day masses. To this day, nearly every schoolchild in Latin America learns stanzas from "Hombres necios que acusáis" [You foolish and unreasoning men],[23] Sor Juana's most popular poem.

Sor Juana's verse spans the sublime and the frivolous and combines the languages of court and convent, Scholasticism and literature, medieval dogma and modern rationalism. A student of symbol and logic, she employed both in structuring works sacred and profane, dramatic and comical. She wrote burlesque sonnets, words for local dance tunes, and occasional poems to accompany gifts, as thank-yous, as entries to the numerous poetry contests, as celebrations of baptisms, birthdays, or the completion for a doctorate, and for inaugurations of churches. For her poems on love, jealousy, quarrels, absence, and yearning, she was favorably compared to the greatest poets of Spain.

Sor Juana's complete works include sixty-five sonnets (including some twenty love sonnets, deemed by many to be among the most beautiful of the seventeenth century); sixty-two *romances* (of a style similar to ballads); and a profusion of *endechas, redondillas, liras, décimas, silvas,* and other metrical forms employed during Spain's literary Golden Age.[24] For dramatic performance, Sor Juana wrote three sacramental *autos* (one-act dramas) and two comedies (one a collaboration). In addition, she composed thirty-two *loas* (preludes to plays) that were sung and performed as pro-

---

[22]Arenal, "Sor Juana Inés de la Cruz: Reclaiming the Mother Tongue," p. 64.

[23]See Selected Poems, below, and Flores and Flores, eds., *The Defiant Muse,* p. 21.

[24]For an explanation of metrical forms in Spanish, see the introduction to Selected Poems, below.

logues to the plays, as well as separately for religious and viceregal celebrations; two *sainetes* (farces) and a *sarao* (celebratory song and dance), performed between the acts of one of the plays; and fifteen or sixteen sets of *villancicos* (carols) for matins. Each of the last-mentioned contained eight or nine songs, elaborations of such religious themes as the Nativity, the Assumption, the Immaculate Conception, and legends of Sts. Joseph, Peter, and Catherine of Alexandria.

In sketching Sor Juana's biography we spoke of the "Allegorical Neptune," the triumphal arch in honor of the arrival of the viceregal couple, the Marquis and Marquise de Mancera. A lesson in statehood, a guide to good government, the corresponding text alludes to the virtues princes and kings ought to possess, and it ascribes the Greco-Roman god Neptune's beneficence to the teachings of his mother, the Egyptian goddess Isis.[25] The viceroy is urged to be praiseworthy both as a husband and as a ruler; welcome is extended the vicereine, and the ruling couple is spoken of as a unit. In her prose commentary Sor Juana expatiates on the complexities of symbolic language as used by the Egyptians, offering cues, in the process, to her own alchemical sympathies; meanings appear in multiple layers and are accessible according to a person's level of insight, intelligence, and initiation.

Sor Juana's 975-verse *First Dream* (referred to in the *Answer* simply as *Dream*) is generally considered the most important philosophical poem in the Spanish language. This symbolic, mirror version of the *Answer* had long been read as a poem of intellectual disillusionment. More recent readings see it as an exploration of "the available modes of human knowledge from the geometrical movements of celestial bodies to the intricate workings of the human body, through induction, logic, and intuition, all revealed as inadequate in the waking world," and also as a refutation of "both the theory and the practice of objectifying women."[26] Critics today celebrate its originality and modernity, admire its statement "in favor of the human spirit's right to unimpeded growth,"[27] and proclaim "its vision not unlike Descartes's . . . a fusion of theology, poetry, and science."[28]

Dream, it should be noted, is the poem that Sor Juana herself

[25]Sor Juana conflates mythologies, drawing a parallel between the Egyptian god of the Nile, Osiris, and the Greco-Roman god of the sea, Neptune.

[26]Bergmann, "Sor Juana Inés de la Cruz: Dreaming in a Double Voice," pp. 163, 159–60.

[27]Trueblood, ed. and trans., *A Sor Juana Anthology*, p. 23.

[28]Arenal, "Where Woman Is Creator of the Wor(l)d," p. 125.

most respected. It is an exaltation of the poet's insatiable thirst to encompass all human knowledge:

> Not being able to grasp
> in a single act of intuition all creation;
> rather by stages, from one concept
> to another ascending step by step . . .
> (OC 1.350:590–94)

Sor Juana combined unparalleled skill–a seeming verbal magic–with a profound and woman-centered vision. Her originality lies in this combination: in the literary forms she gave to her insatiable, gender-conscious, intellectual curiosity. Sor Juana was passionately inquisitive about empirically observed phenomena and cognizant of the changing relationship of human beings to their environment that marked the dawning of the scientific age. She knew and wrote about the ancient pharmaceutical potions of the Greek physician and anatomist Galen (A.D. 130?–201?) and also mentioned indigenous Mexican herbal cures. With visitors from other parts of the Americas and from Europe she pondered and discussed astronomy, mathematics, mechanics, and medicine. She studiously pursued a knowledge of music and painting. All these concerns – her preoccupations and delights – found their way into her poems and prose.

Sor Juana's *Respuesta a Sor Filotea de la Cruz* is often referred to as "autobiographical." It might better be described as a rhetorically structured letter of self-defense. "Self," however, is a term of our time and culture, not hers.[29] In her differently psychological and thoroughly mannered religious age, the "self" she defends cannot be located in an "inner nature" or "consciousness" outwardly expressed. Rather, the author is defending a dearly held intellectual position, which is her concept of how theology can best be done: by studying the arts and sciences and by including women both as subjects of study and teachers of other women. In the following section, we present a detailed consideration of the many elements composing this complex text.

---

[29]Interestingly, the English word "self," which came into use as a substantive with our philosophical and (later) psychological senses in the latter part of the seventeenth century, has no close equivalent in Spanish. Words akin to such terms as "personality," "identity," "the ego," or "the I" can express the concept; but no one Spanish word unites these meanings.

II. La Respuesta / The Answer: A Reading

This section presents essential elements of the immediate context, purpose, and style of Sor Juana's *Answer*. Throughout, we aim to help the reader understand how Sor Juana made use of conventions available to her writing, where she was innovative, and how thoroughly her gendered sense of the world and of language permeates her text.

Sor Juana's Art and Argument

Counterpoint typifies the structure of the *Answer to Sor Filotea de la Cruz*. In keeping with the Baroque literary context of the period and the complex urgency of Sor Juana's purpose, the piece is polyvocal and polysemous—of multiple voices and meanings. Understanding requires that the reader perform several acts of "translation" and exercise a willingness to accept ambiguous complexity.

For many years the essay was read as a relatively straightforward text. Almost nothing the bishop wrote to Sor Juana, however, including his signing of the letter as "Sor Filotea," nor anything Sor Juana answered, particularly regarding her place in the order of things, can be taken wholly at face value. The elaborate quality of the rhetoric makes simple readings insufficient. Letter, legal defense, treatise, and autobiographical essay,[30] the *Answer* displays traditional learning and demonstrates the need for freedom of experimentation and opinion. For educated readers of the time, Sor Juana's methods were familiar, but her message was pioneering; for us, only the message is familiar. We must keep in mind that like a classical ballet, the essay is carefully choreographed and costumed; it is at once sincere and strategic, simple and subtle.

Multiplicity of Meanings. Sor Juana's prismatic method explores and exploits the interplay among words, their etymological roots and cognate forms, their denotations and connotations. For instance, especially in paragraphs 17 and 21 of the *Answer*, Sor Juana highlighted the cluster of Spanish words *seña, señalar, señalada/o* (whose meanings include, respectively, "sign," "signal/signify,"

---

[30]In seventeenth-century Spanish and colonial letters, narratives of individual development were still known as "lives," following classical and early Christian tradition. The use of the term "autobiography" for the writing of the history of a "self" began in the nineteenth century. Conscious of its anachronism, we nevertheless occasionally use the term (see note 29, above).

"significant") that are related to the Latin *signum* ("sign, mark"; "token"; "miracle"). She plays on etymological connections between these words to describe the vulnerability of intelligence and poetic talent. In Christ she saw the quintessential model of intelligence and beauty. By citing the "signs" worked by Christ in the Gospels – "acts of a miraculous nature serving to demonstrate divine power or authority" (OED) – she inveighed against the persecution and vituperation that commonly victimize outstanding or "significant" human beings. Thus, outstanding powers of mind she likened to such "signs" of divine workings, to the miraculous. At the same time, in current terms, she underscores the functions of language as a system of signifiers and as a potent ideological force. Though unfairly fragmented, an excerpt will nevertheless serve as example:

> . . . as for this aptitude at composing verses . . . even should they be sacred verses – what unpleasantness have they not caused me. . . . [A]t times I ponder how it is that a person who achieves high significance – or rather, who is granted significance by God . . . is received as the common enemy. . . . and so they persecute that person. . . . [In Athens] anyone possessing significant qualities and virtues was expelled. . . . [Machiavelli's maxim was] to abhor the person who becomes significant. . . . What else but this could cause that furious hatred of the Pharisees against Christ? . . . O, unhappy eminence, exposed to so many risks! O sign and symbol, set on high as a target of envy and an object to be spoken against! (pars. 17–22)

Through the words and concepts sign/signify/significance, Sor Juana threads together ideas and analogies that are both simple and complex. The ideas concern language, human psychology, theological interpretations, power struggles, and threats to social structure. The analogies include connections drawn between pre-Christian (Hebrew, Greek, Roman) and Christian history and custom, between the Pharisees and the Mexican church hierarchy, between poetry and the accusation of blasphemy, and, not least, between Sor Juana and Christ.

Throughout the *Answer* as a whole, we can only guess at some points, jibes, and arguments Sor Juana makes, for we lack documents that would give us a fuller portrait of her involvement with the intricacies of the power struggles among and between Jesuits, bishops, Spaniards, and *criollos.* We do know about the struggle between Sor Juana and two church authorities (Núñez, the dismissed confessor, and Fernández, the bishop) with whom she had very close ties. But her formally educated contemporaries had an advantage, an everyday familiarity with both the Bible and clas-

Introduction

sical mythology that we lack and that provided them with clues to coded meanings. When Sor Juana cited a passage or alluded to a mythological personage, her readers could contextualize immediately as we cannot, except by study. They would know what came before and after, who was related to whom, the significance of frequently used figures. Therefore, many more implicit meanings were probably understood in the author's time and are not now. On the other hand, some levels of meaning may be clearer to twentieth-century readers than they were to Sor Juana's contemporaries. Both she and we are conscious of discourse as an (en)gendered process – that is, of attitudes about sex roles hidden in speech. We know that "mankind" both includes and hides women. We have learned, as she did, to cross boundaries and read between the lines.

Narrative Modes. Sor Juana disposes the elements of style with such ingenuity that they provide protective covering for her derision of stupidity and her attack on injustice. Too, this reasoned structure is partially obscured by the polite flourishes of Mexican formality and the conceptual wit of Baroque fashion. The classical structuring form follows the rules for writing and speaking set down by Greek and Roman rhetoricians and exemplified with citations from great writers and orators.

Both intensely personal and consciously public, the *Answer* is based on patterns of expression and composition set by the leading male figures of classical antiquity and early Christianity. But it also includes use of narrative modes common to women's religious writing of the sixteenth and seventeenth centuries, the sermon, Renaissance legal and rhetorical discourse, and high literary forms of her day. Polish and intricacy in mixing the style of the Baroque with earlier Christian and classical conventions contribute to the *Answer's* strength and durability.

Sor Juana imitates the traditional nun's *vida* (Life), "obediently" examining and confessing her conscience. She parodies elements of hagiography – saints' lives – which the bishop was accustomed to read and which were expected in writings by nuns. Sor Juana likens herself to St. Teresa of Avila, insisting on the fact that they are both writers and women who rejected marriage. Indeed, there are parallels she did not state: both women deftly maneuvered in and around difficult situations with the church hierarchy and male superiors; both had friends in powerful places. Further, from our modern-day perspective, both have long been honored in Spanish letters. Despite her familiarity with convent style and her specific references to Teresa, there are limits to a comparison between the two. The Spaniard was a mystic; the Mexican, a scholar. Sor Juana did not found monastic houses for women or reform a religious order. She saw the convent as the least noxious of her options, twice saying so and twice finding it necessary to hedge that bold statement with an assurance of her respect for the religious state (pars. 9, 13). It is an intellectual calling, not a mystical or even a spiritual vocation, of which she gives an account. Sor Juana's quest—not unlike the Woolfian room and income of one's own—was for the time and the means necessary for creative reflection. Yet she employs the same stratagems of staged weakness and innocence (pars. 5, 13, 14, 34), of subterfuge, with which writing nuns negotiated ecclesiastic minefields. (See the section "Classical Rhetorical Models," below, for further discussion of the conventions of religious language.)

By her account, Sor Juana's wonder at God's creation comes not through vision or revelation but through empirical observation and deduction; thus the natural, material world provides its own evidence of worth as God's creation. With literary and theatrical flair (and significant topical influence, as Frederick Luciani has shown) she takes us through the tale of her early childhood, skipping her court years. Amazingly, her text raises women's "ways of knowing" to the same level as the noble ancient science of philosophy and the emergent fields that were establishing new scientific principles.

Sor Juana also demonstrates a command of the sermon, one of the most popular forms of the period, in her impassioned reenactment of the scene from Calvary. She implies, in the tradition of the *imitatio Christi* (imitation of Christ), that her suffering was like Christ's, making her judges' charges against her seem as atrocious and deplorable as those hurled at Jesus. Thus, Sor Juana compounds her knowledge of biblical material, presented in sermon form, with the form of classical juridical appeal. Such appeals to emotion, she has learned from her study of classical rhetoric, are "necessary if there are no other means for securing the victory of truth, justice and the public interest."[31] Sor Juana's distinctive "public interest" was the intellectual plight of women in her own time.

The *Answer*, pulling together strands from sermonic, biblical, and legal as well as literary genres, brings the tradition of humanist moralism to Mexican theology and anticipates a later genre, the

---

[31]Quintilian, *Institutio oratoria* VI.i. 7–9, 2:387 in Butler trans. See note to par. 1 and "Classical Rhetorical Models," below.

polemical essay. It is significant that the Spanish writer Baltasar Gracián is the only male literary contemporary whom Sor Juana mentions in the *Answer*. A moralist, he was interested in the ethics of social behavior and associated with the most idealistic and cultured exponents of Hispanic letters. As a stylist and rhetorician he defended the *conceptistas,* poets who displayed intellectual, at times satirical, wit.

Rhetorical Forms. Sor Juana sets the stage for one of her last battles of wits with a battery of precise rhetorical strategies. She knows the rules and conventions governing literary, theological, exegetical (pertaining to exegesis, the detailed explanation of biblical texts), logical, epistolary (pertaining to formal letter writing), and juridical discourse—and she will use them. The essay is in fact and in appearance an epistolary text and follows strict patterns of presentation, well known in her time to those (men) with university training.

Religious Epistolary Address. Readers are liable to find some of the author's stances, especially at the beginning and end of the *Answer,* both mystifying and off-putting. What appear to modern and secular eyes as self-deprecation, exaggerated humility, and convoluted politeness are more accurately understood as conventions of the age, standard modes of address among religious women and men, and courtly manners of a highly stratified colonial society. In Sor Juana's day, formal letter writing was governed by strict rhetorical rules, including Renaissance adaptations of Greek and Latin models. (Vestiges of such rules are quite apparent today in French forms of address in letter writing; early in the twentieth century, formal English-language letters were still ended with the metaphorical "Your humble servant.") Epistolary prose and verse were fashionable literary genres. Writing by nuns and clerics, especially when addressed to their superiors, followed established modes that included such metaphors of humility as "I lowlier than a worm" and, as Sor Juana wrote in a document on the Immaculate Conception of Mary: "I . . . the most insignificant of the slaves of Our Lady the Most Holy Mary" (OC 4.516). Finally, such expressions as "I could give you a very long catalogue of [my verses] . . . but I leave them out in order not to weary you" (par. 28), follow the standard avoidance of *fastidium* (tedium), as required by manuals of epistolary and forensic rhetoric.

Classical Rhetorical Models. The overall organization of the *Answer* is based on classical explanations of "the order to be followed in forensic causes [legal arguments]."[32] It shows Sor Juana's absorption and application of the Greek and Roman teachings of Aristotle, Plato, Cicero, and Quintilian (see annotations to pars. 1, 5, 23, 42). Sor Juana was convinced that in pursuing causes "which present the utmost complication and variety . . . [one had to become thoroughly versed in] the function of *exordium,* the method of the *statement of facts,* the cogency of *proofs,* whether we are confirming our own assertions or refuting those of our opponents, and the force of the *peroration,* whether we have to refresh the memory of the judge . . . or do what is far more effective, stir his emotions."[33] In accord with this model, the basic divisions of the *Answer* are as follows: after the introductory *exordium* (pars. 5–6), into the narration (pars. 7–29); the proofs or arguments (pars. 30–43) precede the concluding peroration (pars. 44–46).[34] Thus, although she is vulnerable to the accusations of her two "fathers" (Núñez, her former confessor, and Bishop Fernández, her erstwhile friend), in the *Answer* Sor Juana spiritedly demonstrates to them that men (triumphant conquerors, par. 43) are in much greater danger than women of falling prey to arrogance and illusions of grandeur, despite common prejudice to the contrary. Presumption and envy are similarly handled.

Quintilian was perhaps the most significant among the great teachers-of-teachers whose advice Sor Juana followed and whose methods she practiced in acquiring her much-prized reading and speaking skills.[35] The first of the seventy-odd citations in the *Answer* (see par. 1) is from his *Institutio oratoria.* So is the strategically cited dictum "Let each one learn, not so much by the precepts of others, *as by following the counsel of his own nature*" (par. 39; emphasis added). With this quote she caps the paragraph that precedes the climactic rhetorical question of the essay:

> If my crime lies in the "Letter Worthy of Athena," was that anything more than a simple report of my opinion, with all the indulgences granted me by our Holy Mother Church? (par. 40)

---

[32]Quintilian, *Institutio oratoria* IV. pars. 3–7, 2:5 in Butler trans.

[33]Ibid.; italics added.

[34]These divisions are identified and discussed in Perelmuter Pérez, "La estructura retórica."

[35]"But although silence and seclusion and absolute freedom of mind are devoutly to be desired, they are not always within our power to attain. Consequently we must not fling aside our book at once, if disturbed . . . " (Quintilian, *Institutio oratoria* X. iii. 28–31, 4:107 in Butler trans.). Even the wording is similar to paragraph 9 of the *Answer.*

24

On this phrasing lies the force not only of her own case, but the claim of all women, of "each one," to interpretive power. To classical teachings of rhetoric and pedagogy she adds the weight of Hebrew and Christian authority, which she emphasizes (following the grammatical gender of Spanish) as maternal. Thus, by following the highly conventional authority of Quintilian, in addition to espousing educational individuality and freedom of opinion, she is able to move the whole edifice of culture under the roof of a "Mother Church" that, she avers, is permission-giving and not withholding. An earlier reference to Christ's "Mother the Synagogue" (par. 23) and the one to "our Holy Mother Church" cited above are part of Sor Juana's recurrent association of motherhood with creativity and wisdom.

Through all these modes of discourse, Sor Juana expresses pain, regret, and anger regarding her personal situation. She praises, begs, rejects, persuades, ridicules, chides, defends, and teaches the bishop and the imaginary jury—her future readers. She plays every role, accused and accuser, subject and superior. She asks the bishop to put himself in her place, and then rhetorically puts herself in his, thus challenging the hierarchical order. Finally, not forgetting her officially inferior position, she insists on her spiritual equality and on exercising her God-given reason, poetic gifts, and free will. In the process, she displays her intellectual peerlessness while mouthing the expected clichés of the rhetoric of feminine ignorance and tendering the requisite offer of retraction, should anything be said that might be condemned as heresy.

The Issues at Stake

To understand the letter Sor Juana wrote in 1691, it is necessary to know something of two other letters preceding the *Answer*. She wrote one; the other, by the bishop of Puebla, Manuel Fernández de Santa Cruz—"Sor Filotea"—was the letter to which she was most immediately replying in the *Answer*. The circumstances surrounding the composition of these two earlier letters were discussed in the sections "Conflict Intensifies" and "The Bishop, the *Answer* and—Silence," above; we return to the letters here to explore their content.

Letter to Her Confessor. The first letter was written by Sor Juana in 1681/82 (i.e., a decade before the *Answer*) but was not recovered until 1980. Sor Juana did not intend it for publication.[36] In it, she addressed her confessor of more than a decade, Antonio Núñez de Miranda, one of the most knowledgeable and influential citizens of New Spain.[37] The letter relieves him of his responsibilities to her for absolution of sins and spiritual guidance – in essence "fires him" – a right every nun had been assured of since the Council of Trent (1545–63). Going beyond personal appeal, Sor Juana's letter criticizes the narrow-mindedness and repressive authoritarianism, the un-Christian and unintelligent dogmatism of the whole imperial establishment, including that of other nuns and laywomen, young and old. The recently recovered letter thus gives us a new view of the political and hierarchical tides Sor Juana had to ride as well as some notion of how she kept them from overwhelming her.

From the first lines of the letter to its conclusion, irony and rhetorical questions heighten Sor Juana's outrage. Specific themes and rhetorical devices (indeed, actual statements and questions) made later in the *Answer* are already posed in this private letter to Núñez: for example, regarding her right to write poetry and to study and her concern for the sanctity of her soul.

This letter of 1681/82 is the source of the most concrete and unadorned information about Sor Juana's activities that we have from her own pen – the "who, what, and when" with regard to support for her Latin and music lessons, the provision of her dowry to enter the convent, her receiving visitors, and the commissioning of several writings such as the *Allegorical Neptune*. Sor Juana attacks Núñez's reputed remark, that had he known she would write poetry, he would have "married her off" rather than put her in the convent. "Indeed, my most beloved Father," she replies, " . . . what direct authority was yours, to dispose either of my per-

---

[36]Fr. Aureliano Tapia Méndez found the letter in the library of the Seminario Arquediocesano de Monterrey (Monterrey Archdiocesan Seminary), among a miscellany of eighteenth-century printed and manuscript reports. He had it printed as *Autodefensa espiritual de Sor Juana* [Sor Juana's Spiritual Self-Defense]. People refer to it variously as the "Monterrey Letter" or the "Letter of Self-Defense." To avoid confusion, we prefer to mention it as the letter of 1681/82 or the letter to her confessor, Núñez. See Paz, 491–502, for a discussion of authenticity and the full text of the letter itself. See also Alatorre, "Para leer," and Moraña, "Orden dogmático."

[37]A prerequisite for receiving the sacrament of Communion, confession entailed the reporting of sins – and, in the seventeenth century especially, even of imagined sins – to a priest. The confessor was to the conscience what the censor was to the written text. Through the act of repentance the soul was purified of sin.

son or my [free] will?" She makes clear that her godfather paid her dowry: Núñez had no such power, although she acknowledges "other affectionate acts and many kindnesses for which I shall be eternally grateful." The personal information given privately to her confessor contrasts sharply with such frequently considered passages as Sor Juana's love for her convent sisters and theirs for her and other selectively anecdotal autobiographical sections of the 1691 *Answer*. Thus, when Sor Juana's two letters are examined together, the *Answer*'s "autobiographical" passages reveal theatrically heightened and fictionally selective motifs and demonstrate the artfully constructed nature of the later, intentionally public essay.

Letter from "Sor Filotea." The second letter necessary for an understanding of the *Answer to Sor Filotea de la Cruz* delivered praise, censure, and admonishment from one "Sor Filotea." As we have seen, Manuel Fernández de Santa Cruz, bishop of Puebla, wrote that letter and signed that pseudonym when he had it printed in 1690 as a preface to Sor Juana's "Letter Worthy of Athena." The *Answer* is a point-by-point retort to the bishop of Puebla, yet few have considered the *Answer* in this light. Much of what Sor Juana says and how she says it was determined by her reaction to his letter.

The central tenet of the bishop's prefatory letter to Sor Juana is that all but divine knowledge should be eschewed, especially by a woman. The humanities are useful only as "slaves" to sacred studies. "Filotea" does not believe women should be barred entirely from learning, so long as learning does not keep women from assuming "a position of obedience" or incline "our sex" to presumptuousness. The bishop (in female disguise) warns Sor Juana:

> I am quite certain that if Your Worship . . . were to form a detailed idea of divine perfections (which is allowed us, even amongst the shadows of our faith), you would at one and the same time find your soul enlightened and your will set aflame and sweetly wounded by the love of God, in order that the Lord, who has so abundantly showered Your Worship with positive favors in the natural world, should not be obliged to grant you only negative ones in the hereafter. (OC 4.696, trans. Amanda Powell)

Accompanying this threat to the salvation of Sor Juana's eternal soul are the bishop's admonitory references to several great (male) religious figures who spurned all worldly learning. By way of answer, Sor Juana will cite other figures, male and female (or the same men, at different periods in their lives), who embraced secular as well as sacred studies. In paragraph 11, she implicitly scolds and ridicules the bishop, demonstrating her complex understanding of the limits to what we today call binary oppositions: "In sum, we see how this Book [the Bible] contains all books, and this Science [of theology] includes all sciences, all of which serve that She may be understood." She protests compartmentalization and argues for the continuity of knowledge, sacred and profane; for the use of reason to strengthen faith; for conciliation of orthodoxy and free will; and for the intellectual parity of women.

In his letter the bishop interweaves acceptance and rejection of verse writing. He posits that Sor Juana had imitated the "meter" of St. Teresa and St. Gregory of Nazianzus;[38] he urges her instead to imitate their religious subject matter. The bishop's assertion makes no sense, specifically because the two saints are not among the poets who influenced Sor Juana's masterful use and innovation of metrical and prosodic form, nor does her prose bear any resemblance to St. Teresa's. Moreover, we may recall that her most important commissions *were* church-related, the subject matter being utterly religious. In the *Answer*, Sor Juana refutes this notion of her lack of religious subject matter: first, by emphasizing the intellectual attention she gives to sacred texts; second, by proving that poetry itself can be inherently sacred. In some of her most forceful pages, bringing her defense to a close, she contests her unfitness, as a woman, to write. Indeed, through citation, both St. Gregory and St. Teresa become witnesses for Sor Juana's side of the argument: Gregory putting forth the view that toleration of one's enemies is as much a victory as vanquishing them; Teresa as a woman officially authorized to write. Clearly, Juana Inés had decided that if she had to tolerate her enemies, she would at least contest their ignorance and their hypocritical dissimulations. At the end of her reply she essentially unveils "Sor Filotea," fully acknowledging the difference in status between her and the bishop: "For in addressing you, my sister, as a nun of the veil, I have forgotten the distance between myself and your most distinguished person, which should not occur were I to see you unveiled" (par. 45).

---

[38]For a study of Sor Juana's versification, see Navarro Tomás, *Los poetas en sus versos,* pp. 163–79.

The Answer as Self-Defense. Sor Juana's *Answer*, then, was a wise refutation of supposed "offenses." In setting up her self-defense, Sor Juana kept the potentially treacherous Inquisition in mind.[39] While it is not known how much real cause she had to fear being called for questioning, nor how directly she had been threatened with such an action, the Holy Office is a presence mentioned four times in the *Answer*. First, in a (semi-?)jest: sins against art are not punished by that institution (par. 5). Second, she wants no trouble—literally, "noise"—with the Holy Office (par. 5). Here, we speculate, she might have continued the sentence with "such as Vieira had." Certainly this is one of the many places where contemporary readers knew more than we; some of them were aware of the Portuguese preacher's difficulties.[40] Later, she implicitly mocks anyone who would suggest that learning is a matter for the Inquisition by mentioning the "very saintly and simple mother superior" who thought so (par. 26). Finally, she issues a brave challenge: if she has been heretical in her theological refutation (the "Letter Worthy of Athena"), as someone has anonymously asserted, then let that nameless coward officially denounce her (par. 40). She is careful to delegitimize vague threats and ill-phrased opinion; from the onset she makes clear her assumption that expressions of opinion, praise or opprobrium, and the pursuit of art itself are immune from punishment.

One aspect of Sor Juana's legal argumentation would certainly serve as a defense in any future danger. Carefully, she places responsibility for publication of the "Letter Worthy of Athena" on the shoulders of the bishop—whether or not we are to believe, as she claims, that her writing down and sending the originally oral refutation was purely an act of obedience. Two other claims about the "Letter Worthy of Athena" are salient and doubly contradictory: she feels, so she declares, both deceived and elated

---

[39]Inquisitional censors scrutinized all "books, pamphlets, and especially plays" to make sure there was nothing unorthodox in them, nothing that went against Catholic dogma. All novels were banned on the premise that they corrupted morals. The aim was to keep Catholics on the straight and narrow and to prevent the spread of Protestantism and Crypto-Judaism. In New Spain "expurgation and emendation rather than outright prohibition usually resulted from this inspection" (Leonard, *Baroque Times in Old Mexico*, p. 104). It was not until the 1960s that the Papal Index, the list of prohibited books—a list which of course changed over time—was abolished.

[40]Vieira moved from great favor to disgrace and expulsion at the Portuguese court; he was at one time persecuted by the Inquisition. Paz briefly discusses Vieira's career in outlining the intense rivalry between Archbishop Aguiar y Seijas and Bishop Fernández (*Sor Juana*, p. 401ff.).

about its publication; she would have both aborted and corrected it had she known it was going to press. Unable to pass up the chance for wordplay, she here uses the plural "presses," which referred also to an instrument of torture: things that went to the press could lead to the presses. Sor Juana thus removes responsibility from herself for the printing. Further, she offers the then-standard retraction that would be required in the event her document were to be called in for scrutiny: anything that goes against church teaching is inadvertent and warrants erasure. She said as much in sending the "Letter Worthy of Athena" in the first place, and she reiterates it here in the *Answer*. While stating firmly the right to hold opinions, as she did in her 1681/82 letter to her confessor, she takes no chances. Interestingly, she employs different tactics in the two letters with respect to being accused. In the earlier, private document of 1681/82, she poses a question and answers it: "Am I perchance a heretic? And if I were, could I become saintly solely through coercion?"[41] In the public *Answer*, she speaks and gives examples of the heresies caused by (male) arrogance, ignorance, and half-knowledge and almost laughs off the suggestion that her writing(s) might be a matter for objection and censorship (pars. 5, 40, 42).

The *Answer* not only responds to the bishop, it also alerts Sor Juana's circle of friends to the dangers she faces. In our reading, further, it declares for posterity her own coming silence – implying in advance what that silence will mean. In answering the bishop's letter, Sor Juana uses the word *castigo* (chastisement, punishment) insistently. Thus she responds to his *stated* threat of damnation and to an *unstated* condemnation, already circulating, that might well have included the spectre of the Inquisition. In the 1681/82 letter of protest, she implicitly declares her intention to continue both cultivating her interest in learning and accepting requests for religious and secular entertainments. In the 1691 letter, she amplifies her arguments and widens the scope of her protest, criticism, and teaching. She performs a sort of counterpreaching, a putting forth of alternative but rational (not mystical) knowledge to the *letrados* (men of letters). And she tacitly announces a change of course: in the face of both friendly admonition and unfriendly threat, she will again take matters into her own hands (pars. 4, 43). She does not here name what that course is to be. In a striking parallel to some of the studious women who collaborated with

---

[41]Quoted ibid., p. 500.

St. Jerome in the fourth and fifth centuries and to whom she refers repeatedly in the *Answer,* Sor Juana will end her life as an ascetic.

A Different Worldview, A Different Law: A Woman-Centered Vision

Sor Juana's worldview was different from ours and different from that of most of her contemporaries. She was intensely aware of women's participation in the creation of culture and curious to learn of new developments in mechanics and astronomy. Lamenting that there were no women in Mexico City of equal learning and sensibility, she found them in the past, establishing precedents from "a host" of outstanding figures:

> . . . I see a Deborah issuing laws, military as well as political, and governing the people among whom there were so many learned men. I see the exceedingly knowledgeable Queen of Sheba, so learned she dares to test the wisdom of the wisest of all wise men with riddles, without being rebuked for it; indeed, on this very account she is to become judge of the unbelievers. I see so many and such significant women: some adorned with the gift of prophecy, like an Abigail; others, of persuasion, like Esther; others, of piety, like Rahab; others, of perseverance, like Anna [Hannah] the mother of Samuel; and others, infinitely more, with other kinds of qualities and virtues. (par. 30)

Catalogues of illustrious women were a popular literary tradition going back to classical times. While the authors of such lists often pointed out that there were many more figures than could be mentioned, none insisted in the same manner and with the same purpose as Sor Juana that active and creative intelligence in women was not the exception but the rule. To counteract the idea of her own rarity and to support her arguments, Sor Juana emphasized the numbers of women of achievement, representative of many more. While she mentions forty-four women individually, she refers to "so many" (par. 30) "and others, infinitely more" (par. 30), a "vast throng" (par. 31) of which "the books are full" (par. 31). Authors of laws, prayers, predictions, translations, prose, and poetry (itself an expression of divinity) all inspired veneration. Over and over again, she sets herself and classical, biblical, and historical women (Isis, the Virgin Mary, and St. Catherine being the most noteworthy) next to and above male divinities, scholars, rulers, fathers, and husbands.

From a position of hard-earned and fast-fading power, selectively citing patristic erudition, Sor Juana proposed a break with the "law of the fathers" as espoused and imposed by her superiors.[42] On many levels, from the most sinful to the most virtuous, the most cowardly to the most brave, the most pagan to the most Christian, Sor Juana draws parallels and situates women next to, above, or in place of men. For instance, men are shown censured as adulterers (par. 43); women are held up as astrologers (par. 31). Teachers are both female and male. She starts and ends with herself as exemplar of the transmutability – rather than the fixity – of the "gendered" attributes of intelligence and learning, as a daughter of St. Jerome and St. Paula:

> . . . I did my best to elevate these studies and direct them to His service, for the goal to which I aspired was the study of Theology. Being a Catholic, I thought it an abject failing not to know everything that can in this life be achieved, through earthly methods, concerning the divine mysteries. And being a nun and not a laywoman, I thought I should, because I was in religious life, profess the study of letters – the more so as the daughter of such as St. Jerome and St. Paula. For it would be a degeneracy for an idiot daughter to proceed from such learned parents. (par. 10)

Silence Redefined, St. Paul Corrected. "Let women keep silence in the churches: for it is not permitted them to speak, but to be subject, as also the law saith. But if they would learn anything, let them ask their husbands at home. For it is a shame for a woman to speak in the church" (1 Corinthians 14:34–35). A main argument throughout the *Answer* demonstrates what Sor Juana considers to be errors committed in applying these words of St. Paul: for centuries authorities had used this biblical dictum to relegate women to silence (pars. 32, 33, 37, 39). Sor Juana exposes the foolishness of the ban and demonstrates the lack of foundation for the imposition of ignorance upon women (pars. 10, 11, 16, 29, 32, 35, 39).[43]

By its end, Sor Juana's document declares the likelihood of her future silence, unless she receives support from her former ally, Bishop Fernández: "Unless your instructions intervene, I shall never in my own defense take up the pen again" (par. 43). There-

---

[42]The extent of Sor Juana's correspondence with pre-Enlightenment intellectuals of Europe is not known, owing to the loss of her letters; what is known is that people interested in science and reason in colonial Mexico and Peru wrote letters to her and visited with her. Their traditional outlook regarding women, however, kept these people from envisioning the same changes she did.

[43]See Scott, "Sor Juana Inés de la Cruz: 'Let Your Women Keep Silence in the Churches.' "

fore, she is careful at the outset to define the meaning of the absence of speech: "I had nearly resolved to leave the matter in silence: yet although silence explains much by the emphasis of leaving all unexplained, because it is a negative thing, one must name the silence, so that what it signifies may be understood" (par. 4). With both seriousness and humor she stresses that, in order to be understoood, she must indicate what her silence will say. Playing on saying / not saying and knowing / not knowing, she skirts direct contention with the powers that be and posits alternative "female" viewpoints.[44] Throughout, she plumbs another silence, the "silence of treachery" – that of those who did not defend Christ, of those who would not speak up for her.[45]

Sor Juana inverts and reassigns the usual gender attributions with regard to the issue of silence. As we have remarked, the *Answer* gives notice of her decision to silence herself. She was intent when writing it, however, on speech: on proving the sanctity of her lifelong pursuit of knowledge. Even St. Paul, she shows, encouraged desirable silence for both sexes: "And in truth . . . the *'Let [them] keep silence'* was meant not only for women, but for all those who are not very competent" (par. 33).

Our reading suggests that at the writing of the *Answer,* after twenty-five years of public service to crown and cross, Sor Juana was garnering only accusatory and menacing threats. (Here, we agree with interpretations such as those of Dorothy Schons and Dario Puccini.) At this point in her life, she seems to have decided it would be best to follow in the footsteps of her learned foremothers and forefathers – Fabiola (par. 31) or Gregory of Nazianzus (par. 42) – and retreat. But she would not do so before setting the record straight, by belittling antifemale rules and edicts – those of the Council of Trent, for instance – as age-old "prejudice and custom."[46] The established order of gender relations was time-bound and relative, she showed, pointing out that even-older and more venerable traditions and viewpoints, wiser and more sacred laws – those of the "great Author," as she calls God (par. 12) – supported her thinking.

---

[44]See Ludmer, "Tricks of the Weak."

[45]See Franco, "Sor Juana Explores Space," and Arenal, "The Convent as Catalyst for Autonomy."

[46]The tenets of the Catholic Reformation were set down at the Council of Trent (1545–63); despite an appeal by religious women for representation, no women's voices were heard at the meetings, where Spanish clerics dominated. Many edicts, nevertheless, prescribed how convents were to be run. In addition to perpetual cloistering (there had been a certain liberty to enter and leave the convent before then), "Holy ignorance" and the limitation especially of the study of Latin to necessary prayers were ruled appropriate for nuns.

✳︎ *The Defense of Education for and by Women.* Sor Juana argues for the existence of an older and more authoritative source in talking about the dangers for women of not having older women to teach them. Cannily, she speaks as though her audience had already accepted that women should be taught in the first place. To dispel the antagonisms excited by criticism she employs jest (pars. 5, 28, 32). She handles the theme of sex and gender at times through direct exposé, at others, she performs a subtle inversion of the expected double standard regarding the dangers of sexual abuse, the portrayal of eroticism in spiritual literature (considered to be as dangerous for men as for women), the significance of socialization for the patterning of masculine and feminine behavior and dress, and the different status of sexuality in ancient cosmology, in the Bible, and in early Christianity. Here, Jesus Christ is beautiful (par. 19); the Virgin Mary is wise (par. 42). Christ's beauty is gazed at by a woman (par. 20); a man inscribes, in terms of the human body, the intelligence of a woman (par. 31). Unexplained inversions of grammatical gender in the Bible are remarked upon (par. 38); the kitchen is the scene of philosophical ferment and scientific experiment (par. 28); women, if only to underscore the prohibitions, are imagined at the university and the pulpit (par. 32).

In the *Answer,* Sor Juana's strongest statement regarding how nuns should spend their time comes indirectly. Dr. Arce, a noted university professor, had expressed regret that cloistered women were forced to waste their intellect memorizing and repeating — reproducing the past — rather than investigating and applying "scientific principles":

> [Our good Arce] relates that he knew two nuns in this City, one . . . who had so thoroughly committed to memory the Divine Office, that . . . she would apply its verses, psalms, and maxims . . . to all her conversations. The other . . . was so adept in reading the Epistles of my father St. Jerome . . . that Arce says: *"I thought that I heard Jerome himself, speaking in Spanish."* . . . [A]nd he grieves that such talents should not have been set to higher studies, guided by principles of science. He never mentions the name of either nun, but he presents them in support of his verdict that the study of sacred letters is not only permissible but most useful and necessary for women, and all the more so for nuns. (par. 41)

Thus, Sor Juana has another authority deplore monastic attitudes about learning. And no wonder: this position directly contradicts what the bishop in his letter held up as desirable.

Reinterpreting "public interests" that have led to the contemporary state of affairs is both Sor Juana's theme and her practice. She limits her explicit criticism to the stifling mindlessness, to the arrogant and error-ridden policies that are harmful to women. But even the crisis of Mexico City – a crisis brought on by inefficiency and bad government as well as natural disasters – may have been on her mind. Tactically, she speaks from a position of weakness in order to claim a different discursive space – for instance, the spaces where women cook (par. 28) and children play games (par. 27) – and she carries on a conceptual "game" to the end of the *Answer*, validating what women know and say.

From the beginning of the *Answer*, as Jean Franco notes, "the transparent fiction of the pseudonym 'Sor Filotea' . . . [permits] an exaggerated deference to the recipient who is supposed to be a powerless woman and thus [exposes] the real power relations behind the egalitarian mask."[47] Under the rhetoric of humility and obedience we read a refusal of her word to those who would keep her voiceless. By the end of the next year, perhaps as a result of a combination of factors, including self-conversion in the face of coercion, disenchantment, and frustration – there are as many interpretations as there are critics – she will turn inward and follow the tradition of the founders of her order. But she has had the last and the lasting word.

As she did in the 1681/82 letter, in the *Answer* Sor Juana uses many tactics to unmask the semantics of repression. She stands her – women's – ground with great and ironic humor: "and I believe this will make you laugh. But in truth, my Lady, what can we women know, save philosophies of the kitchen? . . . [O]ne can philosophize quite well while preparing supper. I often say, when I make these little observations, 'Had Aristotle cooked, he would have written a great deal more' " (par. 28). Sor Juana creates a new "space," cleared from the prohibitions against women's full and free participation in the university, the legal court, the public sphere of intellect and power. Further, she adds to that domain the kitchen, the dormitory, the nursery – places where women teachers can teach girls. She clears the space so that she, and any "competent" woman (her term) can do what all the exemplary women she cites in her *Answer* have done, as seers, writers, lawyers, judges, and so on – exercising abilities for which they have been venerated. In this new and inclusive sphere, nothing – no virtue, no talent, no vice – is to be the exclusive ter-

---

[47]Franco, "Sor Juana Explores Space," p. 44.

rain of either sex. From the beginning to the end of her *Answer,* she goes about exemplifying and persuading in order to prove this point. Notably, she allows even historical, and indeed contemporary women, too, to receive veneration. We can descry much more of her intricate web when we realize that a marked pattern of significant, gender-related issues characterizes the passages that precede and follow the portions of authoritative (particularly biblical) texts she cites, as we show in the notes. She means her examples to resonate with the wider weave of those issues.

In the letter to her confessor, Sor Juana had mentioned St. Jerome's positive attitudes toward the learned women in his circle; in the *Answer,* she takes the opportunity to develop that theme more fully. Jerome was a prominent medieval source for misogynistic argument; thus, her citation of "her holy Father" is strategically drawn. She does not quote the same line of Jerome as the bishop, who emphasizes women's subjection to men. But she does make different use of some of the bishop's examples. While he acknowledges St. Jerome's praise of studious women and separates himself twice from "commonplace censorship" of the practice of letters in women, the bishop's aim is to curtail that very practice. Sor Juana, on the other hand, uses St. Jerome's praise of women like herself to establish a venerable tradition of women's participation in many fields of culture; she also implicitly compares herself to this father of her order.

Sor Juana said, in her letter to Núñez: "If I have read the secular prophets and orators (an impudence of which St. Jerome himself was guilty), I also read the Holy Doctors and Holy Scriptures." When he writes as "Sor Filotea," the bishop cites St. Paul with respect to women's teaching. Sor Juana extends this dialogue, demonstrating that official and popular opinion on the subject of women's talking and teaching is based on old misinterpretations. Without a direct word, but implicitly and by analogy, the *Answer* shames the bishop, her confessor, and all of their cohorts for running the risk of being perfect fools regarding central matters of belief: "A wit once observed, that he who knows no Latin is not an utter fool, but he who does know it has met the prerequisites. And I might add that he is made a perfect fool (if foolishness can attain perfection) by having studied his bit of philosophy and theology and by knowing something of languages. For with that he can be foolish in several sciences and tongues; a great fool cannot be contained in his mother tongue alone" (par. 32). Sor Juana interrogates and exposes her male superiors' behavior toward others, toward scriptural interpretation, toward the acquisition and implementation of learning, toward the unity of knowledge, toward nature, culture, and gender. Most particularly, however, she castigates their myopic views on the role of women as intellectuals.

More than a century before the demise of the Inquisition and the mentality it represented, Sor Juana issued a call for a change in outlook, presenting herself as a test case but representing the intellectual cause of all women. Sor Juana used her art and her religion to be a scholar, and she used her scholarship to create a piece of literary art that defends the sacredness of poetry (as well as of women). She understood the power of language and ideology, and the unstated gender issues embedded in both. That is precisely why, despite the Baroque style of discourse, Sor Juana seems so "modern" and why she continues to rivet our interest.

A Note on the Texts

Asterisks indicate significant words, phrases, or concepts that receive clarifying and contextualizing annotation. Proper names, titles of works, and quotes from textual sources (principally the Old and New Testament Bible, classical authors, and Christian commentators such as St. Jerome) are referenced by line number; they are not signaled by asterisks in the text.

In the English translation, passages given in Latin (chiefly quotations) by Sor Juana are translated and set in italics. The Latin text that Sor Juana cited can be found in italics in the Spanish text. Where surrounding passages of text seem significant to Sor Juana's purpose, these are noted.

The biblical translation used here is the Douay-Rheims English Version of 1609, because it was translated (in many instances quite literally) from the Latin Vulgate Sor Juana used and knew and because its seventeenth-century English gives a flavor closely contemporary with her time.

Respuesta
de la poetisa a la muy ilustre
Sor Filotea de la Cruz

Muy ilustre Señora, mi Señora:

(1)   No mi voluntad, mi poca salud y mi justo temor han suspendido tantos días mi respuesta. ¿Qué mucho si, al primer paso, encontraba para tropezar mi torpe pluma dos imposibles? El primero (y para mí el más riguroso) es saber responder a vuestra doctísima, discretísima, santísima y amorosísima carta. Y si veo que preguntado el Angel de las Escuelas, Santo Tomás, de su silencio con Alberto Magno, su maestro, respondió que callaba porque nada sabía decir digno de Alberto, con
10 cuánta mayor razón callaría, no como el Santo, de humildad, sino que en la realidad es no saber algo digno de vos.* El segundo imposible es saber agradeceros tan excesivo como no esperado favor, de dar a las prensas mis borrones:* merced tan sin medida que aun se le pasara por alto a la esperanza más ambiciosa y al deseo más fantástico; y que ni aun como ente de razón* pudiera caber en mis pensamientos; y en fin, de tal magnitud que no sólo no se puede estrechar a lo limitado de las voces, pero excede a la capacidad del agradecimiento, tanto por grande como por no esperado, que es lo que dijo Quinti-
20 liano: *Minorem spei, maiorem benefacti gloriam pereunt.* Y tal, que enmudecen al beneficiado.

(2)   Cuando la felizmente estéril para ser milagrosamente fecunda, madre del Bautista vio en su casa tan desproporcionada visita como la Madre del Verbo, se le entorpeció el entendimiento y se le suspendió el discurso; y así, en vez de agradecimientos, prorrumpió en dudas y preguntas: *Et unde hoc mihi?*

The Poet's Answer
to the Most Illustrious
Sor Filotea de la Cruz

Most illustrious Lady, my Lady:

It has not been my will, but my scant health and a rightful fear (1)
that have delayed my reply for so many days. Is it to be won-
dered that, at the very first step, I should meet with two obstacles that sent my dull pen stumbling? The first (and to me the most
insuperable) is the question of how to respond to your immense-
ly learned, prudent, devout, and loving letter. For when I consider how the Angelic Doctor, St. Thomas Aquinas, on being asked
of his silence before his teacher Albertus Magnus, responded that
he kept quiet because he could say nothing worthy of Albertus, 10
then how much more fitting it is that I should keep quiet – not
like the Saint from modesty, but rather because, in truth, I am
unable to say anything worthy of you.* The second obstacle is
the question of how to render my thanks for the favor, as excessive as it was unexpected, of giving my drafts and scratches to
the press:* a favor so far beyond all measure as to surpass the
most ambitious hopes or the most fantastic desires, so that as a
rational being* I simply could not house it in my thoughts. In
short, this was a favor of such magnitude that it cannot be
bounded by the confines of speech and indeed exceeds all pow- 20
ers of gratitude, as much because it was so large as because it was
so unexpected. In the words of Quintilian: *"They produce less glory
through hopes, more glory through benefits conferred."* And so much
so, that the recipient is struck dumb.

When the mother of [John] the Baptist – felicitously barren, so (2)
as to become miraculously fertile – saw under her roof so exceed-

39

¿De dónde a mí viene tal cosa? Lo mismo sucedió a Saúl cuando se vio electo y ungido rey de Israel: *Numquid non filius Iemini ego sum de minima tribu Israel, et cognatio mea novissima* 30 *inter omnes de tribu Beniamin? Quare igitur locutus es mihi sermonem istum?* Así yo diré: ¿de dónde, venerable Señora, de dónde a mí tanto favor? ¿Por ventura soy más que una pobre monja, la más mínima criatura del mundo y la más indigna de ocupar vuestra atención? Pues *quare locutus es mihi sermonem istum? Et unde hoc mihi?*

(3)   Ni al primer imposible tengo más que responder que no ser nada digno de vuestros ojos; ni al segundo más que admiraciones, en vez de gracias, diciendo que no soy capaz de agradeceros la más mínima parte de lo que os debo. No es afec-
40 tada modestia,* Señora, sino ingenua verdad de toda mi alma, que al llegar a mis manos, impresa, la carta que vuestra propiedad llamó Atenagórica,* prorrumpí (con no ser esto en mí muy fácil) en lágrimas de confusión, porque me pareció que vuestro favor no era más que una reconvención que Dios hace a lo mal que le correspondo; y que como a otros corrige con castigos,* a mí me quiere reducir a fuerza de beneficios.* Especial favor de que conozco ser su deudora, como de otros infinitos de su inmensa bondad; pero también especial modo de avergonzarme y confundirme: que es más primoroso medio
50 de castigar hacer que yo misma, con mi conocimiento, sea el juez que me sentencie y condene mi ingratitud. Y así, cuando esto considero acá a mis solas, suelo decir: Bendito seáis vos, Señor, que no sólo no quisisteis en manos de otra criatura el juzgarme, y que ni aun en la mía lo pusisteis, sino que lo reservasteis a la vuestra, y me librasteis a mí de mí y de la sentencia que yo misma me daría—que, forzada de mi propio conocimiento, no pudiera ser menos que la condenación—, y vos la reservasteis a vuestra misericordia, porque me amáis más de lo que yo me puedo amar.

(4)   Perdonad, Señora mía, la digresión que me arrebató la fuerza de la verdad; y si la he de confesar toda, también es buscar efugios para huir la dificultad de responder, y casi me he determinado a dejarlo al silencio; pero como éste es cosa negativa, aunque explica mucho con el énfasis de no explicar, es necesario ponerle algún breve rótulo para que se entienda lo

ingly great a guest as the Mother of the Word, her powers of mind were dulled and her speech was halted; and thus, instead of thanks, she burst out with doubts and questions: *"And whence is this to me . . . ?"* The same occurred with Saul when he was chosen 30 and anointed King of Israel: *"Am not I a son of Jemini of the least tribe of Israel, and my kindred the last among all the families of the tribe of Benjamin? Why then hast thou spoken this word to me?"* Just so, I too must say: Whence, O venerable Lady, whence comes such a favor to me? By chance, am I something more than a poor nun, the slightest creature on earth and the least worthy of drawing your attention? Well, *why then hast thou spoken this word to me? And whence is this to me?*

I can answer nothing more to the first obstacle than that I am (3) entirely unworthy of your gaze. To the second, I can offer noth- 40 ing more than amazement, instead of thanks, declaring that I am unable to thank you for the slightest part of what I owe you. It is not false humility,* my Lady, but the candid truth of my very soul, to say that when the printed letter reached my hands – that letter you were pleased to dub "Worthy of Athena"* – I burst into tears (a thing that does not come easily to me), tears of confusion. For it seemed to me that your great favor was nothing other than God's reproof aimed at my failure to return His favors, and while He corrects others with punishments,* He wished to chide me through benefits.* A special favor, this, for which I acknowledge 50 myself His debtor, as I am indebted for infinitely many favors given by His immense goodness; but this is also a special way of shaming and confounding me. For it is the choicest form of punishment to cause me to serve, knowingly, as the judge who condemns and sentences my own ingratitude. And so when I consider this fully, here in solitude, it is my custom to say: Blessed are you, my Lord God, for not only did you forbear to give another creature the power to judge me, nor have you placed that power in my hands. Rather, you have kept that power for yourself and have freed me of myself and of the sentence I would pass on myself, 60 which, forced by my own conscience, could be no less than condemnation. Instead you have reserved that sentence for your great mercy to declare, because you love me more than I can love myself.

My Lady, forgive the digression wrested from me by the power (4) of truth; yet if I must make a full confession of it, this digression is at the same time a way of seeking evasions so as to flee the difficulty of making my answer. And therefore I had nearly resolved to leave the matter in silence; yet although silence ex-

que se pretende que el silencio diga; y si no, dirá nada el silencio, porque ése es su propio oficio: decir nada. Fue arrebatado el Sagrado Vaso de Elección al tercer Cielo,* y habiendo visto los arcanos secretos de Dios dice: *Audivit arcana Dei,*
70 *quae non licet homini loqui.* No dice lo que vio, pero que no lo puede decir; de manera que aquellas cosas que no se pueden decir, es menester decir siquiera que no se pueden decir, para que se entienda que el callar no es no haber qué decir, sino no caber en las voces lo mucho que hay que decir. Dice San Juan que si hubiera de escribir todas las maravillas que obró nuestro Redentor, no cupieran en todo el mundo los libros; y dice Vieyra, sobre este lugar, que en sola esta cláusula dijo más el Evangelista que en todo cuanto escribió; y dice muy bien el Fénix Lusitano* (pero ¿cuándo no dice bien, aun cuando
80 no dice bien?), porque aquí dice San Juan todo lo que dejó de decir y expresó lo que dejó de expresar. Así, yo, Señora mía, sólo responderé que no sé qué responder; sólo agradeceré diciendo que no soy capaz de agradeceros; y diré, por breve rótulo de lo que dejo al silencio, que sólo con la confianza de favorecida y con los valimientos de honrada, me puedo atrever a hablar con vuestra grandeza. Si fuere necedad, perdonadla, pues es alhaja de la dicha,* y en ella ministraré yo más materia a vuestra benignidad y vos daréis mayor forma a mi reconocimiento.

(5) No se hallaba digno Moisés, por balbuciente,* para hablar
90 con Faraón, y, después, el verse tan favorecido de Dios, le infunde tales alientos, que no sólo habla con el mismo Dios, sino que se atreve a pedirle imposibles: *Ostende mihi faciem tuam.* Pues así yo, Señora mía, ya no me parecen imposibles los que puse al principio, a vista de lo que me favorecéis; porque quien hizo imprimir la Carta tan sin noticia mía, quien la intituló, quien la costeó, quien la honró tanto (siendo de todo indigna por sí y por su autora), ¿qué no hará? ¿qué no perdonará? ¿qué dejará de hacer y qué dejará de perdonar? Y así, debajo del supuesto de que hablo con el salvoconducto de vuestros fa-
100 vores y debajo del seguro de vuestra benignidad, y de que me habéis, como otro Asuero, dado a besar la punta del cetro de oro de vuestro cariño en señal de concederme benévola licencia para hablar y proponer* en vuestra venerable presencia, digo que recibo en mi alma vuestra santísima amonestación

plains much by the emphasis of leaving all unexplained, because 70
it is a negative thing, one must name the silence, so that what
it signifies may be understood. Failing that, silence will say nothing, for that is its proper function: to say nothing. The holy Chosen
Vessel was carried off to the third Heaven* and, having seen the
arcane secrets of God, he says: *"That he was caught up into para-
dise, and heard secret words, which it is not granted to man to utter."*
He does not say what he saw, but he says that he cannot say it.
In this way, of those things that cannot be spoken, it must be said
that they cannot be spoken, so that it may be known that silence
is kept not for lack of things to say, but because the many things 80
there are to say cannot be contained in mere words. St. John says
that if he were to write all of the wonders wrought by Our
Redeemer, the whole world could not contain all the books. Vieira
says of this passage that in this one phrase the Evangelist says
more than in all his other writings; and indeed how well the Lusitanian Phoenix* speaks (but when is he not well-spoken, even
when he speaks ill?), for herein St. John says all that he failed to
say and expresses all that he failed to express. And so I, my Lady,
shall answer only that I know not how to answer; I shall thank
you only by saying that I know not how to give thanks; and I shall 90
say, by way of the brief label placed on what I leave to silence,
that only with the confidence of one so favored and with the advantages granted one so honored, do I dare speak to your mag-
nificence. If this be folly, please forgive it; for folly sparkles in
good fortune's crown,* and through it I shall supply further occasion for your goodwill, and you shall better arrange the expression of my gratitude.

Moses, because he was a stutterer,* thought himself unworthy (5)
to speak to Pharaoh. Yet later, finding himself greatly favored by
God, he was so imbued with courage that not only did he speak 100
to God Himself, but he dared to ask of Him the impossible: *"Shew
me thy face."* And so it is with me, my Lady, for in view of the
favor you show me, the obstacles I described at the outset no
longer seem entirely insuperable. For one who had the letter printed, unbeknownst to me, who titled it and underwrote its cost,
and who thus honored it (unworthy as it was of all this, on its
own account and on account of its author), what will such a one
not do? What not forgive? Or what fail to do or fail to forgive?
Thus, sheltered by the assumption that I speak with the safe-
conduct granted by your favors and with the warrant bestowed 110
by your goodwill, and by the fact that, like a second Ahasuerus,
you have allowed me to kiss the top of the golden scepter of your

de aplicar el estudio a Libros Sagrados, que aunque viene en
traje de consejo, tendrá para mí sustancia de precepto; con no
pequeño consuelo de que aun antes parece que prevenía mi
obediencia vuestra pastoral insinuación,* como a vuestra direc-
ción, inferido del asunto y pruebas de la misma Carta.* Bien
110 conozco que no cae sobre ella vuestra cuerdísma advertencia,
sino sobre lo mucho que habréis visto de asuntos humanos que
he escrito; y así, lo que he dicho no es más que satisfaceros
con ella a la falta de aplicación que habréis inferido (con mucha
razón) de otros escritos míos. Y hablando con más especialidad
os confieso, con la ingenuidad que ante vos es debida y con
la verdad y claridad que en mí siempre es natural y costumbre,
que el no haber escrito mucho de asuntos sagrados no ha sido
desafición, ni de aplicación la falta, sino sobra de temor y
reverencia debida a aquellas Sagradas Letras, para cuya in-
120 teligencia yo me conozco tan incapaz y para cuyo manejo soy
tan indigna; resonándome siempre en los oídos, con no pequeño
horror, aquella amenaza y prohibicíon del Señor a los pecadores como yo: *Quare tu enarras iustitias meas, et assumis
testamentum meum per os tuum?* Esta pregunta y el ver que aun
a los varones doctos se prohibía el leer los Cantares hasta que
pasaban de treinta años, y aun el Génesis: éste por su oscuridad,
y aquéllos porque de la dulzura de aquellos epitalamios no
tomase ocasión la imprudente juventud de mudar el sentido
en carnales afectos. Compruébalo mi gran Padre San Jeróni-
130 mo, mandando que sea esto lo último que se estudie, por la
misma razón: *Ad ultimum sine periculo discat Canticum Cantico-
rum, ne si in exordio legerit, sub carnalibus verbis spiritualium nup-
tiarum Epithalamium non intelligens, vulneretur;* y Séneca dice:
Teneris in annis haut clara est fides. Pues ¿cómo me atreviera
yo a tomarlo en mis indignas manos, repugnándolo el sexo,
la edad y sobre todo las costumbres? Y así confieso que muchas
veces este temor me ha quitado la pluma de la mano y ha hecho
retroceder los asuntos hacia el mismo entendimiento de quien
querían brotar; el cual inconveniente no topaba en los asun-
140 tos profanos, pues una herejía contra el arte no la castiga el
Santo Oficio,* sino los discretos con risa y los críticos con censura; y ésta, *iusta vel iniusta, timenda non est,* pues deja comul-
gar y oír misa, por lo cual me da poco o ningún cuidado; porque,

<handwritten>
tono irónico

* el problema con interpretar
  los libros sagrados
</handwritten>

La Respuesta

affection as a sign that you grant me kind license to speak and to plead my case* in your venerable presence, I declare that I receive in my very soul your most holy admonition to apply my study to Holy Scripture; for although it arrives in the guise of counsel, it shall have for me the weight of law. And I take no small consolation from the fact that it seems my obedience, as if at your direction, anticipated your pastoral insinuation,* as may be inferred from the subject matter and arguments of that very Letter.* I recognize full well that your most prudent warning touches not on the letter, but on the many writings of mine on humane matters that you have seen. And thus, all that I have said can do no more than offer that letter to you in recompense for the failure to apply myself which you must have inferred (and reasonably so) from my other writings. And to speak more specifically, I confess, with all the candor due to you and with the truth and frankness that are always at once natural and customary for me, that my having written little on sacred matters has sprung from no dislike, nor from lack of application, but rather from a surfeit of awe and reverence toward those sacred letters, which I know myself to be so incapable of understanding and which I am so unworthy of handling. For there always resounds in my ears the Lord's warning and prohibition to sinners like me, bringing with it no small terror: *"Why dost thou declare my justices, and take my covenant in thy mouth?"* With this question comes the reflection that even learned men were forbidden to read the Song of Songs, and indeed Genesis, before they reached the age of thirty: the latter text because of its difficulty, and the former so that with the sweetness of those epithalamiums, imprudent youth might not be stirred to carnal feelings. My great father St. Jerome confirms this, ordering the Song of Songs to be the last text studied, for the same reason: *"Then at last she may safely read the Song of Songs: if she were to read it at the beginning, she might be harmed by not perceiving that it was the song of a spiritual bridal expressed in fleshly language."* And Seneca says, *"In early years, faith is not yet manifest."* Then how should I dare take these up in my unworthy hands, when sex, and age, and above all our customs oppose it? And thus I confess that often this very fear has snatched the pen from my hand and has made the subject matter retreat back toward that intellect from which it wished to flow; an impediment I did not stumble across with profane subjects, for a heresy against art is not punished by the Holy Office* but rather by wits with their laughter and critics with their censure. And this, *"just or unjust, is not to be feared,"* for one is still permitted to take Com-

según la misma decisión de los que lo calumnian, ni tengo obligación para saber ni aptitud para acertar; luego, si lo yerro, ni es culpa ni es descrédito. No es culpa, porque no tengo obligación; no es descrédito, pues no tengo posibilidad de acertar, y *ad impossibilia nemo tenetur*. Y, a la verdad, yo nunca he escrito sino violentada y forzada y sólo por dar gusto a otros;
150 no sólo sin complacencia, sino con positiva repugnancia, porque nunca he juzgado de mí que tenga el caudal de letras e ingenio que pide la obligación de quien escribe; y así, es la ordinaria respuesta a los que me instan, y más si es asunto sagrado: ¿Qué entendimiento tengo yo, qué estudio, qué materiales, ni qué noticias para eso, sino cuatro bachillerías superficiales?* Dejen eso para quien lo entienda, que yo no quiero ruido con el Santo Oficio, que soy ignorante y tiemblo de decir alguna proposición malsonante o torcer la genuina inteligencia de algún lugar. Yo no estudio para escribir, ni menos para enseñar
160 (que fuera en mí desmedida soberbia), sino sólo por ver si con estudiar ignoro menos. Así lo respondo y así lo siento.
(6)   El escribir nunca ha sido dictamen propio, sino fuerza ajena;* que les pudiera decir con verdad: *Vos me coegistis*. Lo que sí es verdad que no negaré (lo uno porque es notorio a todos, y lo otro porque, aunque sea contra mí, me ha hecho Dios la merced de darme grandísimo amor a la verdad) es que desde que me rayó la primera luz de la razón, fue tan vehemente y poderosa la inclinación a las letras, que ni ajenas represiones — que he tenido muchas —, ni propias reflejas – que he hecho
170 no pocas —, han bastado a que deje de seguir este natural impulso que Dios puso en mí: Su Majestad sabe por qué y para qué; y sabe que le he pedido que apague la luz de mi entendimiento dejando sólo lo que baste para guardar su Ley, pues lo demás sobra, según algunos, en una mujer; y aun hay quien diga que daña. Sabe también Su Majestad que no consiguiendo esto, he intentado sepultar con mi nombre mi entendimiento, y sacrificársele sólo a quien me le dio; y que no otro motivo me entró en religión, no obstante que al desembarazo y quietud que pedía mi estudiosa intención eran repugnantes los ejerci-
180 cios y compañía de una comunidad; y después, en ella, sabe el Señor, y lo sabe en el mundo quien sólo lo debió saber, lo que intenté en orden a esconder mi nombre, y que no me lo

munion and hear Mass, so that it troubles me little if at all. For in such matters, according to the judgment of the very ones who slander me, I have no obligation to know how nor the skill to hit the mark, and thus if I miss it is neither sin nor discredit. No sin, because I had no obligation; no discredit, because I had no possi- *160* bility of hitting the mark, and *"no one is obliged to do the impossible."* And truth to tell, I have never written save when pressed and forced and solely to give pleasure to others, not only without taking satisfaction but with downright aversion, because I have never judged myself to possess the rich trove of learning and wit that is perforce the obligation of one who writes. This, then, is my usual reply to those who urge me to write, and the more so in the case of a sacred subject: What understanding do I possess, what studies, what subject matter, or what instruction, save four profundities of a superficial scholar?* They can leave such things *170* to those who understand them; as for me, I want no trouble with the Holy Office, for I am but ignorant and tremble lest I utter some ill-sounding proposition or twist the true meaning of some passage. I do not study in order to write, nor far less in order to teach (which would be boundless arrogance in me), but simply to see whether by studying I may become less ignorant. This is my answer, and these are my feelings.

My writing has never proceeded from any dictate of my own, (6) but a force beyond me; I can in truth say, *"You have compelled me."* One thing, however, is true, so that I shall not deny it (first *180* because it is already well known to all, and second because God has shown me His favor in giving me the greatest possible love of truth, even when it might count against me). For ever since the light of reason first dawned in me, my inclination to letters was marked by such passion and vehemence that neither the reprimands of others (for I have received many) nor reflections of my own (there have been more than a few) have sufficed to make me abandon my pursuit of this native impulse that God Himself bestowed on me. His Majesty knows why and to what end He did so, and He knows that I have prayed that He snuff out the *190* light of my intellect, leaving only enough to keep His Law. For more than that is too much, some would say, in a woman; and there are even those who say that it is harmful. His Majesty knows too that, not achieving this, I have attempted to entomb my intellect together with my name and to sacrifice it to the One who gave it to me; and that no other motive brought me to the life of Religion, despite the fact that the exercises and companionship of a community were quite opposed to the tranquillity and free-

permitió, diciendo que era tentación; y sí sería. Si yo pudiera
pagaros algo de lo que os debo, Señora mía, creo que sólo os
pagara en contaros esto, pues no ha salido de mi boca jamás,
excepto para quien debió salir.* Pero quiero que con haberos
franqueado de par en par las puertas de mi corazón, hacién-
doos patentes sus más sellados secretos, conozcáis que no des-
dice de mi confianza lo que debo a vuestra venerable persona
190 y excesivos favores.

(7)   *Prosiguiendo en* la narración de mi inclinación, de que os
quiero dar entera noticia, digo que no había cumplido los tres
años de mi edad cuando enviando mi madre a una hermana
mía, mayor que yo, a que se enseñase a leer en una de las que
llaman Amigas,* me llevó a mí tras ella el cariño y la travesura;
y viendo que la daban lección, me encendí yo de manera en
el deseo de saber leer, que engañando, a mi parecer, a la maestra, la dije que mi madre ordenaba me diese lección. Ella no
lo creyó, porque no era creíble; pero, por complacer al donaire,
200 me la dio. Proseguí yo en ir y ella prosiguió en enseñarme, ya
no de burlas, porque la desengañó la experiencia; y supe leer
en tan breve tiempo, que ya sabía cuando lo supo mi madre,
a quien la maestra lo ocultó por darle el gusto por entero y
recibir el galardón por junto; y yo lo callé, creyendo que me
azotarían por haberlo hecho sin orden. Aún vive la que me enseñó (Dios la guarde), y puede testificarlo.

(8)   Acuérdome que en estos tiempos, siendo mi golosina la que
es ordinaria en aquella edad, me abstenía de comer queso, porque oí decir que hacía rudos, y podía conmigo más el deseo
210 de saber que el de comer, siendo éste tan poderoso en los ni-
ños. Teniendo yo después como seis o siete años, y sabiendo
ya leer y escribir, con todas las otras habilidades de labores
y costuras que deprenden las mujeres, oí decir que había
Universidad y Escuelas en que se estudiaban las ciencias, en
Méjico; y apenas lo oí cuando empecé a matar a mi madre con
instantes e importunos ruegos sobre que, mudándome el traje,
me enviase a Méjico, en casa de unos deudos que tenía, para
estudiar y cursar la Universidad;* ella no lo quiso hacer, e hizo
muy bien, pero yo despiqué el deseo en leer muchos libros
220 varios que tenía mi abuelo, sin que bastasen castigos ni reprensiones a estorbarlo; de manera que cuando vine a Méjico, se

dom from disturbance required by my studious bent. And once in the community, the Lord knows – and in this world only he who needs must know it, does – what I did to try to conceal my name and renown from the public; he did not, however, allow me to do this, telling me it was temptation, and so it would have been. If I could repay any part of my debt to you, my Lady, I believe I might do so merely by informing you of this, for these words have never left my mouth save to that one to whom they must be said.* But having thrown wide the doors of my heart and revealed to you what is there under seal of secrecy, I want you to know that this confidence does not gainsay the respect I owe to your venerable person and excessive favors.

To go on with the narration of this inclination of mine, of (7) which I wish to give you a full account: I declare I was not yet three years old when my mother sent off one of my sisters, older than I, to learn to read in one of those girls' schools that they call *Amigas.** Affection and mischief carried me after her; and when I saw that they were giving her lessons, I so caught fire with the desire to learn that, deceiving the teacher (or so I thought), I told her that my mother wanted her to teach me also. She did not believe this, for it was not to be believed; but to humor my whim she gave me lessons. I continued to go and she continued to teach me, though no longer in make-believe, for the experience undeceived her. I learned to read in such a short time that I already knew how by the time my mother heard of it. My teacher had kept it from my mother to give delight with a thing all done and to receive a prize for a thing done well. And I had kept still, thinking I would be whipped for having done this without permission. The woman who taught me (may God keep her) is still living, and she can vouch for what I say.

I remember that in those days, though I was as greedy for treats (8) as children usually are at that age, I would abstain from eating cheese, because I heard tell that it made people stupid, and the desire to learn was stronger for me than the desire to eat – powerful as this is in children. Later, when I was six or seven years old and already knew how to read and write, along with all the other skills like embroidery and sewing that women learn, I heard that in Mexico City there were a University and Schools where they studied the sciences. As soon as I heard this I began to slay my poor mother with insistent and annoying pleas, begging her to dress me in men's clothes and send me to the capital, to the home of some relatives she had there, so that I could enter the University and study.* She refused, and was right in doing

sacrificies for education

200

220

230

240

admiraban, no tanto del ingenio, cuanto de la memoria y noticias que tenía en edad que parecía que apenas había tenido tiempo para aprender a hablar.

(9)   Empecé a deprender gramática, en que creo no llegaron a veinte las lecciones que tomé;* y era tan intenso mi cuidado, que siendo así que en las mujeres −y más en tan florida juventud− es tan apreciable el adorno natural del cabello, yo me cortaba de él cuatro o seis dedos, midiendo hasta dónde 230 llegaba antes, e imponiéndome ley de que si cuando volviese a crecer hasta allí no sabía tal o tal cosa que me había propuesto deprender en tanto que crecía, me lo había de volver a cortar en pena de la rudeza. Sucedía así que él crecía y yo no sabía lo propuesto, porque el pelo crecía aprisa y yo aprendía despacio, y con efecto le cortaba en pena de la rudeza: que no me parecía razón que estuviese vestida de cabellos cabeza que estaba tan desnuda de noticias, que era más apetecible adorno. Entréme religiosa, porque aunque conocía que tenía el estado cosas (de las accesorias hablo, no de las formales), muchas 240 repugnantes a mi genio,* con todo, para la total negación que tenía al matrimonio,* era lo menos desproporcionado y lo más decente que podía elegir en materia de la seguridad que deseaba de mi salvación;* a cuyo primer respeto (como al fin más importante) cedieron y sujetaron la cerviz todas las impertinencillas de mi genio, que eran de querer vivir sola; de no querer tener ocupación obligatoria que embarazase la libertad de mi estudio, ni rumor de comunidad que impidiese el sosegado silencio de mis libros. Esto me hizo vacilar algo en la determinación, hasta que alumbrándome personas doctas de que 250 era tentación, la vencí con el favor divino, y tomé el estado que tan indignamente tengo. Pensé yo que huía de mí misma, pero ¡miserable de mí! trájeme a mí conmigo y traje mi mayor enemigo en esta inclinación, que no sé determinar si por prenda o castigo me dio el Cielo, pues de apagarse o embarazarse con tanto ejercicio que la religión tiene, reventaba como pólvora, y se verificaba en mí el *privatio est causa appetitus*.

(10)   Volví (mal dije, pues nunca cesé); proseguí, digo, a la estudiosa tarea (que para mí era descanso en todos los ratos que sobraban a mi obligación) de leer y más leer, de estudiar y más 260 estudiar, sin más maestro que los mismos libros. Ya se ve cuán

so; but I quenched my desire by reading a great variety of books that belonged to my grandfather, and neither punishments nor scoldings could prevent me. And so when I did go to Mexico City, people marveled not so much at my intelligence as at my memory and the facts I knew at an age when it seemed I had scarcely had time to learn to speak.

I began to study Latin, in which I believe I took fewer than (9) twenty lessons.* And my interest was so intense, that although in women (and especially in the very bloom of youth) the natural adornment of the hair is so esteemed, I would cut off four to six 250 fingerlengths of my hair, measuring how long it had been before. And I made myself a rule that if by the time it had grown back to the same length I did not know such and such a thing that I intended to study, then I would cut my hair off again to punish my dull-wittedness. And so my hair grew, but I did not yet know what I had resolved to learn, for it grew quickly and I learned slowly. Then I cut my hair right off to punish my dull-wittedness, for I did not think it reasonable that hair should cover a head that was so bare of facts—the more desirable adornment. I took the veil because, although I knew I would find in religious life many 260 things that would be quite opposed to my character* (I speak of accessory rather than essential matters), it would, given my ab- solute unwillingness to enter into marriage,* be the least unfit- ting and the most decent state I could choose, with regard to the assurance I desired of my salvation.* For before this first concern (which is, at the last, the most important), all the impertinent lit- tle follies of my character gave way and bowed to the yoke. These were wanting to live alone and not wanting to have either obliga- tions that would disturb my freedom to study or the noise of a community that would interrupt the tranquil silence of my books. 270 These things made me waver somewhat in my decision until, be- ing enlightened by learned people as to my temptation, I van- quished it with divine favor and took the state I so unworthily hold. I thought I was fleeing myself, but—woe is me!—I brought myself with me, and brought my greatest enemy in my inclina- tion to study, which I know not whether to take as a Heaven-sent favor or as a punishment. For when snuffed out or hindered with every [spiritual] exercise known to Religion, it exploded like gun- powder; and in my case the saying *privation gives rise to appetite* was proven true. 280

I went back (no, I spoke incorrectly, for I never stopped)—I went (10) on, I mean, with my studious task (which to me was peace and rest in every moment left over when my duties were done) of read-

duro es estudiar en aquellos carácteres sin alma, careciendo de la voz viva y explicación del maestro; pues todo este trabajo sufría yo muy gustosa por amor de las letras. ¡Oh, si hubiese sido por amor de Dios, que era lo acertado, cuánto hubiera merecido! Bien que yo procuraba elevarlo cuanto podía y dirigirlo a su servicio, porque el fin a que aspiraba era a estudiar Teología,* pareciéndome menguada inhabilidad, siendo católica, no saber todo lo que en esta vida se puede alcanzar, por medios naturales, de los divinos misterios; y que siendo
270 monja y no seglar, debía, por el estado eclesiástico, profesar letras; y más siendo hija de un San Jerónimo y de una Santa Paula, que era degenerar de tan doctos padres ser idiota la hija. Esto me proponía yo de mí misma y me parecía razón; si no es que era (y eso es lo más cierto) lisonjear y aplaudir a mi propia inclinación, proponiéndola como obligatorio su propio gusto.

(11)   *Con esto proseguí, dirigiendo siempre, como he dicho, los pasos de mi estudio a la cumbre de la Sagrada Teología; pareciéndome preciso, para llegar a ella, subir por los escalones
280 de las ciencias y artes humanas; porque ¿cómo entenderá el estilo de la Reina de las Ciencias quien aun no sabe el de las ancilas? ¿Cómo sin Lógica sabría yo los métodos generales y particulares con que está escrita la Sagrada Escritura? ¿Cómo sin Retórica entendería sus figuras, tropos y locuciones? ¿Cómo sin Física,* tantas cuestiones naturales de las naturalezas de los animales de los sacrificios, donde se simbolizan tantas cosas ya declaradas, y otras muchas que hay? ¿Cómo si el sanar Saúl al sonido del arpa de David fue virtud y fuerza natural de la música, o sobrenatural que Dios quiso poner en David?
290 ¿Cómo sin Aritmética se podrán entender tantos cómputos de años, de días, de meses, de horas, de hebdómadas tan misteriosas como las de Daniel, y otras para cuya inteligencia es necesario saber las naturalezas, concordancias y propiedades de los números? ¿Cómo sin Geometría se podrán medir el Arca Santa del Testamento y la Ciudad Santa de Jerusalén, cuyas misteriosas mensuras hacen un cubo con todas sus dimensiones, y aquel repartimiento proporcional de todas sus partes tan maravilloso? ¿Cómo sin Arquitectura, el gran Templo de Salomón, donde fue el mismo Dios el artífice que dio la dis-

ing and still more reading, study and still more study, with no teacher besides my books themselves. What a hardship it is to learn from those lifeless letters, deprived of the sound of a teacher's voice and explanations; yet I suffered all these trials most gladly for the love of learning. Oh, if only this had been done for the love of God, as was rightful, think what I should have merited! Nevertheless I did my best to elevate these studies and direct them 290 to His service, for the goal to which I aspired was the study of Theology.* Being a Catholic, I thought it an abject failing not to know everything that can in this life be achieved, through earthly methods, concerning the divine mysteries. And being a nun and not a laywoman, I thought I should, because I was in religious life, profess the study of letters – the more so as the daughter of such as St. Jerome and St. Paula: for it would be a degeneracy for an idiot daughter to proceed from such learned parents. I argued in this way to myself, and I thought my own argument quite reasonable. However, the fact may have been (and this seems most 300 likely) that I was merely flattering and encouraging my own inclination, by arguing that its own pleasure was an obligation.

I went on in this way, always directing each step of my studies, (11) as I have said, toward the summit of Holy Theology; but it seemed to me necessary to ascend by the ladder of the humane arts and sciences in order to reach it; for who could fathom the style of the Queen of Sciences without knowing that of her handmaidens? Without Logic, how should I know the general and specific methods by which Holy Scripture is written? Without Rhetoric, how should I understand its figures, tropes, and locutions? Or 310 how, without Physics or Natural Science, understand all the questions that naturally arise concerning the varied natures of those animals offered in sacrifice, in which a great many things already made manifest are symbolized, and many more besides? How should I know whether Saul's cure at the sound of David's harp was owing to a virtue and power that is natural in Music or owing, instead, to a supernatural power that God saw fit to bestow on David? How without Arithmetic might one understand all those mysterious reckonings of years and days and months and hours and weeks that are found in Daniel and elsewhere, which 320 can be comprehended only by knowing the natures, concordances, and properties of numbers? Without Geometry, how could we take the measure of the Holy Ark of the Covenant or the Holy City of Jerusalem, each of whose mysterious measurements forms a perfect cube uniting their dimensions, and each displaying that most marvelous distribution of the proportions of every part?

importance of science in studying theology

300 posición y la traza, y el Sabio Rey sólo fue sobrestante que la
ejecutó; donde no había basa sin misterio, columna sin sím-
bolo, cornisa sin alusión, arquitrabe sin significado; y así de
otras sus partes, sin que el más mínimo filete estuviese sólo
por el servicio y complemento del Arte, sino simbolizando cosas mayores? ¿Cómo sin grande conocimiento de reglas y partes
de que consta la Historia se entenderán los libros historiales?*
Aquellas recapitulaciones en que muchas veces se pospone en
la narración lo que en el hecho sucedió primero. ¿Cómo sin
grande noticia de ambos Derechos* podrán entenderse los
310 libros legales?* ¿Cómo sin grande erudición tantas cosas de
historias profanas, de que hace mención la Sagrada Escritura;
tantas costumbres de gentiles, tantos ritos, tantas maneras de
hablar? ¿Cómo sin muchas reglas y lección de Santos Padres
se podrá entender la oscura locución de los Profetas? Pues sin
ser muy perito en la Música, ¿cómo se entenderán aquellas
proporciones musicales y sus primores que hay en tantos lugares, especialmente en aquellas peticiones que hizo a Dios
Abraham, por las Ciudades,* de que si perdonaría habiendo
cincuenta justos, y de este número bajó a cuarenta y cinco, que
320 es sesquinona y es como de mi a re; de aquí a cuarenta, que
es sesquioctava y es como de re a mi; de aquí a treinta,
que es sesquitercia, que es la del diatesarón; de aquí a veinte,
que es la proporción sesquiáltera, que es la del diapente; de
aquí a diez, que es la dupla, que es el diapasón; y como no
hay más proporciones armónicas no pasó de ahí? Pues ¿cómo
se podrá entender esto sin Música?* Allá en el Libro de Job
le dice Dios: *Numquid coniungere valebis micantes stellas Pleia-
das, aut gyrum Arcturi poteris dissipare? Numquid producis Luci-
ferum in tempore suo, et Vesperum super filios terrae consurgere
330 facis?*, cuyos términos, sin noticia de Astrología, será imposible entender. Y no sólo estas nobles ciencias; pero no hay arte
mecánica que no se mencione. Y en fin, cómo el Libro* que
comprende todos los libros, y la Ciencia* en que se incluyen
todas las ciencias, para cuya inteligencia todas sirven; y después
de saberlas todas (que ya se ve que no es fácil, ni aun posible)
pide otra circunstancia más que todo lo dicho, que es una con-
tinua oración y pureza de vida, para impetrar de Dios aquella
purgación de ánimo e iluminación de mente que es menester

Without the science of Architecture, how understand the mighty Temple of Solomon—where God Himself was the Draftsman who set forth His arrangement and plan, and the Wise King was but the overseer who carried it out; where there was no foundation without its mystery, nor column without its symbol, nor cornice without its allusion, nor architrave without its meaning, and likewise for every other part, so that even the very least fillet served not only for the support and enhancement of Art, but to symbolize greater things? How, without a thorough knowledge of the order and divisions by which History is composed, is one to understand the Historical Books*—as in those summaries, for example, which often postpone in the narration what happened first in fact? How, without command of the two branches of Law,* should one understand the Books of Law?* Without considerable erudition, how should we understand the great many matters of profane history that are mentioned by Holy Scripture: all the diverse customs of the Gentiles, all their rituals, all their manners of speech? Without knowing many precepts and reading widely in the Fathers of the Church, how could one understand the obscure sayings of the Prophets? Well then, and without being expert in Music, how might one understand those musical intervals and their perfections that occur in a great many passages—especially in Abraham's petitions to God on behalf of the Cities,* beseeching God to spare them if there were found fifty righteous people within? And the number fifty Abraham reduced to forty-five, which is sesquinonal [10 to 9] or like the interval from mi to re; this in turn he reduced to forty, which is the sesquioctave [9 to 8] or like the interval from re to mi; thence he went down to thirty, which is sesquitertia, or the interval of the diatessaron [the perfect fourth]; thence to twenty, the sesquialtera or the diapente [the fifth]; thence to ten, the duple, which is the diapason [the interval and consonance of the octave]; and because there are no more harmonic intervals, Abraham went no further. How could all this be understood without knowledge of Music?* Why, in the very Book of Job, God says to him: *"Shalt thou be able to join together the shining stars the Pleiades, or canst thou stop the turning about of Arcturus? Canst thou bring forth the day star in its time, and make the evening star to rise upon the children of the earth?"* Without knowledge of Astronomy, these terms would be impossible to understand. Nor are these noble sciences alone represented; indeed, not one of the mechanical arts escapes mention. In sum, we see how this Book* contains all books, and this Science* includes all sciences, all of which serve that She may

330

340

350

360

[handwritten annotation] explains why it is necessary for her to study all the sciences to understand theology

para la inteligencia de cosas tan altas; y si esto falta, nada sirve
340 de lo demás.

(12)   Del Angélico Doctor Santo Tomás dice la Iglesia estas
palabras: *In difficultatibus locorum Sacrae Scripturae ad oratio-
nem ieiunium adhibebat. Quin etiam sodali suo Frati Reginaldo
dicere solebat, quidquid sciret, non tam studio, aut labore suo
peperisse, quam divinitus traditum accepisse.* Pues yo, tan distante de la virtud y las letras, ¿cómo había de tener ánimo para
escribir? Y así por tener algunos principios granjeados, estudiaba continuamente diversas cosas, sin tener para alguna particular inclinación, sino para todas en general; por lo cual, el
350 haber estudiado en unas más que en otras, no ha sido en mí
elección, sino que el acaso de haber topado más a mano libros
de aquellas facultades les ha dado, sin arbitrio mío, la preferen-
cia. Y como no tenía interés que me moviese, ni límite de tiempo que me estrechase el continuado estudio de una cosa por
la necesidad de los grados, casi a un tiempo estudiaba diversas cosas o dejaba unas por otras; bien que en eso observaba
orden, porque a unas llamaba estudio y a otras diversión; y
en éstas descansaba de las otras: de donde se sigue que he estudiado muchas cosas y nada sé, porque las unas han embaraza-
360 do a las otras. Es verdad que esto digo de la parte práctica en
las que la tienen, porque claro está que mientras se mueve la
pluma descansa el compás y mientras se toca el arpa sosiega
el órgano, *et sic de caeteris;* porque como es menester mucho
uso corporal para adquirir hábito, nunca le puede tener per-
fecto quien se reparte en varios ejercicios; pero en lo formal
y especulativo sucede al contrario, y quisiera yo persuadir a
todos con mi experiencia a que no sólo no estorban, pero se
ayudan dando luz y abriendo camino las unas para las otras,
por variaciones y ocultos engarces – que para esta cadena
370 universal les puso la sabiduría de su Autor –, de manera que
parece se corresponden y están unidas con admirable trabazón
y concierto. Es la cadena que fingieron los antiguos que salía
de la boca de Júpiter,* de donde pendían todas las cosas es-
labonadas unas con otras. Así la demuestra el R. P. Atanasio
Quirquerio en su curioso libro *De Magnete.* Todas las cosas salen de Dios, que es el centro a un tiempo y la circunferencia
de donde salen y donde paran todas las líneas criadas.

be understood. And once each science is mastered (which we see 370
is not easy, or even possible), She demands still another condi-
tion beyond all I have yet said, which is continual prayer and purity of life, to entreat God for that cleansing of the spirit and
illumination of the mind required for an understanding of such
high things. And if this be lacking, all the rest is useless.

The Church says these words of the Angelic Doctor, St. Thomas (12)
Aquinas: *"At the difficult passages of Holy Scripture, he added fast-*
ing to prayer. And he used to say to his companion Brother Reginald
that he owed all his knowledge not so much to study or hard work,
but rather he had received it from God." How then should I, so far 380
from either virtue or learning, find the courage to write? And so,
to acquire a few basic principles of knowledge, I studied con-
stantly in a variety of subjects, having no inclination toward any
one of them in particular but being drawn rather to all of them
generally. Therefore, if I have studied some things more than
others it has not been by my choice, but because by chance the
books on certain subjects came more readily to hand, and this
gave preference to those topics, without my passing judgment in
the matter. I held no particular interest to spur me, nor had I any
limit to my time compelling me to reduce the continuous study 390
of one subject, as is required in taking a degree. Thus almost at
one sitting I would study diverse things or leave off some to take
up others. Yet even in this I maintained a certain order, for some
subjects I called my study and others my diversion, and with the
latter I would take my rest from the former. Hence, I have studied
many things but know nothing, for one subject has interfered with
another. What I say is true regarding the practical element of those
subjects that require practice, for clearly the compass must rest
while the pen is moving, and while the harp is playing the organ
is still, *and likewise with all things.* Much bodily repetition is needed 400
to form a habit, and therefore a person whose time is divided
among several exercises will never develop one perfectly. But in
formal and speculative arts the opposite is true, and I wish I might
persuade everyone with my own experience: to wit, that far from
interfering, these subjects help one another, shedding light and
opening a path from one to the next, by way of divergences and
hidden links – for they were set in place so as to form this universal chain by the wisdom of their great Author. Thus it appears
that they correspond each one to another and are united with a
wondrous bond and harmonious agreement. This is the very chain 410
the ancients believed to come forth from the mouth of Jupiter,*
whence hung all things, each linked to the next. The Reverend

(13)   Yo de mí puedo asegurar que lo que no entiendo en un autor de una facultad, lo suelo entender en otro de otra que parece
380 muy distante; y esos propios, al explicarse, abren ejemplos
metafóricos de otras artes: como cuando dicen los lógicos que
el medio se ha con los términos como se ha una medida con
dos cuerpos distantes, para conferir si son iguales o no; y que
la oración del lógico anda como la línea recta, por el camino
más breve, y la del retórico se mueve, como la corva, por el
más largo, pero van a un mismo punto los dos; y cuando dicen
que los expositores* son como la mano abierta y los
escolásticos* como el puño cerrado. Y así no es disculpa, ni
por tal la doy, el haber estudiado diversas cosas, pues éstas
390 antes se ayudan, sino que el no haber aprovechado ha sido in-
eptitud mía y debilidad de mi entendimiento, no culpa de la
variedad. Lo que sí pudiera ser descargo mío es el sumo trabajo
no sólo en carecer de maestro,* sino de condiscípulos con
quienes conferir y ejercitar lo estudiado, teniendo sólo por
maestro un libro mudo, por condiscípulo un tintero insensi-
ble; y en vez de explicación y ejercicio, muchos estorbos, no
sólo los de mis religiosas obligaciones (que éstas ya se sabe cuán
útil y provechosamente gastan el tiempo) sino de aquellas cosas accesorias de una comunidad: como estar yo leyendo y an-
400 tojárseles en la celda vecina tocar y cantar; estar yo estudiando
y pelear dos criadas y venirme a constituir juez de su penden-
cia; estar yo escribiendo y venir una amiga a visitarme, ha-
ciéndome muy mala obra con muy buena voluntad, donde es
preciso no sólo admitir el embarazo, pero quedar agradecida
del perjuicio. Y esto es continuamente, porque como los ratos
que destino a mi estudio son los que sobran de lo regular de
la comunidad, esos mismos les sobran a las otras para venirme
a estorbar; y sólo saben cuánta verdad es ésta los que tienen
experiencia de vida común, donde sólo la fuerza de la voca-
410 ción puede hacer que mi natural esté gustoso, y el mucho amor
que hay entre mí y mis amadas hermanas, que como el amor
es unión, no hay para él extremos distantes.
(14)   En esto sí confieso que ha sido inexplicable mi trabajo; y así
no puedo decir lo que con envidia oigo a otros: que no les ha
costado afán el saber. ¡Dichosos ellos! A mí, no el saber (que
aún no sé), sólo el desear saber me le ha costado tan grande

Athanasius Kircher demonstrates this in his curious book *On the Magnet*. All things proceed from God, who is at once the center and circumference, whence all lines are begotten and where they have their end.

For my part, I can say with certainty that what I do not under- (13) stand in one author on a certain subject, I usually understand in another author who treats what appears to be a very distant sub- ject. And in turn these very authors, once understood, can un- 420 lock the metaphorical examples employed in still other arts: as when the logicians say, to compare whether terms are equal, that the middle term is to the major and minor terms as a measuring rod is to two distant bodies; or that the argument of the logician moves like a straight line by the shortest path, while that of the rhetorician moves like a curved line by the longest path, but both end at last at the same point; or when it is said that the Expositors* are like an open hand, while the Scholastics* are like a closed fist. And thus it serves as no excuse, nor do I intend it as such, that I have studied diverse things, for indeed these aid one another. 430 Rather, my lack of profit in it is the fault of my ineptitude and the weakness of my mind, not the fault of variety. What could, however, serve to excuse me would be the great trial I have un- dergone in lacking not only a teacher,* but schoolfellows with whom to review and practice what had been studied. For my only teacher was a mute book, my only schoolfellow an unfeeling ink- well. And instead of explanations and exercises I had interrup- tions, posed not only by my religious duties (for it is well known how usefully and beneficially these take up one's time), but by all those other things incidental to life in a community: as when 440 I would be reading and the nuns in the next cell would have a notion to sing and play; or I would be reading and two maid- servants, arguing, would come to appoint me arbiter in their dis- pute; again, as I was writing, a friend would come to visit me, doing me a very bad turn with very good intentions, so that one must not only make way for the interruption but give thanks for the harm done. And it is always so, for the times I devote to study are usually those left over when observance of the Rule of the community is fulfilled, and the same time is left to the other nuns to come and interrupt me. The truth of this can be known only 450 to those who have experienced life in community, where the strength of my vocation alone assures that my nature can find enjoyment, together with the great love that exists between me and my dear sisters. For as love itself is union, it admits no dis- tant extremes.

The Answer

59

*how all her studies /citations made her credible → a man his well-studied would have been considered brilliant

que pudiera decir con mi Padre San Jerónimo (aunque no con su aprovechamiento): *Quid ibi laboris insumpserim, quid sustinuerim difficultatis, quoties desperaverim, quotiesque cessaverim*
420 *et contentione discendi rursus inceperim; testis est conscientia, tam mea, qui passus sum, quam eorum qui mecum duxerunt vitam.* Menos los compañeros y testigos (que aun de ese alivio he carecido), lo demás bien puedo asegurar con verdad. ¡Y que haya sido tal esta mi negra inclinación, que todo lo haya vencido!

(15)   Solía sucederme que, como entre otros beneficios, debo a Dios un natural tan blando y tan afable y las religiosas me aman mucho por él (sin reparar, como buenas, en mis faltas) y con esto gustan mucho de mi compañía, conociendo esto y movi-
430 da del grande amor que las tengo, con mayor motivo que ellas a mí, gusto más de la suya: así, me solía ir los ratos que a unas y a otras nos sobraban, a consolarlas y recrearme con su conversación.* Reparé que en este tiempo hacía falta a mi estudio, y hacía voto de no entrar en celda alguna si no me obligase a ello la obediencia o la caridad: porque, sin este freno tan duro, al de sólo propósito le rompiera el amor; y este voto (conociendo mi fragilidad) le hacía por un mes o por quince días; y dando cuando se cumplía, un día o dos de treguas, lo volvía a renovar, sirviendo este día, no tanto a mi descanso (pues nunca
440 lo ha sido para mí el no estudiar) cuanto a que no me tuviesen por áspera, retirada e ingrata al no merecido cariño de mis carísimas hermanas.

(16)   *Bien se deja en esto conocer cuál es la fuerza de mi inclinación. Bendito sea Dios que quiso fuese hacia las letras y no hacia otro vicio, que fuera en mí casi insuperable; y bien se infiere también cuán contra la corriente han navegado (o por mejor decir, han naufragado) mis pobres estudios. Pues aún falta por referir lo más arduo de las dificultades; que las de hasta aquí sólo han sido estorbos obligatorios y casuales, que
450 indirectamente lo son; y faltan los positivos que directamente han tirado a estorbar y prohibir el ejercicio. ¿Quién no creerá, viendo tan generales aplausos,* que he navegado viento en popa y mar en leche, sobre las palmas de las aclamaciones comunes? Pues Dios sabe que no ha sido muy así, porque entre las flores de esas mismas aclamaciones se han levantado y

In this respect, I do confess that the trial I have undergone has (14) been beyond all telling; and thus I cannot confirm what I have, with envy, heard others say: that learning has cost them no drudgery. How lucky they are! For me, it has not been knowledge (for I still know nothing) but the desire to know that has cost me so 460 dear that I might truly say, like my good Father St. Jerome (though not with the benefit he offers): *"What efforts I spent on that task, what difficulties I had to face, how often I despaired, how often I gave up and then in my eagerness to learn began again, my own knowledge can witness from personal experience and those can testify who were then living with me."* Save for the mention of companions and witnesses (for I have lacked even this mitigation), I can in all truth affirm the rest of his words. And to think that this, my wicked inclination, should be such, that it has vanquished all before it!

It has often befallen me – for among other favors I owe to God (15) a nature that is mild and affable; and the nuns, good creatures that they are, love me very much on this account and take no note of my failings, and so they delight in my company. Knowing this, and moved by the great love I bear them with more cause than theirs for me, I take even greater delight in their company. – And so, as I say, in the times they and I have not been occupied, I have often gone to offer them comfort and to find recreation in their conversation.* I began to notice that I was stealing this time away from my studies, and I made a vow not to step into another nun's cell unless I were thus obliged by obedience or charity to 480 do so; for unless I reined myself in this harshly, love would burst the restraint exerted by my intent alone. Thus, knowing my own weakness, I would hold to this vow for a month or a fortnight; and when it was done, I gave myself a truce of a day or two before I renewed it. That day would serve not so much to give me rest (for to desist from study has never been restful for me), but so that I might not be thought gruff, withdrawn, and ungrateful in the face of the undeserved affection of my most beloved sisters.

*This shows all too well just how great is the strength of my (16) inclination. May God be praised that He inclined me to letters 490 and not some other vice, which would have been, in my case, nearly insurmountable. And from this, too, it may well be inferred just how my poor studies have found their way (or, to be more exact, have foundered) in steering against the current. For I have yet to tell the most strenuous of my difficulties. Those accounted for to this point have been no more than hindrances caused by my obligations or by chance, posed indirectly; they are not purposeful obstacles directly aimed at impeding and prohibiting my

despertado tales áspides de emulaciones y persecuciones, cuantas no podré contar, y los que más nocivos y sensibles para mí han sido, no son aquéllos que con declarado odio y malevolencia me han perseguido, sino los que amándome y
460 deseando mi bien* (y por ventura, mereciendo mucho con Dios por la buena intención), me han mortificado y atormentado más que los otros, con aquel: *No conviene a la santa ignorancia que deben, este estudio; se ha de perder, se ha de desvanecer en tanta altura con su misma perspicacia y agudeza.* * ¿Qué me habrá costado resistir esto? ¡Rara especie de martirio donde yo era el mártir y me era el verdugo!*

(17)   Pues por la —en mí dos veces infeliz*— habilidad de hacer versos, aunque fuesen sagrados, ¿qué pesadumbres no me han dado o cuáles no me han dejado de dar? Cierto, señora mía,
470 que algunas veces me pongo a considerar que el que se señala* —o le señala Dios, que es quien sólo lo puede hacer— es recibido como enemigo común, porque parece a algunos que usurpa los aplausos que ellos merecen o que hace estanque de las admiraciones a que aspiraban, y así le persiguen.

(18)   Aquella ley políticamente bárbara de Atenas, por la cual salía desterrado de su república el que se señalaba en prendas y virtudes porque no tiranizase con ellas la libertad pública, todavía dura, todavía se observa en nuestros tiempos, aunque no hay ya aquel motivo de los atenienses; pero hay otro, no
480 menos eficaz aunque no tan bien fundado, pues parece máxima del impío Maquiavelo: que es aborrecer al que se señala porque desluce a otros. Así sucede y así sucedió siempre.

(19)   *Y si no, ¿cuál fue la causa de aquel rabioso odio de los fariseos contra Cristo, habiendo tantas razones para lo contrario? Porque si miramos su presencia,* ¿cuál prenda más amable que aquella divina hermosura? ¿Cuál más poderosa para arrebatar los corazones? Si cualquiera belleza humana tiene jurisdicción sobre los albedríos y con blanda y apetecida violencia los sabe sujetar, ¿qué haría aquélla con tantas prerrogati-
490 vas y dotes soberanos? ¿Qué haría, qué movería y qué no haría y qué no movería aquella incomprensible beldad, por cuyo hermoso rostro, como por un terso cristal se estaban transparentando los rayos de la Divinidad? ¿Qué no movería aquel semblante, que sobre incomparables perfecciones en lo

training. Who would not think, upon hearing such widespread applause,* that I had sailed before the wind with a sea smooth 500 as glass, upon the cheers of universal acclaim? Yet God Himself knows it has not quite been so, because among the blossoms of that very acclaim there have roused themselves and reared up the asps of rivalry and persecution, more than I could possibly count. And the most venomous and hurtful to me have not been those who with explicit hatred and ill-will have persecuted me, but those persons, loving me and desiring my good* (and, there-fore, greatly deserving before God for their good intentions), who have mortified and tormented me more than any others, with these words: *"All this study is not fitting, for holy ignorance is your* 510 *duty; she shall go to perdition, she shall surely be cast down from such heights by that same wit and cleverness."** How was I to bear up against this? A strange martyrdom indeed, where I must be both martyr and my own executioner!*

Well, as for this aptitude at composing verses – which is dou- (17) bly unfortunate,* in my case, even should they be sacred verses – what unpleasantness have they not caused me, and indeed do they not still cause? Truly, my Lady, at times I ponder how it is that a person who achieves high significance* – or rather, who is grant-ed significance by God, for He alone can do this – is received as 520 the common enemy. For that person seems to others to usurp the applause they deserve or to draw off and dam up the admiration to which they had aspired, and so they persecute that person.

That politically barbarous law of Athens remains in effect, (18) whereby anyone possessing significant qualities and virtues was expelled from the republic to prevent his using them for the sub-jugation of public liberty; it is still observed in our own times, though no longer for the same reason the Athenians held. But now there is another motive, no less potent though less well founded, for it resembles a maxim of that impious Machiavelli: to abhor 530 the person who becomes significant because that one tarnishes the fame of others.

What else but this could cause that furious hatred of the (19) Pharisees against Christ, when there were so many reasons to feel the opposite? If we consider Christ's bodily form, what quality could be more worthy of love than His divine beauty? What could bear off our hearts more powerfully? For if any human beauty whatsoever can hold sway over our fancies and enthrall them with gentle and ravishing force, then what indeed might that other beauty accomplish, with so many sovereign powers and perfec- 540 tions? What could it do and move us to do, what could it not do

humano, señalaba iluminaciones de divino? Si el de Moisés, de sólo la conversación con Dios, era intolerable* a la flaqueza de la vista humana, ¿qué sería el del mismo Dios humanado? Pues si vamos a las demás prendas, ¿cuál más amable que aquella celestial modestia, que aquella suavidad y blandura

500 derramando misericordias en todos sus movimientos, aquella profunda humildad y mansedumbre, aquellas palabras de vida eterna y eterna sabiduría? Pues ¿cómo es posible que esto no les arrebatara las almas, que no fuesen enamorados y elevados tras él?

(20) Dice la Santa Madre y madre mía Teresa,* que después que vio la hermosura de Cristo quedó libre de poderse inclinar a criatura alguna, porque ninguna cosa veía que no fuese fealdad, comparada con aquella hermosura. Pues ¿cómo en los hombres hizo tan contrarios efectos? Y ya que como toscos y

510 viles no tuvieran conocimiento ni estimación de sus perfecciones, siquiera como interesables ¿no les moviera sus propias conveniencias y utilidades en tantos beneficios como les hacía, sanando los enfermos, resucitando los muertos, curando los endemoniados? Pues ¿cómo no le amaban? ¡Ay Dios, que por eso mismo no le amaban, por eso mismo le aborrecían! Así lo testificaron ellos mismos.

(21) Júntanse en su concilio y dicen: *Quid facimus, quia hic homo multa signa facit?* ¿Hay tal causa? Si dijeran: éste es un malhechor, un transgresor de la ley, un alborotador que con en-

520 gaños alborota el pueblo, mintieran, como mintieron cuando lo decían; pero eran causales más congruentes a lo que solicitaban, que era quitarle la vida; mas dar por causal que hace cosas señaladas, no parece de hombres doctos, cuales eran los fariseos. Pues así es, que cuando se apasionan los hombres doctos prorrumpen en semejantes inconsecuencias. En verdad que sólo por eso salió determinado que Cristo muriese. Hombres, si es que así se os puede llamar, siendo tan brutos, ¿por qué es esa tan cruel determinación? No responden más sino que *multa signa facit.* ¡Válgame Dios, que el hacer cosas

530 señaladas es causa para que uno muera! Haciendo reclamo este *multa signa facit* a aquel: *radix Iesse, qui stat in signum populorum,* y al otro: *in signum cui contradicetur.* ¿Por pues signo? ¡Pues muera! ¿Señalado? ¡Pues padezca, que eso es el premio de quien se señala!

or fail to move us to do, that unfathomable beauty through whose fair face, as through a polished glass, there shone unclouded the brilliant beams of Divinity? What could that countenance not inspire, in which far beyond incomparable human perfections there shone luminous signs of divine radiance? If the face of Moses, after no more than a conversation with God, became intolerable* to the frailty of human sight, what must occur with the very face of God Himself made human? And if we go on to His other qualities, what could be more worthy of love than that heavenly 550 modesty, that gentle softness pouring out mercies in all His movements, that depth of humility and meekness, those words of eternal life and eternal wisdom? Then how could this fail to bear off every soul? How could any fail to follow, loving and uplifted, behind Him?

Our Holy Mother, my own mother Teresa,* says that from the (20) time she beheld the beauty of Christ she was freed of the possibility of inclination toward any earthly creature, for she could see nothing that was not ugliness compared to such beauty. Then how could it work such opposite effects in men? And since, being crude 560 and base men, they could form no understanding nor measure of His perfections, why then in mere self-interest were they not moved by their own advantage and by the profit to them entailed in the many benefits He proffered, when He made the sick healthy, revived the dead, and cast out devils from those possessed? How then could they not love Him? Dear God, it was for this very reason they did not love Him. It was for this that they despised him!

They gathered in their council and declared: *"What do we, for* (21) *this man doth many miracles?"* Can such a thing be cause for accu- 570 sation? If they had said, "This man is a malefactor, a transgressor against the law, a troublemaker who with his deceits stirs up the people," they would have lied; indeed, they did lie when they said those very things. Yet those accusations at least presented cause more suited to the end they proposed, which was to take His life. No, to state as cause that He worked miracles seems unfitting in learned men, and such were the Pharisees. But this is the way of things, for when learned men fall prey to passion they burst out illogically in just this fashion. In truth, it was concluded for this reason alone that Christ must die. O men – if such you may 580 be called, being so brutish – why do you reach such a cruel decision? They answer only, *"He doth many miracles."* May God preserve me if working signs and miracles is cause that one should die! This saying, *"He doth signs and miracles"* calls forth that earli-

(22)   *Suelen en la eminencia de los templos colocarse por adorno unas figuras de los Vientos y de la Fama, y por defenderlas
de las aves, las llenan todas de púas; defensa parece y no es
sino propiedad forzosa: no puede estar sin púas que la pun-
cen quien está en alto. Allí está la ojeriza del aire; allí es el
540 rigor de los elementos; allí despican la cólera los rayos; allí es
el blanco de piedras y flechas. ¡Oh infeliz altura, expuesta a
tantos riesgos! ¡Oh signo que te ponen por blanco de la envidia
y por objeto de la contradicción! Cualquiera eminencia, ya sea
de dignidad, ya de nobleza, ya de riqueza, ya de hermosura,
ya de ciencia, padece esta pensión; pero la que con más rigor
la experimenta es la del entendimiento. Lo primero, porque
es el más indefenso, pues la riqueza y el poder castigan a quien
se les atreve, y el entendimiento no, pues mientras es mayor
es más modesto y sufrido y se defiende menos. Lo segundo
550 es porque, como dijo doctamente Gracián, las ventajas en el
entendimiento lo son en el ser.* No por otra razón es el ángel
más que el hombre que porque entiende más; no es otro el
exceso que el hombre hace al bruto, sino sólo entender; y así
como ninguno quiere ser menos que otro, así ninguno confiesa
que otro entiende mas, porque es consecuencia del ser más.
Sufrirá uno y confesará que otro es más noble que él, que es
más rico, que es más hermoso y aun que es más docto; pero
que es más entendido apenas habrá quien lo confiese: *Rarus
est, qui velit cedere ingenio.* Por eso es tan eficaz la batería con-
560 tra esta prenda.
(23)   *Cuando los soldados hicieron burla, entretenimiento y
diversión de Nuestro Señor Jesucristo, trajeron una púrpura
vieja y una caña hueca y una corona de espinas para coronarle
por rey de burlas. Pues ahora, la caña y la púrpura eran afren-
tosas, pero no dolorosas; pues ¿por qué sólo la corona es doloro-
sa? ¿No basta que, como las demás insignias, fuese de escarnio
e ignominia, pues ése era el fin? No, porque la sagrada cabeza
de Cristo y aquel divino cerebro eran depósito de la sabiduría; y cerebro sabio en el mundo no basta que esté escarneci-
570 do, ha de estar también lastimado y maltratado; cabeza que
es erario de sabiduría no espere otra corona que de espinas.
¿Cuál guirnalda espera la sabiduría humana si ve la que obtu-
vo la divina? Coronaba la soberbia romana las diversas hazañas

er *"root of Jesse, who standeth for an ensign of the people"* and that other *"for a sign which shall be contradicted."* For a sign? Then let him die! Of significance? He must suffer, for that is the prize given one who is thought significant!

Figures of the Winds and of Fame are often placed on the top- (22) most heights of temples as adornments; to defend them from the 590 birds, these images are covered with barbs. This would seem to be a defense, yet it is not, but rather a requisite attribute; for a figure thus standing on high must needs feel those barbs. Up there are felt the grudges of the wind, the severity of the elements. There the rage of the lightning thrusts. Up there is the target of stones and arrows. O, unhappy eminence, exposed to so many risks! O sign and symbol, set on high as a target of envy and an object to be spoken against! These are the wages suffered by eminence, whether of dignity, or nobility, or wealth, or beauty, or learning; but it is high intelligence that experiences all this with greatest 600 force. For in the first place, intelligence lacks defense: wealth and power punish those who confront them, while intelligence does not. Indeed, the greater it is, the more modest and long-suffering intelligence becomes and defends itself less. Secondly, this is be- cause, as Gracián said with great erudition, "The advantages of intelligence are advantages of being." The angel is superior to man for no other reason than that the angel is more intelligent; man surpasses the beast in no other way but intelligence. And thus, as no one wants to be less than another, no one will admit that another is more intelligent, for that follows logically from the 610 other's *being* more. One will suffer the admission that another is nobler than himself, wealthier, more beautiful, and even more learned; but there are few indeed who will admit that another possesses superior powers of mind: *"It is the rare man who will con- cede greater intelligence* [to his friend]." That is why weaponry is so effective against this particular talent.

how people rarely admit that another is more intelligent

*When the soldiers made a mockery, an entertainment, and a (23) diversion of Our Lord Jesus Christ, they brought an old purple cloak and a hollow staff and a crown of thorns to mock Him as king of fools. Now, the cloak and staff were insulting, but they 620 did not cause pain. Why should the crown alone be painful? Was it not enough that, like the other insignia, it should be an emblem of scorn and mockery, since that was their aim? No, because the sacred head of Christ and His divine mind were the storehouse of wisdom. And in this world it is not enough that the wise mind be scorned; it must needs be wounded and beaten. The head that is a treasury of wisdom can hope for no other crown than thorns.

de sus capitanes también con diversas coronas: ya con la cívica al que defendía al ciudadano; ya con la castrense al que entraba en los reales enemigos; ya con la mural al que escalaba el muro; ya con la obsidional al que libraba la ciudad cercada o el ejército sitiado o el campo o en los reales; ya con la naval, ya con la oval, ya con la triunfal otras hazañas, según refieren
580 Plinio y Aulo Gelio; mas viendo yo tantas diferencias de coronas, dudaba de cuál especie sería la de Cristo, y me parece que fue obsidional, que (como sabéis, señora) era la más honrosa y se llamaba obsidional de *obsidio,* que quiere decir cerco; la cual no se hacía de oro ni de plata, sino de la misma grama o yerba que cría el campo en que se hacía la empresa. Y como la hazaña de Cristo fue hacer levantar el cerco al Príncipe de las Tinieblas, el cual tenía sitiada toda la tierra, como lo dice en el libro de Job: *Circuivi terram et ambulavi per eam* y de él dice San Pedro: *Circuit, quaerens quem devoret;* y vino nuestro
590 caudillo y le hizo levantar el cerco: *nunc princeps huius mundi eiicietur foras,* así los soldados le coronaron no con oro ni plata, sino con el fruto natural que producía el mundo que fue el campo de la lid, el cual, después de la maldición, *spinas et tribulos germinabit tibi,* no producía otra cosa que espinas; y así fue propísima corona de ellas en el valeroso y sabio vencedor con que le coronó su madre la Sinagoga;* saliendo a ver el doloroso triunfo, como al del otro Salomón festivas, a éste llorosas las hijas de Sión,* porque es el triunfo de sabio obtenido con dolor y celebrado con llanto, que es el modo de triunfar la
600 sabiduría; siendo Cristo, como rey de ella, quien estrenó la corona, porque santificada en sus sienes, se quite el horror a los otros sabios y entiendan que no han de aspirar a otro honor.
(24)   Quiso la misma Vida ir a dar la vida a Lázaro difunto;* ignoraban los discípulos el intento y le replicaron: *Rabbi, nunc quaerebant te Iudaei lapidare, et iterum vadis illuc?* Satisfizo el Redentor el temor: *Nonne duodecim sunt horae diei?* Hasta aquí, parece que temían porque tenían el antecedente de quererle apedrear porque les había reprendido llamándoles ladrones y no pastores de las ovejas. Y así, temían que si iba a lo mismo
610 (como las reprensiones, aunque sean tan justas, suelen ser mal reconocidas), corriese peligro su vida; pero ya desengañados y enterados de que va a dar vida a Lázaro, ¿cuál es la razón

What wreath can human learning hope for if it sees what is bestowed on the divine? Roman pomp crowned the varied feats of their captains with crowns that were equally varied: the civic 630 crown to one who saved the life of a fellow citizen; the castrensian crown to one who stormed the enemy's camps; the mural crown to one who scaled the walls; the obsidional crown to one who freed the besieged city, an encircled army, or the battlefield or encampment. They rewarded other feats with the naval crown, the oval crown, and the triumphal crown, according to Pliny and Aulus Gellius. But upon seeing so many and diverse crowns, I pondered which sort the crown given to Christ might be; and I think it must be the obsidional crown, which (as you know, my Lady) conferred the greatest honor and was called "obsidional" 640 from *obsidio*, which means "siege." This crown was made neither of gold nor silver, but of the very grasses growing in the field where the brave deed was carried out. And Christ's feat was to raise the siege of the Prince of Darkness, who had encircled the entire earth, as Satan himself says in the Book of Job: *"I have gone round about the earth, and walked through it"*; and as St. Peter says of him: *"Your adversary [the devil] goeth about seeking whom he may devour."* And our Chieftain came, and made Satan raise the siege: *"Now shall the prince of this world be cast out."* Thus, the soldiers crowned Him with neither gold nor silver, but with the plant 650 springing up throughout the world, which was their field of battle. For after the curse, *"Thorns and thistles shall it bring forth to thee,"* this world produced nothing but thorns. And so it was meet and right that His Mother the Synagogue* should crown the brave and wise conquerer with those very thorns. The daughters of Zion went out weeping to see this sorrowful triumph,* as they went gaily to see Solomon triumphant; for the triumph of the wise is won with sorrow and celebrated with tears. This is the way that wisdom triumphs. It was Christ the King of Wisdom who first wore that crown, so that seeing it sanctified upon His brow, all 660 other men of learning might lose their horror of it, and know they need aspire to no other honor.

Our very Life saw fit to go and give new life to dead Lazarus.* (24) The disciples did not know what he intended, and they argued with Him: *"Rabbi, the Jews but now sought to stone thee: and goest thou thither again?"* And the Redeemer made full reply to their foreboding: *"Are there not twelve hours of the day?"* Up to this point in the text, it seems the disciples were afraid because they bore in mind the precedent that some had tried to stone Him because He had rebuked them, calling them thieves and not shepherds of 670

que pudo mover a Tomás para que tomando aquí los alientos que en el huerto Pedro: *Eamus et nos, ut moriamur cum eo.* ¿Qué dices, apóstol santo? A morir no va el Señor, ¿de qué es el recelo? Porque a lo que Cristo va no es a reprender, sino a hacer una obra de piedad, y por esto no le pueden hacer mal. Los mismos judíos* os podían haber asegurado, pues cuando los reconvino queriéndole apedrear: *Multa bona opera ostendi vo-*
620 *bis ex patre meo, propter quod eorum opus me lapidatis?,* le respondieron: *De bono opere non lapidamus te, sed de blasphemia.* Pues si ellos dicen que no le quieren apedrear por las buenas obras y ahora va a hacer una tan buena como dar la vida a Lázaro, ¿de qué es el recelo o por qué? ¿No fuera mejor decir: Vamos a gozar el fruto del agradecimiento de la buena obra que va a hacer nuestro Maestro: a verle aplaudir y rendir gracias al beneficio; a ver las admiraciones que hacen del milagro? Y no decir, al parecer una cosa tan fuera del caso como es: *Eamus et nos, ut moriamur cum eo.* Mas ¡ay! que el Santo temió como
630 discreto y habló como apóstol. ¿No va Cristo a hacer un milagro? Pues ¿qué mayor peligro? Menos intolerable es para la soberbia oír las reprensiones, que para la envidia ver los milagros. En todo lo dicho, venerable señora, no quiero (ni tal desatino cupiera en mí) decir que me han perseguido por saber, sino sólo porque he tenido amor a la sabiduría y a las letras, no porque haya conseguido ni uno ni otro.*

(25)   Hallábase el Príncipe de los Apóstoles, en un tiempo, tan distante de la sabiduría como pondera aquel enfático: *Petrus vero sequebatur eum a longe;* tan lejos de los aplausos de docto quien
640 tenía el título de indiscreto: *Nesciens quid diceret;* y aun examinado del conoçimiento de la sabiduría dijo él mismo que no había alcanzado la menor noticia: *Mulier, nescio quid dicis. Mulier, non novi illum.* Y ¿qué le sucede? Que teniendo estos créditos de ignorante, no tuvo la fortuna, sí las aflicciones, de sabio. ¿Por qué? No se dio otra causal sino: *Et hic cum illo erat.* Era afecto a la sabiduría, llevábale el corazón, andábase tras ella, preciábase de seguidor y amoroso de la sabiduría; y aunque era tan *a longe* que no le comprendía ni alcanzaba, bastó para incurrir sus tormentos. Ni faltó soldado de fuera que no le
650 afligiese, ni mujer doméstica que no le aquejase.* Yo confieso que me hallo muy distante de los términos de la sabiduría y

flocks. And so the disciples feared that if He went back to do the same thing (as rebukes, however just they may be, tend to be ill-received), He would be in danger of His life. But once disabused of the error—knowing that He was going to restore life to Lazarus—what could then stir Thomas, taking courage just as Peter did in the garden, to say: *"Let us also go, that we may die with Him"*? What are you saying, blessed Apostle? The Lord does not go to die; then what is your misgiving? For Christ goes not to rebuke but to perform an act of mercy, and they can do no ill to Him for that. The Jews themselves* could have assured you of this. 680 For when He reproached them for wanting to stone Him, saying, *"Many good works I have shewed you from my Father; for which of those works do you stone me?"* they answered Him: *"For a good work we stone thee not, but for blasphemy."* If the Jews declare that they do not wish to stone Him for good works, and if now He goes to work such great good as to give new life to Lazarus, on what account or to what purpose do you feel such misgiving? Would you not better say, "Let us go taste the fruits of gratitude for the good work our Master will perform; let us go see Him praised and thanked for the favor He gives; let us see how they marvel 690 at His miracle," rather than saying a thing so apparently out of place as *"Let us also go, that we may die with Him"*? But alas, our Saint had the fears of a wise man, and he spoke like a true apostle. Does Christ not set out to work a miracle, a sign? Well then, what greater danger can He risk? Less intolerable is it for pride to hear itself rebuked than for envy to see miracles performed. In all that I have said, my Lady, I do not wish (nor would I be capable of such foolishness) to claim that I have been persecuted because of my knowledge, but rather only because of my love for learning and letters, and not because I had attained either one 700 or the other.*

The Prince of the Apostles once found himself a long way in- (25) deed from Knowledge, as is remarked in the emphatic *"But Peter followed afar off."* A long way from receiving praise as a learned man was he, who once bore the title of unknowing: *"not knowing what he said."* And indeed, when faced with an examination concerning his acquaintance with Knowledge, he himself said he had not acquired the least notion: *"Woman, I know not what thou sayest. Woman, I am not [one of them]."* And what befalls him? Possessing this reputation for ignorance, he reaps none of the rewards but 710 suffers all the afflictions of the learned. And why? No other reason is given, save: *"This man also was with him."* Peter was fond of Knowledge, which bore away his heart; and he followed after,

que la he deseado seguir, aunque *a longe*. Pero todo ha sido acercarme más al fuego de la persecución, al crisol del tormento; y ha sido con tal extremo que han llegado a solicitar que se me prohiba el estudio.*

(26) Una vez lo consiguieron con una prelada muy santa y muy cándida que creyó que el estudio era cosa de Inquisición y me mandó que no estudiase.* Yo la obedecí (unos tres meses que duró el poder ella mandar) en cuanto a no tomar libro, que 660 en cuanto a no estudiar absolutamente, como no cae debajo de mi potestad, no lo pude hacer, porque aunque no estudiaba en los libros, estudiaba en todas las cosas que Dios crió, sirviéndome ellas de letras, y de libro toda esta máquina universal.* Nada veía sin refleja; nada oía sin consideración, aun en las cosas más menudas y materiales; porque como no hay criatura, por baja que sea, en que no se conozca el *me fecit Deus*, no hay alguna que no pasme el entendimiento, si se considera como se debe. Así yo, vuelvo a decir, las miraba y admiraba todas; de tal manera que de las mismas personas con quienes 670 hablaba, y de lo que me decían, me estaban resaltando mil consideraciones: ¿De dónde emanaría aquella variedad de genios e ingenios,* siendo todos de una especie? ¿Cuáles serían los temperamentos y ocultas cualidades que lo ocasionaban? Si veía una figura, estaba combinando la proporción de sus líneas y mediándola con el entendimiento y reduciéndola a otras diferentes. Paseábame algunas veces en el testero de un dormitorio nuestro (que es una pieza muy capaz) y estaba observando que siendo las líneas de sus dos lados paralelas y su techo a nivel, la vista fingía que sus líneas se inclinaban una a otra 680 y que su techo estaba más bajo en lo distante que en lo próximo: de donde infería que las líneas visuales corren rectas, pero no paralelas, sino que van a formar una figura piramidal. Y discurría si sería ésta la razón que obligó a los antiguos a dudar si el mundo era esférico o no. Porque, aunque lo parece, podía ser engaño de la vista, demostrando concavidades donde pudiera no haberlas.

(27) Este modo de reparos en todo me sucedía y sucede siempre, sin tener yo arbitrio en ello, que antes me suelo enfadar porque me cansa la cabeza; y yo creía que a todos sucedía esto 690 mismo y el hacer versos, hasta que la experiencia me ha mos-

calling himself a follower and a lover of Knowledge. And though he followed so *"afar off"* that he neither understood nor attained Knowledge, still this sufficed to incur its torments. The soldier from without would not hesitate to afflict him, nor the maidservant within-doors fail to trouble him.* I confess that I am far indeed from the terms of Knowledge and that I have wished to follow it, though *"afar off."* But all this has merely led me closer 720
to the flames of persecution, the crucible of affliction; and to such extremes that some have even sought to prohibit me from study.*

They achieved this once, with a very saintly and simple mother (26)
superior who believed that study was an affair for the Inquisition and ordered that I should not read.* I obeyed her (for the three months or so that her authority over us lasted) in that I did not pick up a book. But with regard to avoiding study absolutely, as such a thing does not lie within my power, I could not do it. For although I did not study in books, I studied all the things that God created, taking them for my letters, and for my book all the 730
intricate structures of this world.* Nothing could I see without reflecting upon it, nothing could I hear without pondering it, even to the most minute, material things. For there is no creature, however lowly, in which one cannot recognize the great *"God made me";* there is not one that does not stagger the mind if it receives due consideration. And so, I repeat, I looked and marveled at all things, so that from the very persons with whom I spoke and from what they said to me, a thousand speculations leapt to my mind: Whence could spring this diversity of character and intelligence* among individuals all composing one single species? What tem- 740
peraments, what hidden qualities could give rise to each? When I noticed a shape, I would set about combining the proportions of its lines and measuring it in my mind and converting it to other proportions. I sometimes walked back and forth along the fore-wall of one of our dormitories (which is a very large room), and I began to observe that although the lines of its two sides were parallel and the ceiling was flat, yet the eye falsely perceived these lines as though they approached each other and the ceiling as though it were lower in the distance than close by; from this I inferred that visual lines run straight, but not parallel, and that 750
they form a pyramidal figure. And I conjectured whether this might be the reason the ancients were obliged to question whether the world is spherical or not. Because even though it seems so, this could be a delusion of the eye, displaying concavities where there were none.

This kind of observation has been continual in me and is so to (27)

trado lo contrario; y es de tal manera esta naturaleza o costumbre,* que nada veo sin segunda consideración. Estaban en mi presencia dos niñas jugando con un trompo, y apenas yo vi el movimiento y la figura, cuando empecé, con esta mi locura,* a considerar el fácil moto de la forma esférica, y cómo duraba el impulso ya impreso e independiente de su causa, pues distante la mano de la niña, que era la causa motiva, bailaba el trompillo; y no contenta con esto, hice traer harina y cernerla para que, en bailando el trompo encima, se conociese

700 si eran círculos perfectos o no los que describía con su movimiento; y hallé que no eran sino unas líneas espirales que iban perdiendo lo circular cuanto se iba remitiendo el impulso. Jugaban otras a los alfileres (que es el más frívolo juego que usa la puerilidad); yo me llegaba a contemplar las figuras que formaban; y viendo que acaso se pusieron tres en triángulo, me ponía a enlazar uno en otro, acordándome de que aquélla era la figura que dicen tenía el misterioso anillo de Salomón,* en que habiá unas lejanas luces y representaciones de la Santísima Trinidad, en virtud de lo cual obraba tantos prodigios

710 y maravillas; y la misma que dicen tuvo el arpa de David, y que por eso sanaba Saúl a su sonido; y casi la misma conservan las arpas en nuestros tiempos.

(28)   Pues ¿qué os pudiera contar, Señora, de los secretos naturales que he descubierto estando guisando? Veo que un huevo se une y fríe en la manteca o aceite y, por contrario, se despedaza en el almíbar; ver que para que el azúcar se conserve fluida basta echarle una muy mínima parte de agua en que haya estado membrillo u otra fruta agria; ver que la yema y clara de un mismo huevo son tan contrarias, que en los unos, que sir-

720 ven para el azúcar, sirve cada una de por sí y juntos no. Por no cansaros con tales frialdades,* que sólo refiero por daros entera noticia de mi natural y creo que os causará risa; pero, señora, ¿qué podemos saber las mujeres sino filosofías de cocina? Bien dijo Lupercio Leonardo, que bien se puede filosofar y aderezar la cena. Y yo suelo decir viendo estas cosillas: Si Aristóteles hubiera guisado, mucho más hubiera escrito. Y prosiguiendo en mi modo de cogitaciones,* digo que esto es tan continuo en mí, que no necesito de libros; y en una ocasión que, por un grave accidente de estómago, me prohibie-

this day, without my having control over it; rather, I tend to find it annoying, because it tires my head. Yet I believed this happened to everyone, as with thinking in verse, until experience taught me otherwise. This trait, whether a matter of nature or custom,* is such that nothing do I see without a second thought. Two little 760 girls were playing with a top in front of me, and no sooner had I seen the motion and shape than I began, with this madness of mine,* to observe the easy movement of the spherical form and how the momentum lasted, now fixed and set free of its cause; for even far from its first cause, which was the hand of the girl, the little top went on dancing. Yet not content with this, I ordered flour to be brought and sifted on the floor, so that as the top danced over it, we could know whether its movement described perfect circles or no. I found they were not circular, but rather spiral lines that lost their circularity as the top lost its momentum. Other girls 770 were playing at spillikins (the most frivolous of all childhood games). I drew near to observe the shapes they made, and when I saw three of the straws by chance fall in a triangle, I fell to intertwining one with another, recalling that this was said to be the very shape of Solomon's mysterious ring,* where distantly there shone bright traces and representations of the Most Blessed Trinity, by virtue of which it worked great prodigies and marvels. And they say David's harp had the same shape, and thus was Saul cured by its sound; to this day, harps have almost the same form.

Well, and what then shall I tell you, my Lady, of the secrets (28) of nature that I have learned while cooking? I observe that an egg becomes solid and cooks in butter or oil, and on the contrary that it dissolves in sugar syrup. Or again, to ensure that sugar flow freely one need only add the slightest bit of water that has held quince or some other sour fruit. The yolk and white of the very same egg are of such a contrary nature that when eggs are used with sugar, each part separately may be used perfectly well, yet they cannot be mixed together. I shall not weary you with such inanities,* which I relate simply to give you a full account of my nature, and I believe this will make you laugh. But in truth, my 790 Lady, what can we women know, save philosophies of the kitchen? It was well put by Lupercio Leonardo [sic] that one can philosophize quite well while preparing supper. I often say, when I make these little observations, "Had Aristotle cooked, he would have written a great deal more." And so to go on with the mode of my cogitations:* I declare that all this is so continual in me that I have no need of books. On one occasion, because of a severe stomach ailment, the doctors forbade me to study. I spent sev-

730 ron los médicos el estudio, pasé así algunos días, y luego les propuse que era menos dañoso el concedérmelos, porque eran tan fuertes y vehementes mis cogitaciones, que consumían más espíritus en un cuarto de hora que el estudio de los libros en cuatro días; y así se redujeron a concederme que leyese; y más, Señora mía, que ni aun el sueño se libró* de este continuo movimiento de mi imaginativa; antes suele obrar en él más libre y desembarazada, confiriendo con mayor claridad y sosiego las especies que ha conservado del día, arguyendo, haciendo versos, de que os pudiera hacer un catálogo muy grande, y de

740 algunas razones y delgadezas que he alcanzado dormida mejor que despierta, y las dejo por no cansaros,* pues basta lo dicho para que vuestra discreción y trascendencia penetre y se entere perfectamente en todo mi natural y del principio, medios y estado de mis estudios.

(29)   Si éstos, Señora, fueran méritos (como los veo por tales celebrar en los hombres), no lo hubieran sido en mí porque obro necesariamente. Si son culpa, por la misma razón creo que no la he tenido;* mas, con todo, vivo siempre tan desconfiada de mí, que ni en esto ni en otra cosa me fío de mi juicio;

750 y así remito la decisión a ese soberano talento, sometiéndome luego a lo que sentenciare, sin contradicción ni repugnancia,* pues esto no ha sido más de una simple narración de mi inclinación a las letras.

(30)   *Confieso también que con ser esto verdad tal que, como he dicho, no necesitaba de ejemplares,* con todo no me han dejado de ayudar los muchos que he leído, así en divinas como en humanas letras. Porque veo a una Débora dando leyes, así en lo militar como en lo político, y gobernando el pueblo donde había tantos varones doctos. Veo una sapientísima reina de

760 Sabá, tan docta que se atreve a tentar con enigmas la sabiduría del mayor de los sabios, sin ser por ello reprendida, antes por ello será juez de los incrédulos. Veo tantas y tan insignes mujeres: unas adornadas del don de profecía, como una Abigaíl; otras de persuasión, como Ester; otras, de piedad, como Rahab; otras de perseverancia, como Ana, madre de Samuel; y otras infinitas, en otras especies de prendas y virtudes.

(31)   Si revuelvo a los gentiles, lo primero que encuentro es con las Sibilas, elegidas de Dios para profetizar los principales mis-

eral days in that state, and then quickly proposed to them that
it would be less harmful to allow me my books, for my cogita-   800
tions were so strenuous and vehement that they consumed more
vitality in a quarter of an hour than the reading of books could
in four days. And so the doctors were compelled to let me read.
What is more, my Lady, not even my sleep has been free* of this
ceaseless movement of my imagination. Rather, my mind oper-
ates in sleep still more freely and unobstructedly, ordering with
greater clarity and ease the events it has preserved from the day,
presenting arguments and composing verses. I could give you a
very long catalogue of these, as I could of certain reasonings and
subtle turns I have reached far better in my sleep than while   810
awake; but I leave them out in order not to weary you.* I have
said enough for your judgment and your surpassing eminence to
comprehend my nature with clarity and full understanding,
together with the beginnings, the methods, and the present state
of my studies.

If studies, my Lady, be merits (for indeed I see them extolled   (29)
as such in men), in me they are no such thing: I study because
I must. If they be a failing, I believe for the same reason that the
fault is none of mine.* Yet withal, I live always so wary of myself that neither in this nor in anything else do I trust my own   820
judgment. And so I entrust the decision to your supreme skill and
straightway submit to whatever sentence you may pass, posing
no objection or reluctance,* for this has been no more than a simple account of my inclination to letters.

*I confess also that, while in truth this inclination has been such   (30)
that, as I said before, I had no need of exemplars,* nevertheless
the many books that I have read have not failed to help me, both
in sacred as well as secular letters. For there I see a Deborah is-
suing laws, military as well as political, and governing the people
among whom there were so many learned men. I see the exceed-   830
ingly knowledgeable Queen of Sheba, so learned she dares to test
the wisdom of the wisest of all wise men with riddles, without being rebuked for it; indeed, on this very account she is to become
judge of the unbelievers. I see so many and such significant wom-
en: some adorned with the gift of prophecy, like an Abigail; others,
of persuasion, like Esther; others, of piety, like Rahab; others, of
perseverance, like Anna [Hannah] the mother of Samuel; and
others, infinitely more, with other kinds of qualities and virtues.

If I consider the Gentiles, the first I meet are the Sibyls, chosen   (31)
by God to prophesy the essential mysteries of our Faith in such   840
learned and elegant verses that they stupefy the imagination.* I

famous women of society

terios de nuestra Fe; y en tan doctos y elegantes versos que
770 suspenden la admiración.* Veo adorar por diosa de las ciencias a una mujer como Minerva, hija del primer Júpiter y maestra de toda la sabiduría de Atenas. Veo una Pola Argentaria,
que ayudó a Lucano, su marido, a escribir la gran Batalla Far-
sálica. Veo a la hija del divino Tiresias, más docta que su padre.
Veo a una Cenobia, reina de los Palmirenos, tan sabia como
valerosa. A una Arete, hija de Aristipo, doctísima. A una Nicostrata, inventora de las letras y eruditísima en las griegas. A una
Aspasia Milesia que enseñó filosofía y retórica y fue maestra
del filósofo Pericles. A una Hipasia que enseñó astrología y
780 leyó mucho tiempo en Alejandría. A una Leoncia, griega, que
escribió contra el filósofo Teofrasto y le convenció. A una Jucia,
a una Corina, a una Cornelia; y en fin a toda la gran turba de
las que merecieron nombres, ya de griegas, ya de musas, ya
de pitonisas; pues todas no fueron más que mujeres doctas,
tenidas y celebradas y también veneradas de la antigüedad por
tales. Sin otras infinitas, de que están los libros llenos, pues
veo aquella egipciaca Catarina, leyendo y convenciendo todas
las sabidurías de los sabios de Egipto. Veo una Gertrudis leer,
escribir y enseñar. Y para no buscar ejemplos fuera de casa,
790 veo una santísima madre mía, Paula, docta en las lenguas
hebrea, griega y latina y aptísima para interpretar las Escrituras.* ¿Y qué más que siendo su cronista un Máximo Jerónimo, apenas se hallaba el Santo digno de serlo, pues con aquella
viva ponderación y enérgica eficacia con que sabe explicarse
dice: Si todos los miembros de mi cuerpo fuesen lenguas, no
bastarían a publicar la sabiduría y virtud de Paula. Las mismas alabanzas le mereció Blesila, viuda; y las mismas la es-
clarecida virgen Eustoquio, hijas ambas de la misma Santa; y
la segunda, tal, que por su ciencia era llamada Prodigio del
800 Mundo. Fabiola, romana, fue también doctísima en la Sagrada Escritura. Proba Falconia, mujer romana, escribió un
elegante libro con centones de Virgilio, de los misterios de Nuestra Santa Fe. Nuestra reina Doña Isabel, mujer del décimo Alfonso, es corriente que escribió de astrología. Sin otras que
omito por no trasladar lo que otros han dicho (que es vicio que
siempre he abominado), pues en nuestros tiempos está flore-
ciendo la gran Cristina Alejandra, Reina de Suecia, tan docta

see a woman such as Minerva, daughter of great Jupiter and mistress of all the wisdom of Athens, adored as goddess of the sciences. I see one Polla Argentaria, who helped Lucan, her husband, to write the *Battle of Pharsalia.* I see the daughter of the divine Tiresias, more learned still than her father. I see, too, such a woman as Zenobia, queen of the Palmyrians, as wise as she was courageous. Again, I see an Arete, daughter of Aristippus, most learned. A Nicostrata, inventor of Latin letters and most erudite in the Greek. An Aspasia Miletia, who taught philosophy and 850 rhetoric and was the teacher of the philosopher Pericles. An Hypatia, who taught astrology and lectured for many years in Alexandria. A Leontium, who won over the philosopher Theophrastus and proved him wrong. A Julia, a Corinna, a Cornelia; and, in sum, the vast throng of women who merited titles and earned renown: now as Greeks, again as Muses, and yet again as Pythonesses. For what were they all but learned women, who were considered, celebrated, and indeed venerated as such in Antiquity? Without mentioning still others, of whom the books are full; for I see the Egyptian Catherine, lecturing and refuting all the learn- 860 ing of the most learned men of Egypt. I see a Gertrude read, write, and teach. And seeking no more examples far from home, I see my own most holy mother Paula, learned in the Hebrew, Greek, and Latin tongues and most expert in the interpretation of the Scriptures.* What wonder then can it be that, though her chronicler was no less than the unequaled Jerome, the Saint found himself scarcely worthy of the task, for with that lively gravity and energetic effectiveness with which only he can express himself, he says: "If all the parts of my body were tongues, they would not suffice to proclaim the learning and virtues of Paula." Blessil- 870 la, a widow, earned the same praises, as did the luminous virgin Eustochium, both of them daughters of the Saint herself [Paula]; and indeed Eustochium was such that for her knowledge she was hailed as a World Prodigy. Fabiola, also a Roman, was another most learned in Holy Scripture. Proba Falconia, a Roman woman, wrote an elegant book of centos, joining together verses from Virgil, on the mysteries of our holy Faith. Our Queen Isabella, wife of Alfonso X, is known to have written on astrology – without mentioning others, whom I omit so as not merely to copy what others have said (which is a vice I have always detested): Well 880 then, in our own day there thrive the great Christina Alexandra, Queen of Sweden, as learned as she is brave and generous; and too those most excellent ladies, the Duchess of Aveyro and the Countess of Villaumbrosa.

como valerosa y magnánima, y las Excelentísimas señoras Duquesa de Aveyro y Condesa de Villaumbrosa.

(32)   El venerable Doctor Arce (digno profesor de Escritura por su virtud y letras), en su *Studioso Bibliorum* excita esta cuestión: *An liceat foeminis sacrorum Bibliorum studio incumbere? eaque interpretari?* Y trae por la parte contraria muchas sentencias de santos, en especial aquello del Apóstol: *Mulieres in Ecclesiis taceant, non enim permittitur eis loqui,* etc. Trae después otras sentencias, y del mismo Apóstol aquel lugar ad Titum: *Anus similiter in habitu sancto, bene docentes,* con interpretaciones de los Santos Padres; y al fin resuelve, con su prudencia, que el leer públicamente en las cátedras y predicar en los púlpitos,
820 no es lícito a las mujeres; pero que el estudiar, escribir y enseñar privadamente, no sólo les es lícito, pero muy provechoso y útil; claro está que esto no se debe entender con todas, sino con aquellas a quienes hubiere Dios dotado de especial virtud y prudencia y que fueren muy provectas y eruditas y tuvieren el talento y requisitos necesarios para tan sagrado empleo. Y esto es tan justo que no sólo a las mujeres, que por tan ineptas están tenidas, sino a los hombres, que con sólo serlo piensan que son sabios, se había de prohibir la interpretación de las Sagradas Letras, en no siendo muy doctos y virtuosos
830 y de ingenios dóciles y bien inclinados; porque de lo contrario creo yo que han salido tantos sectarios y que ha sido la raíz de tantas herejías; porque hay muchos que estudian para ignorar, especialmente los que son de ánimos arrogantes, inquietos y soberbios, amigos de novedades en la Ley (que es quien las rehusa); y así hasta que por decir lo que nadie ha dicho dicen una herejía, no están contentos. De éstos* dice el Espíritu Santo: *In malevolam animam non introibit sapientia.* A éstos, más daño les hace el saber que les hiciera el ignorar. Dijo un discreto que no es necio entero el que no sabe latín, pero
840 el que lo sabe está calificado. Y añado yo que le perfecciona (si es perfección la necedad) el haber estudiado su poco de filosofía y teología y el tener alguna noticia de lenguas, que con eso es necio en muchas ciencias y lenguas: porque un necio grande no cabe en sólo la lengua materna.

(33)   A éstos, vuelvo a decir, hace daño el estudiar, porque es poner espada en manos del furioso;* que siendo instrumento nobilísi-

The venerable Dr. Arce (worthy professor of Scripture, known (32) for his virtue and learning), in his *For the Scholar of the Bible,* raises this question: *"Is it permissible for women to apply themselves to the study, and indeed the interpretation, of the Holy Bible?"* And in opposition he presents the verdicts passed by many saints, particularly the words of [Paul] the Apostle: *"Let women keep silence in* 890 *the churches: for it is not permitted them to speak,"* etc. Arce then presents differing verdicts, including this passage addressed to Titus, again spoken by the Apostle: *"The aged women, in like manner, in holy attire [. . .] teaching well";* and he gives other interpretations from the Fathers of the Church. Arce at last resolves, in his prudent way, that women are not allowed to lecture publicly in the universities or to preach from the pulpits, but that studying, writing, and teaching privately is not only permitted but most beneficial and useful to them.* Clearly, of course, he does not mean by this that all women should do so, but only those whom 900 God may have seen fit to endow with special virtue and prudence, and who are very mature and erudite and possess the necessary talents and requirements for such a sacred occupation. And so just is this distinction that not only women, who are held to be so incompetent, but also men, who simply because they are men think themselves wise, are to be prohibited from the interpretation of the Sacred Word, save when they are most learned, virtuous, of amenable intellect and inclined to the good. For when the reverse is true, I believe, numerous sectarians are produced, and this has given rise to numerous heresies. For there are many who 910 study only to become ignorant, especially those of arrogant, restless, and prideful spirits, fond of innovations in the Law (the very thing that rejects all innovation). And so they are not content until, for the sake of saying what no one before them has said, they speak heresy. Of such men as these* the Holy Spirit says: *"For wisdom will not enter into a malicious soul."* For them, more harm is worked by knowledge than by ignorance. A wit once observed that he who knows no Latin is not an utter fool, but he who does know it has met the prerequisites. And I might add that he is made a perfect fool (if foolishness can attain perfection) by having 920 studied his bit of philosophy and theology and by knowing something of languages. For with that he can be foolish in several sciences and tongues; a great fool cannot be contained in his mother tongue alone.

To such men, I repeat, study does harm, because it is like putting a sword in the hands of a madman:* though the sword be the noblest of instruments for defense, in his hands it becomes

mo para la defensa, en sus manos es muerte suya y de muchos. Tales fueron las Divinas Letras en poder del malvado Pelagio y del protervo Arrio, del malvado Lutero y de los demás
850 heresiarcas, como lo fue nuestro Doctor (nunca fue nuestro ni doctor) Cazalla; a los cuales hizo daño la sabiduría porque, aunque es el mejor alimento y vida del alma, a la manera que en el estómago mal acomplexionado y de viciado calor, mientras mejores los alimentos que recibe, más áridos, fermentados y perversos son los humores que cría, así estos malévolos, mientras más estudian, peores opiniones engendran; obstrúyeseles el entendimiento con lo mismo que había de alimentarse, y es que estudian mucho y digieren poco, sin proporcionarse al vaso limitado de sus entendimientos. A esto dice el Apóstol:
860 *Dico enim per gratiam quae data est mihi, omnibus qui sunt inter vos: Non plus sapere quam oportet sapere, sed sapere ad sobrietatem: et unicuique sicut Deus divisit mensuram fidei.* Y en verdad no lo dijo el Apóstol a las mujeres, sino a los hombres; y que no es sólo para ellas el *taceant*, * sino para todos los que no fueren muy aptos. Querer yo saber tanto o más que Aristóteles o que San Agustín, si no tengo la aptitud de San Agustín o de Aristóteles, aunque estudie más que los dos, no sólo no lo conseguiré sino que debilitaré y entorpeceré la operación de mi flaco entendimiento con la desproporción del objeto.

(34)   ¡Oh si todos —y yo la primera, que soy una ignorante— * nos tomásemos la medida al talento antes de estudiar, y lo peor es, de escribir con ambiciosa codicia de igualar y aun de exceder a otros, qué poco ánimo nos quedara y de cuántos errores nos excusáramos y cuántas torcidas inteligencias que andan por ahí no anduvieran! Y pongo las mías en primer lugar, pues si conociera, como debo, esto mismo no escribiera. Y protesto que sólo lo hago por obedeceros; con tanto recelo, que me debéis más en tomar la pluma con este temor, que me debiérades si os remitiera más perfectas obras. Pero, bien que va a
880 vuestra corrección; borradlo, rompedlo y reprendedme, que eso apreciaré yo más que todo cuanto vano aplauso me pueden otros dar: *Corripiet me iustus in misericordia, et increpabit: oleum autem peccatoris non impinguet caput meum.*

(35)   Y volviendo a nuestro Arce, digo que trae en confirmación de su sentir aquellas palabras de mi Padre San Jerónimo *(ad*

his own death and that of many others. This is what the Divine Letters became in the hands of that wicked Pelagius and of the perverse Arius, of that wicked Luther, and all the other heretics, like our own Dr. Cazalla (who was never either our own nor a doctor). Learning harmed them all, though it can be the best nourishment and life for the soul. For just as an infirm stomach, suffering from diminished heat, produces more bitter, putrid, and perverse humors the better the food that it is given, so too these evil persons give rise to worse opinions the more they study. Their understanding is obstructed by the very thing that should nourish it, and the fact is they study a great deal and digest very little, failing to measure their efforts to the narrow vessel of their understanding. In this regard the Apostle has said: *"For I say, by the grace that is given me, to all that are among you, not to be more wise than it behoveth to be wise, but to be wise unto sobriety, and according as God hath divided to every one the measure of faith."* And in truth the Apostle said this not to women but to men, and the *"Let [them] keep silence"* was meant not only for women,* but for all those who are not very competent. If I wish to know as much as or more than Aristotle or St. Augustine, but I lack the ability of a St. Augustine or an Aristotle, then I may study more than both of them together, but I shall not only fail to reach my goal: I shall weaken and stupefy the workings of my feeble understanding with such a disproportionate aim.

Oh, that all men—and I, who am but an ignorant woman, first of all*—might take the measure of our abilities before setting out to study and, what is worse, to write, in our jealous aspiration to equal and even surpass others. How little boldness would we summon, how many errors might we avoid, and how many distorted interpretations now noised abroad should be noised no further! And I place my own before all others, for if I knew all that I ought, I would not so much as write these words. Yet I protest that I do so only to obey you; and with such misgiving that you owe me more for taking up my pen with all this fear than you would owe me were I to present you with the most perfect works. But withal, it is well that this goes to meet with your correction: erase it, tear it up, and chastise me, for I shall value that more than all the vain applause others could give me. *"The just man shall correct me in mercy, and shall reprove me: but let not the oil of the sinner fatten my head."*

And returning to our own Arce, I observe that in support of his views he presents these words of my father St. Jerome (in the letter *To Leta, on the Education of Her Daughter*), where he says: *"[Her]*

Laetam, de institutione filiae), donde dice: *Adhuc tenera lingua psalmis dulcibus imbuatur. Ipsa nomina per quae consuescit paulatim verba contexere; non sint fortuita, sed certa, et coacervata de industria. Prophetarum videlicet, atque Apostolorum, et omnis ab*

890 *Adam Patriarcharum series, de Matthaeo, Lucaque descendat, ut dum aliud agit, futurae memoriae praeparetur. Reddat tibi pensum quotidie, de Scripturarum floribus carptum.* Pues si así quería el Santo que se educase una niña que apenas empezaba a hablar, ¿qué querrá en sus monjas y en sus hijas espirituales? Bien se conoce en las referidas Eustoquio y Fabiola y en Marcela, su hermana, Pacátula y otras a quienes el Santo honra en sus epístolas, exhortándolas a este sagrado ejercicio, como se conoce en la citada epístola donde noté yo aquel *reddat tibi pensum,* que es reclamo y concordante del *bene docentes* de San

900 Pablo; pues el *reddat tibi* de mi gran Padre da a entender que la maestra de la niña ha de ser la misma Leta su madre.

(36)   * ¡Oh cuántos daños se excusaran en nuestra república si las ancianas fueran doctas como Leta, y que supieran enseñar como manda San Pablo y mi Padre San Jerónimo! Y no que por defecto de esto y la suma flojedad en que han dado en dejar a las pobres mujeres,* si algunos padres desean doctrinar más de lo ordinario a sus hijas les fuerza la necesidad y falta de ancianas sabias, a llevar maestros hombres a enseñar a leer, escribir y contar, a tocar y otras habilidades, de que no pocos

910 daños resultan, como se experimentan cada día en lastimosos ejemplos de desiguales consorcios, porque con la inmediación del trato y la comunicación del tiempo, suele hacerse fácil lo que no se pensó ser posible. Por lo cual, muchos quieren más dejar bárbaras e incultas a sus hijas que no exponerlas a tan notorio peligro como la familiaridad con los hombres, lo cual se excusara si hubiera ancianas doctas, como quiere San Pablo, y de unas en otras fuese sucediendo el magisterio como secede en el de hacer labores* y lo demás que es costumbre.

(37)   Porque ¿qué inconveniente tiene que una mujer anciana, doc-

920 ta en letras y de santa conversación y costumbres, tuviese a su cargo la educación de las doncellas? Y no que éstas o se pierden por falta de doctrina o por querérsela aplicar por tan peligrosos medios cuales son los maestros hombres, que cuando no hubiera más riesgo que la indecencia de sentarse al lado

childish tongue must be imbued with the sweet music of the Psalms. [. . .] The very words from which she will get into the way of forming sentences should not be taken at haphazard but be definitely chosen and arranged on purpose. For example, let her have the names of the prophets and the apostles, and the whole list of patriarchs from Adam downwards, as Matthew and Luke give it. She will then be doing two things at the same time, and will remember them afterwards. [. . .] Let her every day repeat to you a portion of the Scriptures as her fixed task." Very well, if the Saint wished a little girl, scarcely beginning to speak, to be instructed thus, what must he desire for his 980 nuns and spiritual daughters? We see this most clearly in the women already mentioned – Eustochium and Fabiola – and also in Marcella, the latter's sister; in Pacatula, and in other women whom the Saint honors in his epistles, urging them on in this holy exercise. This appears in the letter already cited, where I noted the words *"let her repeat to you . . ."* which serve to reclaim and confirm St. Paul's description, "teaching well." For the *"let her repeat the task to you"* of my great Father makes clear that the little girl's teacher must be Leta herself, the girl's mother.

   Oh, how many abuses would be avoided in our land if the older (36) women were as well instructed as Leta and knew how to teach as is commanded by St. Paul and my father St. Jerome! Instead, for lack of such learning and through the extreme feebleness in which they are determined to maintain our poor women, if any parents then wish to give their daughters more extensive Christian instruction than is usual, necessity and the lack of learned older women oblige them to employ men as instructors to teach reading and writing, numbers and music, and other skills. This leads to considerable harm, which occurs every day in doleful instances of these unsuitable associations. For the immediacy of such con- 1000 tact and the passage of time all too frequently allow what seemed impossible to be accomplished quite easily. For this reason, many parents prefer to let their daughters remain uncivilized and untutored, rather than risk exposing them to such notorious peril as this familiarity with men. Yet all this could be avoided if there were old women of sound education, as St. Paul desires, so that instruction could be passed from the old to the young just as is done with sewing* and all the customary skills.

   For what impropriety can there be if an older woman, learned (37) in letters and holy conversation and customs, should have in her 1010 charge the education of young maids? Better so than to let these young girls go to perdition, either for lack of any Christian teaching or because one tries to impart it through such dangerous

de una mujer verecunda (que aun se sonrosea de que la mire a la cara su propio padre) un hombre tan extraño a tratarla con casera familiaridad y a tratarla con magistral llaneza, el pudor del trato con los hombres y de su conversación basta para que no se permitiese. Y no hallo yo que este modo de enseñar de
930 hombres a mujeres pueda ser sin peligro, si no es en el severo tribunal de un confesionario o en la distante docencia de los púlpitos o en el remoto conocimiento de los libros, pero no en el manoseo de la inmediación.* Y todos conocen que esto es verdad; y con todo, se permite sólo por el defecto de no haber ancianas sabias; luego es grande daño el no haberlas. Esto debían considerar los que atados al *Mulieres in Ecclesia taceant,* blasfeman de que las mujeres sepan y enseñen; como que no fuera el mismo Apóstol el que dijo: *bene docentes.* Demás de que aquella prohibición cayó sobre lo historial que refiere Eu-
940 sebio, y es que en la Iglesia primitiva se ponían las mujeres a enseñar las doctrinas unas a otras en los templos; y este rumor confundía cuando predicaban los apóstoles y por eso se les mandó callar; como ahora sucede, que mientras predica el predicador no se reza en alta voz.

(38)   No hay duda de que para inteligencia de muchos lugares* es menester mucha historia, costumbres, ceremonias, proverbios y aun maneras de hablar de aquellos tiempos en que se escribieron, para saber sobre qué caen y a qué aluden algunas locuciones de las divinas letras.* *Scindite corda vestra, et non*
950 *vestimenta vestra,* ¿no es alusión a la ceremonia que tenían los hebreos de rasgar los vestidos, en señal de dolor, como lo hizo el mal pontífice cuando dijo que Cristo había blasfemado?* Muchos lugares del Apóstol sobre el socorro de las viudas* ¿no miraban también a las costumbres de aquellos tiempos? Aquel lugar de la mujer fuerte:* *Nobilis in portis vir eius* ¿no alude a la costumbre de estar los tribunales de los jueces en las puertas de las ciudades? El *dare terram Deo* ¿no significaba hacer algún voto? *Hiemantes* ¿no se llamaban los pecadores públicos, porque hacían penitencia a cielo abierto, a diferencia de los
960 otros que la hacían en un portal? Aquella queja de Cristo al fariseo de la falta de ósculo y lavatorio de pies* ¿no se fundó en la costumbre que de hacer estas cosas tenían los judíos? Y otros infinitos lugares no sólo de las letras divinas sino tam-

means as male teachers. For if there were no greater risk than the simple indecency of seating a completely unknown man at the side of a bashful woman (who blushes if her own father should look her straight in the face), allowing him to address her with household familiarity and to speak to her with intimate authority, even so the modesty demanded in interchange with men and in conversation with them gives sufficient cause to forbid this. *1020* Indeed, I do not see how the custom of men as teachers of women can be without its dangers, save only in the strict tribunal of the confessional, or the distant teachings of the pulpit, or the remote wisdom of books; but never in the repeated handling that occurs in such immediate and tarnishing contact.* And everyone knows this to be true. Nevertheless, it is permitted for no better reason than the lack of learned older women; therefore, it does great harm not to have them. This point should be taken into account by those who, tied to the _"Let women keep silence in the churches,"_ curse the idea that women should acquire knowledge *1030* and teach, as if it were not the Apostle himself who described them _"teaching well."_ Furthermore, that prohibition applied to the case related by Eusebius: to wit, that in the early Church, women were set to teaching each other Christian doctrine in the temples. The murmur of their voices caused confusion when the apostles were preaching, and that is why they were told to be silent. Just so, we see today that when the preacher is preaching, no one prays aloud.

There can be no doubt that in order to understand many passages,* one must know a great deal of the history, customs, rituals, proverbs, and even the habits of speech of the times in which they were written, in order to know what is indicated and what alluded to by certain sayings in divine letters.* _"Rend your hearts, and not your garments"_ – is that not an allusion to the Hebrews' ritual of tearing their clothing as a sign of grief, as was done by the evil high priest when he said that Christ had blasphemed?* Do not many passages by the Apostle [Paul], on the aid and comfort of widows,* refer to the customs of his times? Or that passage concerning the strong woman,* _"Her husband is honourable in the gates,"_ does it not allude to the custom of placing the judges' *1050* tribunals at the city gates? The saying _"Give land to God,"_ does it not stand for making some vow? Was not the term _hiemantes_ used for public sinners, because they made their penance out of doors, unlike others who did penance in a doorway? The complaint of Christ to the Pharisee who failed to greet Him with the kiss of peace or the washing of feet,* is that not based on the Jewish

(38)
1040

bién de las humanas,* que se topan a cada paso, como el *adorate purpuram*, que significaba obedecer al rey; el *manumittere eum*, que significa dar libertad, aludiendo a la costumbre y ceremonia de dar una bofetada al esclavo para darle libertad. Aquel *intonuit coelum*, de Virgilio, que alude al agüero de tronar ha-
970 cia occidente, que se tenía por bueno. Aquel *tu nunquam leporem edisti*, de Marcial, que no sólo tiene el donaire de equívoco en el *leporem*, sino la alusión a la propiedad que decían tener la liebre. Aquel proverbio: *Maleam legens, quae sunt domi obliviscere*, que alude al gran peligro del promontorio de Laconia. Aquella respuesta de la casta matrona al pretensor molesto, de: *por mí no se untarán los quicios, ni arderán las teas*, para decir que no quería casarse, aludiendo a la ceremonia de untar las puertas con manteca y encender las teas nupciales en los matrimonios; como si ahora dijéramos: por mí no se gastarán
980 arras ni echará bendiciones el cura.* Y así hay tanto comento de Virgilio y de Homero y de todos los poetas y oradores. Pues fuera de esto, ¿qué dificultades no se hallan en los lugares sagrados, aun en lo gramatical, de ponerse el plural por singular,* de pasar de segunda a tercera persona,* como aquello de los Cantares: *osculetur me osculo oris sui: quia meliora sunt ubera tua vino?* Aquel poner los adjetivos en genitivo, en vez de acusativo,* como *Calicem salutaris accipiam?* Aquel poner el femenino por masculino; y, al contrario, llamar adulterio a cualquier pecado?*

(39)   Todo esto pide más lección de lo que piensan algunos que, de meros gramáticos, o cuando mucho con cuatro términos de Súmulas,* quieren interpretar las Escrituras y se aferran del *Mulieres in Ecclesiis taceant*, sin saber cómo se ha de entender. Y de otro lugar: *Mulier in silentio discat;* siendo este lugar más en favor que en contra de las mujeres, pues manda que aprendan, y mientras aprenden claro está que es necesario que callen.* Y también está escrito: *Audi Israel, et tace;* donde se habla con toda la colección de los hombres y mujeres, y a todos se manda callar, porque quien oye y aprende es mucha
1000 razón que atienda y calle. Y si no, yo quisiera que estos intérpretes y expositores de San Pablo me explicaran cómo entienden aquel lugar: *Mulieres in Ecclesia taceant*. Porque o lo han de entender de lo material de los púlpitos y cátedras, o de lo

custom of doing these things? And so it is with infinitely many more passages, not only in divine but in humane letters* as well, which are met at every turn, like the phrase *"Honor the purple,"* which meant "Obey the king"; or the phrase *"to put a hand to him,"* which meant "to emancipate," referring to the custom and ritual of giving a slave a slap to set him at liberty. Again, Virgil's *"The heavens thundered,"* alluding to the augury of thunder toward the west, which was thought a good omen. There is Martial's *"You never ate hare,"* which shows not only the wordplay in *leporem* (which means both "hare" and "jest"), but also a reference to a quality the hare was said to possess. There is the proverb, *"To sail the shores of Malia is to forget all the things of home,"* which refers to the great peril of the promontory of Laconia. The response of the chaste matron to an unwanted suitor, *"No doorframes shall be annointed on my account, nor shall the torches burn,"* to say that she would not marry, alludes to the ritual of annointing the doorways with oil and lighting nuptial torches at weddings; just so, we might say today, "On my account shall no dowry coins be spent, nor shall the priest give his blessing."* And in this vein, much commentary can be made on Virgil and Homer and all the poets and orators. Very well, and in addition to all this, what difficulties do we not find in sacred texts, even in matters of grammar – putting the plural in place of the singular,* or moving from second to third person,* like the passage in the Song of Songs: *"Let him kiss me with the kiss of his mouth: for thy breasts are better than wine"*? Or putting the adjectives in the genitive case, instead of the accusative,* as in *"I will take the chalice of salvation"*? Or again, putting the feminine in place of the masculine; or, on the contrary, calling every sin adultery?*

All this requires more study than is supposed by certain men who, as mere grammarians or, at most, armed with four terms from the principles of logic,* wish to interpret the Scriptures and cling to the *"Let women keep silence in the churches,"* without knowing how to understand it rightly. So it is with another passage, *"Let the woman learn in silence";* for this passage is more in favor of than against women, as it says that they *should* learn, and while they are learning, obviously, they must needs keep quiet.* And it is also written, *"Hear, O Israel, and be silent,"* where the whole congregation of men and women are addressed, and all are told to be quiet, for whoever listens and learns has good reason to take heed and keep still. If this be not so, I would like these interpreters and expounders of St. Paul to explain to me how they understand the passage, *"Let women keep silence in the churches."* For they must

formal de la universalidad de los fieles, que es la Iglesia. Si lo entienden de lo primero (que es, en mi sentir, su verdadero sentido, pues vemos que, con efecto, no se permite en la Iglesia que las mujeres lean públicamente ni prediquen), ¿por qué reprenden a las que privadamente estudian? Y si lo entienden de lo segundo y quieren que la prohibición del Apóstol sea 1010 trascendentalmente, que ni en lo secreto se permita escribir ni estudiar a las mujeres, ¿cómo vemos que la Iglesia ha permitido que escriba una Gertrudis, una Teresa, una Brígida, la monja de Agreda y otras muchas? Y si me dicen que éstas eran santas, es verdad, pero no obsta a mi argumento; lo primero, porque la proposición de San Pablo es absoluta y comprende a todas las mujeres sin excepción de santas, pues también en su tiempo lo eran Marta y María, Marcela, María madre de Jacob, y Salomé, y otras muchas que había en el fervor de la primitiva Iglesia, y no las exceptúa; y ahora vemos que la Iglesia 1020 permite escribir a las mujeres santas y no santas, pues la de Agreda y María de la Antigua no están canonizadas y corren sus escritos; y ni cuando Santa Teresa y las demás escribieron, lo estaban: luego la prohibición de San Pablo sólo miró a la publicidad de los púlpitos, pues si el Apóstol prohibiera el escribir, no lo permitiera la Iglesia. Pues ahora, yo no me atrevo a enseñar – que fuera en mí muy desmedida presunción –; y el escribir, mayor talento que el mío requiere y muy grande consideración. Así lo dice San Cipriano: *Gravi consideratione indigent, quae scribimus.* Lo que sólo he deseado 1030 es estudiar para ignorar menos: que, según San Agustín, unas cosas se aprenden para hacer y otras para sólo saber: *Discimus quaedam, ut sciamus; quaedam, ut faciamus.* Pues ¿en qué ha estado el delito,* si aun lo que es lícito a las mujeres, que es enseñar escribiendo, no hago yo porque conozco que no tengo caudal para ello, siguiendo el consejo de Quintiliano: *Noscat quisque, et non tantum ex alienis praeceptis, sed ex natura sua capiat consilium?*

(40)   Si el crimen está en la Carta Atenagórica, ¿fue aquélla más que referir sencillamente mi sentir con todas las venias que 1040 debo a nuestra Santa Madre Iglesia?* Pues si ella, con su santísima autoridad, no me lo prohibe, ¿por qué me lo han de prohibir otros? ¿Llevar una opinión contraria de Vieyra fue en mí

understand it either materially, to mean the pulpit and the lecture hall, or formally, to mean the community of all believers, which is to say the Church. If they understand it in the first sense (which is to my way of thinking its true sense, for we can see that indeed it is not permitted by the Church for women to read publicly or to preach), why then do they rebuke those women who study in private? And if they understand it in the second sense and wish to extend the Apostle's prohibition to all instances without exception, so that not even in private may women write or study, then how is it that we see the Church has allowed a Gertrude, a Teresa, a Brigid, the nun of Agreda, and many other women to write? And if they tell me that these women all were saintly, true enough, but that in no way hinders my argument. First, because St. Paul's proposition is absolute and includes all women with no exception made for saints; for saintly, too, in their own day were Martha and Mary, and Marcella, and Mary the mother of Jacob, and Salome, and many other women who took part in the zeal of the early Church, yet Paul makes no exception for them. And in our own time we see that the Church permits writing by women saints and those who are not saints alike; for the nun of Agreda and María de la Antigua are not canonized, yet their writings go from hand to hand. Nor when Sts. Teresa and the others were writing, had they yet been canonized. Therefore, St. Paul's prohibition applied only to public speech from the pulpit; for if the Apostle were to prohibit all writing, then the Church could not permit it. Very well now, I am not so bold as to teach, which would be most unsuitably presumptuous of me; and to write requires more talent than is mine and the greatest deliberation. So says St. Cyprian: *"That which we write requires solemn deliberation."* All that I have desired has been to study, so as to become less ignorant. For according to St. Augustine, some things are learned so as to act on them, and others simply for the sake of knowing them: *"We learn certain things in order to know them; others in order to do them."* Then where is my transgression,* if I refrain even from that which is permissible for women – to teach by writing – because I know myself to lack the abundant talent needed for it, following Quintilian's counsel: *"Let each one learn, not so much by the precepts of others, as by following the counsel of his own nature"?*

If my crime lies in the "Letter Worthy of Athena," was that anything more than a simple report of my opinion, with all the indulgences granted me by our Holy Mother Church?* For if She, with her most holy authority, does not forbid my writing, why must others forbid it? Is it bold of me to oppose Vieira, yet not

atrevimiento, y no lo fue en su Paternidad llevarla contra los tres Santos Padres de la Iglesia? Mi entendimiento tal cual ¿no es tan libre como el suyo, pues viene de un solar? ¿Es alguno de los principios de la Santa Fe, revelados,* su opinión, para que la hayamos de creer a ojos cerrados? Demás que yo ni falté al decoro que a tanto varón se debe, como acá ha faltado su defensor, olvidado de la sentencia de Tito Lucio: *Artes com-*

1050 *mittatur decor;* ni toqué a la Sagrada Compañía* en el pelo de la ropa; ni escribí más que para el juicio de quien me lo insinuó; y según Plinio, *non similis est conditio publicantis, et nominatim dicentis.* Que si creyera se había de publicar, no fuera con tanto desaliño como fue. Si es, como dice el censor,* herética, ¿por qué no la delata? y con eso él quedará vengado y yo contenta, que aprecio, como debo, más el nombre de católica y de obediente hija de mi Santa Madre Iglesia, que todos los aplausos de docta. Si está bárbara —que en eso dice bien—, ríase, aunque sea con la risa que dicen del conejo,* que yo no

1060 le digo que me aplauda, pues como yo fui libre para disentir de Vieyra, lo será cualquiera para disentir de mi dictamen.

(44) Pero ¿dónde voy, Señora mía? Que esto no es de aquí, ni es para vuestros oídos, sino que como voy tratando de mis impugnadores, me acordé de las cláusulas de uno que ha salido ahora, e insensiblemente se deslizó la pluma al quererle responder en particular, siendo mi intento hablar en general. Y así, volviendo a nuestro Arce, dice que conoció en esta ciudad dos monjas:* la una en el convento de Regina, que tenía el Breviario de tal manera en la memoria, que aplicaba con gran-

1070 dísima prontitud y propiedad sus versos, salmos y sentencias de homilías de los santos, en las conversaciones. La otra, en el convento de la Concepción, tan acostumbrada a leer las Epístolas de mi Padre San Jéronimo, y locuciones del Santo, de tal manera que dice Arce: *Hieronymum ipsum hispane loquentem audire me existimarem.* Y de ésta dice que supo, después de su muerte, había traducido dichas Epístolas en romance; y se duele de que tales talentos no se hubieran empleado en mayores estudios con principios científicos, sin decir los nombres de la una ni de la otra, aunque las trae para con-

1080 firmación de su sentencia, que es que no sólo es lícito, pero utilísimo y necesario a las mujeres el estudio de las sagradas

so for that <u>Reverend Father</u> to oppose the three holy Fathers of
the Church? <u>Is my mind</u>, such as it is, less free than his, though
it derives from the same source? Is his opinion to be taken as one
of the principles of the Holy Faith made manifest,* that we must
believe it blindly? Besides which, I have not in the slightest way
fallen short of that respect owed such a great man, as his defender
has done in this instance, forgetting the observation of Titus Lucius, *"Respect befits the arts."* Nor did I so much as graze the hem
of the blessed Society.* Nor did I write for anyone other than the   *1150*
person who suggested it to me; and according to Pliny, *"The situation of one who publishes a thing is different from that of one who
speaks it by name."* For had I thought the letter was to be published,
it would not have appeared as unkempt as it was. If it is heretical, as the critic says,* why does he not denounce it? Thus he
would find revenge and I contentment, <u>for I more greatly value,</u>
<u>as I ought, the name of Catholic and obedient daughter of my Holy</u>
<u>Mother Church than any praise that might befall me as a scholar.</u>
If the letter be crude – as he rightly says it is – then let him laugh
at it, though he laugh falsely with what they call rabbit's laugh-   *1160*
ter.* I do not say that he should praise me, for just as I was free
to disagree with Vieira, <u>any person shall be free to disagree with</u>
<u>my judgment.</u>

But where am I bound, my Lady? For none of this is pertinent   (41)
here; nor meant for your ears; instead, as I was speaking of my
detractors, I recalled the phrases of one such who has recently
appeared, and all unwittingly my pen strayed in a desire to reply
to him specifically, although my intention is to speak generally.
And so, to return to our good Arce: he relates that he knew two
nuns in this City,* one of them in the Convent of Regina, who   *1170*
had so thoroughly committed to memory the Divine Office that
with the greatest alacrity and propriety she would apply its verses,
psalms, and maxims from the homilies of the saints to all her con-
versations. The other, in the Convent of the Conception, was so
adept in reading the Epistles of my father St. Jerome, and so well
versed in his sayings, that Arce says: *"I thought that I heard Jerome himself, speaking in Spanish."* Of the second nun, Arce says
that he learned, after her death, that she had translated those very
Epistles into the Spanish language; and he grieves that such talents
should not have been set to higher studies, guided by principles   *1180*
of science. He never mentions the name of either nun, but he
presents them in support of his verdict that the study of sacred
letters is not only permissible but most useful and necessary for
women, and all the more so for nuns. This is the same end to

letras, y mucho más a las monjas, que es lo mismo a que vuestra discreción me exhorta y a que concurren tantas razones.

(42) Pues si vuelvo los ojos a la tan perseguida habilidad de hacer versos —que en mí es tan natural, que aun me violento para que esta carta no lo sean, y pudiera decir aquello de *Quidquid conabar dicere, versus erat*—, viéndola condenar a tantos tanto y acriminar, he buscado muy de propósito cuál sea el daño que puedan tener, y no le he hallado; antes sí los veo aplaudidos
1090 en las bocas de las Sibilas; santificados en las plumas de los Profetas, especialmente del Rey David, de quien dice el gran expositor y amado Padre mío,* dando razón de las mensuras de sus metros: *In morem Flacci et Pindari nunc iambo currit, nunc alcaico personat, nunc sapphico tumet, nunc semipede ingreditur.* Los más de los libros sagrados están en metro, como el Cántico de Moisés; y los de Job, dice San Isidoro, en sus Etimologías, que están en verso heroico. En los Epitalamios los escribió Salomón; en los Trenos, Jeremías. Y así dice Casiodoro: *Omnis poetica locutio a Divinis scripturis sumpsit exordium.* Pues nues-
1100 tra Iglesia Católica no sólo no los desdeña, mas los usa en sus Himnos y recita los de San Ambrosio, Santo Tomás, de San Isidoro y otros. San Buenaventura les tuvo tal afecto que apenas hay plana suya sin versos. San Pablo bien se ve que los había estudiado, pues los cita, y traduce el de Arato: *In ipso enim vivimus, et movemur, et sumus,* y alega el otro de Parménides: *Cretenses semper mendaces, malae bestiae pigri.* San Gregorio Nacianceno disputa en elegantes versos las cuestiones de Matrimonio y la de la Virginidad. Y ¿qué me canso? La Reina de la Sabiduría y Señora nuestra, con sus sagrados labios,
1110 entonó el Cántico de la *Magnificat;* y habiéndola traído por ejemplar, agravio fuera traer ejemplos profanos, aunque sean de varones gravísimos y doctísimos, pues esto sobra para prueba; y el ver que, aunque como la elegancia hebrea no se pudo estrechar a la mensura latina, a cuya causa el traductor sagrado,* más atento a lo importante del sentido, omitió el verso, con todo, retienen los Salmos el nombre y divisiones de versos; pues ¿cuál es el daño que pueden tener ellos en sí? Porque el mal uso no es culpa del arte, sino del mal profesor que los vicia, haciendo de ellos lazos del demonio; y esto en todas
1120 las facultades y ciencias sucede.

which I am urged by your discretion, and wherein so many arguments concur.

*Now, if I turn my eyes to my much-maligned skill at writing (42) in verse – so natural to me that indeed I must force myself not to write this very letter in rhyme, and I could observe as another did, *"Whatever I tried to say came out in verse";* seeing this facility *1190* for writing poems condemned by so many and so vilified, I have sought quite deliberately to discover what harm there might be in them, and I cannot. Rather, I see them praised in the mouths of the Sibyls and sanctified by the pens of the Prophets, especially that of King David, of whom the great expositor, my own beloved Father,* says in scanning the measures of his meters: *"In the style of Horace and Pindar, now it runs in iambics, now it resounds in the alcaic measure, now it swells in sapphics, now in half-feet it moves slowly forward."* The greater part of our sacred books are written in meter, like the Canticle of Moses; and most of Job, ac- *1200* cording to the *Etymologies* of St. Isidore, is in heroic verse. Solomon wrote poetry in the *Epithalamia,* as did Jeremiah in his Lamentations. Cassiodorus says the following: *"All poetic speech had its origins in the Holy Scriptures."* Indeed, our own Catholic Church, far from spurning verses, employs them in her hymns and recites those of St. Ambrose, St. Thomas, St. Isidore, and others. St. Bonaventure was so fond of them that scarcely a page of his lacks verses. It is clear that St. Paul had studied them, for he cites them, and translates the following from Aratus: *"For in him we live, and move, and are";* and he quotes another, from Par- *1210* menides: *"The Cretians* [sic] *are always liars, evil beasts, slothful bellies."* St. Gregory of Nazianzus debates in elegant verses the questions of matrimony and virginity. And why should I grow weary? Our Lady, the Queen of Knowledge, with her blessed lips intoned the Canticle of the *Magníficat;* and once having presented her as an exemplar, it would be injurious to present profane examples, be they the verses of men ever so solemn and learned, for that would exceed the needs of proof. And we see that although the elegance of the Hebrew could not be bound in the Latin meter, so that the sacred translator,* heeding more closely the essence of the *1220* meaning, was obliged to omit the verse, yet still the Psalms retain the name and divisions of verses. Then what harm can verses cause in and of themselves? For their misuse is no fault of the art, but of the bad practitioner who debases them, fashioning devil's snares of them. And this occurs in all the faculties and sciences.

And if the evil lies in their being used by a woman, we have (43) just seen how many women have used them most laudably; then

The Answer   95

(43)   Pues si está el mal en que los use una mujer, ya se ve cuántas los han usado loablemente; pues ¿en qué está el serlo yo? Confieso desde luego mi ruindad y vileza; pero no juzgo que se habrá visto una copla mía indecente. Demás, que yo nunca he escrito cosa alguna por mi voluntad, sino por ruegos y preceptos ajenos; de tal manera, que no me acuerdo haber escrito por mi gusto sino es un papelillo que llaman *El Sueño*. Esa carta que vos, Señora mía, honrasteis tanto,* la escribí con más repugnancia que otra cosa; y así porque era de cosas sagradas a quienes (como he dicho) tengo reverente temor, como porque parecía querer impugnar, cosa a que tengo aversión natural. Y creo que si pudiera haber prevenido el dichoso destino a que nacía —pues, como a otro Moisés, la arrojé expósita a las aguas del Nilo del silencio, donde la halló y acarició una princesa como vos—; creo, vuelvo a decir, que si yo tal pensara, la ahogara antes entre las mismas manos en que nacía, de miedo de que pareciesen a la luz de vuestro saber los torpes borrones de mi ignorancia. De donde se conoce la grandeza de vuestra bondad, pues está aplaudiendo vuestra voluntad lo que precisamente ha de estar repugnando vuestro clarísimo entendimiento. Pero ya que su ventura la arrojó a vuestras puertas, tan expósita y huérfana que hasta el nombre le pusisteis vos, pésame que, entre más deformidades, llevase también los defectos de la prisa; porque así por la poca salud que continuamente tengo, como por la sobra de ocupaciones en que me pone la obediencia, y carecer de quien me ayude a escribir, y estar necesitada a que todo sea de mi mano y porque, como iba contra mi genio y no quería más que cumplir con la palabra a quien no podía desobedecer, no veía la hora de acabar; y así dejé de poner discursos enteros y muchas pruebas que se me ofrecían, y las dejé por no escribir más; que, a saber que se había de imprimir, no las hubiera dejado, siquiera por dejar satisfechas algunas objeciones que se han excitado, y pudiera remitir, pero no seré tan desatenta que ponga tan indecentes objetos a la pureza de vuestros ojos, pues basta que los ofenda con mis ignorancias, sin que los remita a ajenos atrevimientos. Si ellos por sí volaren por allá (que son tan livianos que sí harán), me ordenaréis lo que debo hacer; que, si no es interviniendo vuestros preceptos, lo que es por mi defensa nunca

what evil lies in my being one? I confess straightway my rough and uncouth nature; but I wager not a soul has seen an indecent verse of mine. What is more, I have never written a single thing 1230 of my own volition, but rather only in response to the pleadings and commands of others; so much so that I recall having written nothing at my own pleasure save a trifling thing they call the *Dream.* The letter that you so honored,* my Lady, I wrote with greater abhorrence than anything else. This was because it treated sacred matters for which (as I have said) I hold such reverent dread; and, too, because it would appear to be an attempt at refutation, to which I have a natural aversion. And I believe that, could I have foreseen the happy destiny for which it was born — for I cast it out, like a second Moses, as a foundling upon the waters 1240 of the Nile of silence, where it was discovered and cherished by a princess no less than yourself — I believe, as I was saying, that were I to have imagined any such thing, I should first have drowned it with these very hands to which it was born, for fear that the dull-witted scribbles of my ignorance should appear before the light of your knowledge. Thus we know the extent of your noble beneficence; for your goodwill applauds precisely what your most brilliant discernment should repudiate. But now that the letter's fate has cast it before your doors, a foundling so orphaned that its very name was bestowed by you, I regret that among all 1250 its many deformities it displays the defects of hasty composition. This is so as much on account of the poor health that is always mine as of the surfeit of tasks that obedience requires of me and the lack of anyone to help me with writing, so that it must all be done in my own hand. And while the task went against my character, yet I wanted nothing more than to keep my word to one whom I could not disobey, so that I thought I should never be done with it. And thus I left out entire arguments and a great many proofs that occurred to me, omitting them so as to be done writing. Had I known it was to be printed, I would not have left 1260 them out, were it only for the sake of satisfying a few objections that have arisen. And I could submit the latter to you; but I shall not be so careless as to set such indecent objects before the purity of your eyes, for it is enough that I offend them with my stupidities, without submitting them to the effronteries of others. If of their own account these go flying about (for they are so flighty that they will do so), you must order how I should proceed. Unless your instructions intervene, I shall never in my own defense take up the pen again.* For it seems to me that one who, by the very act of concealing his identity, acknowledges error needs no 1270

1160 tomaré la pluma,* porque me parece que no necesita de que
otro le responda, quien en lo mismo que se oculta conoce su
error, pues, como dice mi Padre San Jerónimo, *bonus sermo
secreta non quaerit*, y San Ambrosio: *latere criminosae est con-
scientiae*. Ni yo me tengo por impugnada, pues dice una regla
del Derecho: *Accusatio non tenetur si non curat de persona, quae
produxerit illam*. Lo que sí es de ponderar es el trabajo que le
ha costado el andar haciendo traslados. ¡Rara demencia: can-
sarse más en quitarse el crédito que pudiera en granjearlo! Yo,
Señora mía, no he querido responder; aunque otros lo han
1170 hecho, sin saberlo yo: basta que he visto algunos papeles, y
entre ellos uno que por docto os remito y porque el leerle os
desquite parte del tiempo que os he malgastado en lo que yo
escribo. Si vos, Señora, gustáredes de que yo haga lo contrario
de lo que tenía propuesto a vuestro juicio y sentir, al menor
movimiento de vuestro gusto cederá, como es razón, mi dictamen que, como os he dicho, era de callar, porque aunque dice
San Juan Crisóstomo: *calumniatores convincere oportet, interroga-
tores docere*, veo que también dice San Gregorio: *Victoria non
minor est, hostes tolerare, quam hostes vincere;* y que la pacien-
1180 cia vence tolerando y triunfa sufriendo. Y si entre los gentiles
romanos era costumbre, en la más alta cumbre de la gloria de
sus capitanes —cuando entraban triunfando de las naciones,
vestidos de púrpura y coronadas de laurel, tirando el carro,
en vez de brutos, coronadas frentes de vencidos reyes, acom-
pañados de los despojos de las riquezas de todo el mundo y
adornada la milicia vencedora de las insignias de sus hazañas,
oyendo los aplausos populares en tan honrosos títulos y
renombres como llamarlos Padres de la Patria, Columnas del
Imperio, Muros de Roma, Amparos de la República y otros
1190 nombres gloriosos—, que en este supremo auge de la gloria
y felicidad humana fuese un soldado, en voz alta diciendo al
vencedor, como con sentimiento suyo y orden del Senado: Mira
que eres mortal; mira que tienes tal y tal defecto; sin perdonar los más vergonzosos, como sucedió en el triunfo de César,
que voceaban los más viles soldados a sus oídos: *Cavete roma-
ni, adducimus vobis adulterum calvum*. Lo cual se hacía porque
en medio de tanta honra no se desvaneciese el vencedor, y porque el lastre de estas afrentas hiciese contrapeso a las velas

one to make accusation. As my father St. Jerome says, *"Honest words seek no quiet retreat"*; and St. Ambrose, *"It is the nature of a guilty conscience to hide away."* Nor do I consider myself to be impugned, for as a rule of Law maintains, *"An accusation cannot be upheld if it fails to pay heed to the character of the person who made it."* But what is worthy of wonder is the labor it has cost him to go about making copies. An odd dementia it is to wear oneself out more in avoiding credit than one could in earning it! My Lady, I have not wished to reply, though others have done so without my knowledge. It is enough that I have seen certain 1280 papers, among them one I send to you because it is learned, and because reading it will restore to you a portion of your time that I have wasted with what I am writing. If by your wisdom and sense, my Lady, you should be pleased for me to do other than what I propose, then as is only right, to the slightest motion of your pleasure I shall cede my own decision, which was as I have told you to keep still. For although St. John Chrysostom says, *"One's slanderers must be proven wrong, and one's questioners must be taught,"* I see too that St. Gregory says, *"It is no less a victory to tolerate one's enemies than to defeat them,"* and that patience 1290 defeats by tolerance and triumphs by suffering. Indeed, it was the custom among the Roman Gentiles, for their captains at the very height of glory—when they entered triumphing over other nations, clothed in purple and crowned with laurel; with their carts drawn by the crowned brows of vanquished kings rather than by beasts of burden; accompanied by the spoils of the riches of all the world, before a conquering army decorated with the emblems of its feats; hearing the crowd's acclaim in such honorable titles and epithets as Fathers of the Fatherland, Pillars of the Empire, Ramparts of Rome, Refuge of the Republic, and other glori- 1300 ous names—it was the custom, at this supreme apex of pride and human felicity, that a common soldier should cry aloud to the conqueror, as if from his own feeling and at the order of the Senate: "Behold, how you are mortal; behold, for you have such and such a failing." Nor were the most shameful excused; as at the triumph of Caesar, when the most contemptible soldiers shouted in his ears, *"Beware, Romans, for we bring before you the bald adulterer."* All of this was done so that in the midst of great honor the conqueror might not puff up with pride, and that the ballast of these affronts might prove a counterweight to the sails of so much 1310 praise, so that the ship of sound judgment should not founder in the winds of acclaim. If, as I say, all this was done by mere Gentiles, guided only by the light of Natural Law, then for us as Cath-

de tantos aplausos, para que no peligrase la nave del juicio entre
1200 los vientos de las aclamaciones. Si esto, digo, hacían unos gentiles, con sola la luz de la Ley Natural, nosotros, católicos, con un precepto de amar a los enemigos, ¿qué mucho haremos en tolerarlos? Yo de mí puedo asegurar que las calumnias algunas veces me han mortificado, pero nunca me han hecho daño, porque yo tengo por muy necio al que teniendo ocasión de merecer, pasa el trabajo y pierde el mérito, que es como los que no quieren conformarse al morir y al fin mueren sin servir su resistencia de excusar la muerte, sino de quitarles el mérito de la conformidad, y de hacer mala muerte la muerte que
1210 podía ser bien. Y así, Señora mía, estas cosas creo que aprovechan más que dañan, y tengo por mayor el riesgo de los aplausos en la flaqueza humana, que suelen apropiarse lo que no es suyo, y es menester estar con mucho cuidado y tener escritas en el corazón aquellas palabras del Apóstol: *Quid autem habes quod non accepisti? Si autem accepisti, quid gloriaris quasi non acceperis?*, para que sirvan de escudo que resista las puntas de las alabanzas, que son lanzas que, en no atribuyéndose a Dios, cuyas son, nos quitan la vida y nos hacen ser ladrones de la honra de Dios y usurpadores de los talentos que nos entre-
1220 gó y de los dones que nos prestó y de que hemos de dar estrechísima cuenta. Y así, Señora, yo temo más esto que aquello; porque aquello, con sólo un acto sencillo de paciencia, está convertido en provecho; y esto, son menester muchos actos reflexos de humildad y propio conocimiento para que no sea daño. Y así, de mí lo conozco y reconozco que es especial favor de Dios el conocerlo, para saberme portar en uno y en otro con aquella sentencia de San Agustín: *Amico laudanti credendum non est, sicut nec inimico detrahenti.* Aunque yo soy tal que las más veces lo debo de echar a perder o mezclarlo con tales defectos e im-
1230 perfecciones, que vicio lo que de suyo fuera bueno. Y así, en lo poco que se ha impreso mío, no sólo mi nombre, pero ni el consentimiento para la impresión ha sido dictamen propio, sino libertad ajena que no cae debajo de mi dominio, como lo fue la impresión de la carta Atenagórica; de suerte que solamente unos *Ejercicios de la Encarnación* y unos *Ofrecimientos de los Dolores,* se imprimieron con gusto mío por la pública devoción, pero sin mi nombre; de los cuales remito algunas

La Respuesta

olics, who are commanded to *love* our enemies, is it any great matter for us to tolerate them? For my part, I can testify that these detractions have at times been a mortification to me, but they have never done me harm. For I think that man very foolish who, having the opportunity to earn due merit, undertakes the labor and then forfeits the reward. This is like people who do not want to resign themselves to death. In the end they die all the same, with their resistance serving not to exempt them from dying, but only to deprive them of the merit of conformity to God's will, and thus to give them an evil death when it could have been blessed. And so, my Lady, I think these detractions do more good than harm. I maintain that a greater risk to human frailty is worked by praise, which usually seizes what does not belong to it, so that one must proceed with great care and have inscribed in one's heart these words of the Apostle: *"Or what hast thou that thou hast not received? And if thou hast received, why dost thou glory, as if thou hadst not received it?"* For these words should serve as a shield to deflect the prongs of praises, which are spears that, when not attributed to God to whom they belong, take our very lives and make us thieves of God's honor and usurpers of the talents that He bestowed on us, and of the gifts He lent us, for which we must one day render Him a most detailed account. And so, good Lady, I fear applause far more than slander. For the slander, with just one simple act of patience, is turned to a benefit, whereas praise requires many acts of reflection and humility and self-knowledge if it is not to cause harm. And so, for myself I know and own that this knowledge is a special favor from God, enabling me to conduct myself in the face of one as in the other, following that dictum of St. Augustine: *"One must believe neither the friend who speaks praises nor the enemy who reviles."* Although I am such a one as most times must either let the opportunity go to waste, or mix it with such failings and flaws that I spoil what left to itself would have been good. And so, with the few things of mine that have been printed, the appearance of my name – and, indeed, permission for the printing itself – have not followed my own decision, but another's liberty that does not lie under my control, as was the case with the "Letter Worthy of Athena." So you see, only some little *Exercises for the Annunciation* and certain *Offerings for the Sorrows* were printed at my pleasure for the prayers of the public, but my name did not appear. I submit to you a few copies of the same, so that you may distribute them (if you think it seemly) among our sisters the nuns of your blessed community and others in this City. Only one copy remains of the *Sorrows*, because

The Answer 1320 1330 1340 1350

copias, porque (si os parece) los repartáis entre nuestras hermanas las religiosas de esa santa comunidad y demás de esa
1240 ciudad. De los *Dolores* va sólo uno porque se han consumido ya y no pude hallar más. Hícelos sólo por la devoción de mis hermanas, años ha, y después se divulgaron; cuyos asuntos son tan improporcionados a mi tibieza como a mi ignorancia, y sólo me ayudó en ellos ser cosas de nuestra gran Reina: que no sé qué se tiene el que en tratando de María Santísima se enciende el corazón más helado. Yo quisiera, venerable Señora mía, remitiros obras dignas de vuestra virtud y sabiduría; pero como dijo el Poeta:*

1250   *Ut desint vires, tamen est laudanda voluntas:*
         hac ego contentos, auguror esse Deos.

(44)   Si algunas otras cosillas escribiere, siempre irán a buscar el sagrado de vuestras plantas y el seguro de vuestra corrección, pues no tengo otra alhaja con que pagaros, y en sentir de Séneca, el que empezó a hacer beneficios se obligó a continuarlos; y así os pagará a vos vuestra propia liberalidad, que sólo así puedo yo quedar dignamente desempeñada, sin que caiga en mí aquello del mismo Séneca: *Turpe est beneficiis vinci.* Que
1260 es bizarría del acreedor generoso dar al deudor pobre, con que pueda satisfacer la deuda. Así lo hizo Dios con el mundo imposibilitado de pagar: diole a su Hijo propio para que se le ofreciese por digna satisfacción.*

(45)   *Si el estilo, venerable Señora mía, de esta carta, no hubiere sido como a vos es debido, os pido perdón de la casera familiaridad o menos autoridad de que tratándoos como a una religiosa de.velo, hermana mía, se me ha olvidado la distancia de vuestra ilustrísima persona, que a veros yo sin velo, no sucediera así;* pero vos, con vuestra cordura y benignidad,
1270 supliréis o enmendaréis los términos, y si os pareciere incongruo el *Vos* de que yo he usado* por parecerme que para la reverencia que os debo es muy poca reverencia la *Reverencia,* mudadlo en el que os pareciere decente a lo que vos merecéis, que yo no me he atrevido a exceder de los límites de vuestro estilo ni a romper el margen de vuestra modestia.

(46)   Y mantenedme en vuestra gracia, para impetrarme la divi-

they have all been given away and I could find no more. I made them only for the prayers of my sisters, many years ago, and then they became more widely known. Their subjects are as disproportionate to my lukewarm ability as to my ignorance, and 1360 I was helped in writing them only by the fact that they dealt with matters of our great Queen; I know not why it is that in speaking of the Most Blessed Mary, the most icy heart is set aflame. It would please me greatly, my venerable Lady, to send you works worthy of your virtue and wisdom, but as the Poet* remarked:

Even when strength is lacking, still the intention must be praised.
I surmise the gods would be content with that.

If ever I write any more little trifles, they shall always seek (44) haven at your feet and the safety of your correction, for I have no other jewel with which to repay you. And in the opinion of 1370 Seneca, he who has once commenced to confer benefits becomes obliged to continue them. Thus you must be repaid by your own generosity, for only in that way can I be honorably cleared of my debt to you, lest another statement, again Seneca's, be leveled against me: *"It is shameful to be outdone in acts of kindness."* For it is magnanimous for the generous creditor to grant a poor debtor some means of satisfying the debt. Thus God behaved toward the world, which could not possibly repay Him: He gave His own Son, that He might offer Himself as a worthy amends.*

If the style of this letter, my venerable Lady, has been less than (45) your due, I beg your pardon for its household familiarity or the lack of seemly respect. For in addressing you, my sister, as a nun of the veil, I have forgotten the distance between myself and your most distinguished person, which should not occur were I to see you unveiled.* But you, with your prudence and benevolence, will substitute or emend my terms; and if you think unsuitable the familiar terms of address I have employed* – because it seems to me that given all the reverence I owe you, "Your Reverence" is very little reverence indeed – please alter it to whatever you think suitable. For I have not been so bold as to exceed the limits set by the 1390 style of your letter to me, nor to cross the border of your modesty.

And hold me in your own good grace, so as to entreat divine grace (46) on my behalf; of the same, may the Lord grant you great increase,

na, de que os conceda el Señor muchos aumentos y os guarde, como le suplico y he menester. De este convento de N. Padre San Jerónimo de Méjico, a primero día del mes de marzo de mil seiscientos y noventa y un años. B. V. M. vuestra más

1280 favorecida

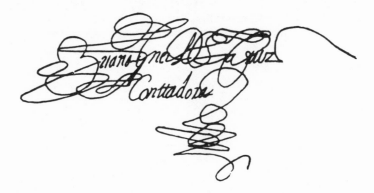

and may He keep you, as I beg of Him and as I am needful. Written at the Convent of our Father St. Jerome in Mexico City, this first day of March of the year 1691. Receive the embrace of your most greatly favored,

Sor Juana Inés de la Cruz

Annotations to
La Respuesta / The Answer

In preparing these notes, we sought to maintain the emphasis on gender that informs both Sor Juana's text and our edition of it. We have provided sufficient information to help students and general readers appreciate the sphere of intellectual concerns within which Sor Juana (SJ) wrote. Exhaustive treatment of her many classical, biblical, historical, and other references is beyond the scope of this work. See "A Note on the Texts," above.

Sor Filotea de la Cruz is the pseudonym of Manuel Fernández de Santa Cruz, the powerful and influential bishop of Puebla (1637–99). Literally, "Philo-thea" (from the Greek) means Lover-of-God; thus the whole name means Sister Lover-of-God of the Cross. Both the bishop preceding Fernández in Puebla and St. Francis de Sales, a French bishop and reformer whom Fernández greatly admired, had used the name to address nuns. Sor Juana was well aware she was answering to a male authority. On how and why the letter was written, see "The Issues at Stake" in Pt. II of the Introduction, above.

(1) l. 8 the Angelic Doctor, St. Thomas Aquinas: 1225–74. "The greatest figure of Scholasticism . . . held that faith and reason constitute two harmonious realms" (CE). According to the *Golden Legend,* Thomas's teacher, Albertus Magnus, defended the "silent" Thomas from schoolfellows who derided him (DCLL). SJ thus implicitly draws a parallel between Thomas and herself, between Albertus and the bishop (who ought therefore to defend her), and between the ignorant schoolfellows and her detractors. Such parallels between herself and illustrious figures, both male and female, appear throughout the text.

ll. 12–13 in truth . . . worthy of you: See note on "false humility," par. 3, below, and "Sor Juana's Art and Argument," in Pt. II of the Introduction, above.

ll. 14–16 the favor . . . of giving . . . to the press / favor, de dar a las prensas: For commentary on wordplay contained here, see "The Answer as Self-Defense" in Pt. II of Introduction, above.

l. 18 a rational being / ente de razón: From *ens rationis,* a Scholastic term, used here in the service of Baroque word-games. The bishop is placed in the realm often ascribed to women (the irrational), and Sor Juana in that of reason. The bishop has praised her unreasonably. Thus from the beginning, both playfully and seriously, SJ identifies herself with rational rather than supernatural religiosity.

l. 22 Quintilian: Marcus Fabius Quintilianus, A.D. c. 35–c. 95, the Roman rhetorician. SJ begins and ends this work by citing him, an indication of the profound influence on her of his *Institutio oratoria* [On the Education of an Orator], "a survey of education, literature, the principles of rhetoric and the life and training of the orator" (CE). Quintilian was rediscovered in the Renaissance, and his name became synonymous with "teacher." SJ clearly studied him and applied his rhetorical methods in structuring her arguments in the *Answer* (see Perelmuter Pérez).

ll. 22–23 "They produce less . . . benefits conferred": SJ gives the Latin phrase as *Minorem spei, maiorem benefacti gloriam pereunt.* The closest source in Quintilian's *Institutio* would seem to be III.vii.13, *Minores opes fuerunt, maiorem bene factis gloriam parit:* "The glory of good deeds may be enhanced by the smallness of their resources" (Butler trans., p. 471). SJ's Latin here is idiosyncratic, and she may be quoting from memory. See par. 9, below, for SJ's account of her opportunity to learn Latin.

(2) ll. 29–30 "And whence is this to me . . . ?": Luke 1:43. In many of the biblical passages from which SJ selects her citations, women are of great significance. Luke 1 recounts the Visitation of Mary to Elizabeth, making much of the mother's role in naming the child. Verses 1:46–56, known as the *Magnificat,* are attributed to Mary; SJ will allude to it at the end of the *Answer* by way of summarizing her contention that poetry is sacred and that women have employed the form magnificently.

From the outset of the *Answer,* through the text and its intertexts (passages alluded to, which her contemporaries would recognize), SJ emphasizes Mary and the mystery of the Incarnation. SJ explored this interest through Thomistic thought (the philosophy of St. Thomas Aquinas, reaching back through Albertus Magnus to Aristotle), which countered the Neoplatonic emphasis on the Crucifixion and Resurrection. (See first note, par. 1, above; Montross, *Virtue or Vice?* and Arenal, "Sor Juana Inés de la Cruz: Reclaiming the Mother Tongue.")

ll. 31–33 "Am not I . . . this word to me?": 1 Samuel 9:21. According to his vision, the prophet Samuel recognizes and selects Saul to be the first king of Israel. SJ continues to underscore the structure of the power relationships underlying her situation and to make her subtextual appeal to the protection of the teacher/prophet/prelate: SJ is to the bishop as Thomas is to Albert and Saul to Samuel.

(3) l. 43 false humility: The rhetoric of humility, standardly used by male and female religious, was intensified by a rhetoric of femininity (see Weber). Writing nuns used a strategy of affected modesty and (at times ironic) self-deprecation (see "Rhetorical Forms" in "Sor Juana's Art and Argument," Pt. II, Introduction, above).

ll. 44–45 that letter . . . "Worthy of Athena": Athena is the Greek goddess of wisdom. The letter is SJ's 1690 critique of a sermon by the celebrated Portuguese Jesuit Antonio Vieira (1608–97). The bishop had titled her letter thus and published it, SJ says, without her knowledge or permission. Vieira's "Maundy [or Holy] Thursday Sermon" (for the day Jesus washed his disciples' feet) saw in Christ's encouragement of the love of human beings for each other the highest example of God's love. SJ countered that the greatest love lay, rather, in God's withholding his love in order to allow for the exercise of effort and will. For contextualizing information, see "The Issues at Stake" in Pt. II of the Introduction, above.

ll. 48–49 and while . . . punishments: This echoes SJ's request (1681/82 letter to confessor) that "punishment" be gentle, loving, and in God's hands. Implicitly SJ carries on the argument regarding God's greatest favors that occupied the "Letter Worthy of Athena" (*Carta atenagórica*) and stresses God's ultimate authority, above that of her (chastising) male superiors.

ll. 49–50 chide me through benefits: Again, SJ continues the "Athenagoric" argument. See also poem 58, ll. 1–4:

Sweet lover and the soul's beloved, [i.e., Christ]
Highest good I yearn to reach,
Who with benefits and favors
Punishes our faults . . .

(4) ll. 73–74 the holy Chosen Vessel . . . third Heaven: St. Paul is referred to as the "holy chosen vessel" in Acts 9:15. The Spanish St. Teresa interpreted the rapture that carried St. Paul to the "third heaven" as a *vuelo del espíritu*, or "flight of the spirit" (in *Las moradas* [Sixth Mansion, chap. 5]); SJ instead offers a theological exegesis, explaining rationally the limits of speech. Consistently drawing parallels with regard to gender, SJ in this one echoes Mary's status as a "chosen vessel."

Annotations to La Respuesta / The Answer

ll. 75–76 "That he was caught up . . . ": 2 Corinthians 12:4. SJ cites the same chapter in par. 6 (see below). In choosing this second part of St. Paul's Epistles to the Corinthians, SJ is able safely to echo the first part (1 Corinthians; a section interestingly titled, in the BAC Bible, "Abuses in Need of Reform"). SJ opposes her rational religiosity to St. Teresa's mystical spirituality (as she will again, at the end of the *Answer*).

l. 83 Vieira: See note to par. 3, above. Two volumes of Antonio Vieira's sermons, translated into Spanish, were dedicated to Aguiar y Seijas, archbishop of Mexico. Here SJ tacitly juxtaposes herself (the "Mexican Phoenix") to Vieira (the "Lusitanian Phoenix") and cites a phrase she admires while alluding to his sometimes ill-used eloquence (as in the sermon that motivated her critique, which in turn caused such a stir). Her critique may have been aimed against Aguiar y Seijas in the first place, or at least against him as well; it was certainly read that way in her own time. Throughout the *Answer*, SJ will defend freedom of opinion for men and women.

ll. 85–86 Lusitanian Phoenix: I.e., Vieira. Lusitania is the ancient name for Portugal; "phoenix" was an encomiastic term used in this period to honor writers (SJ herself was dubbed "phoenix").

ll. 94–95 folly sparkles . . . crown: I.e. (ironically), "my stupidity is a blessing in disguise."

(5) l. 98 Moses . . . stutterer: In Exodus 4:10, Moses complains to God that he is "not eloquent" and has "impediment and slowness of tongue" and therefore is not a fit emissary to Pharaoh. His brother Aaron is appointed to speak for him (see Exodus 4:10–16).

ll. 101–2 "Shew me thy face": Exodus 33:20

l. 111 Ahaseurus: or Assuerus; King Xerxes I of Persia, 486–465 B.C. SJ compares the bishop/Filotea to King Ahasuerus (in the biblical Book of Esther) and, so doing, implicitly likens herself to Queen Esther, who saved her people with the king's "safe-conduct" and permission. SJ here gives a biblical context for the *Answer*'s challenge to sexual politics, for her consistent turning of the tables. Note that Ahasuerus had banished Queen Vashti for not being properly subservient, fearing that other women might in turn fail to honor and submit to their husbands (Esther 1:20). Subsequently, however, the king listens and in fact "obeys" Esther. In 5:2 he extends his scepter, she touches it, and he asks to know her petition. (In a suppressed version, Apocryphal Additions D12, he puts his scepter against her neck and kisses her, saying "Speak to me.") Esther's wisdom and wiles will save the Jews from extinction (see Esther 1, 4 [15:9–15], 5:2, 8:7).

l. 114 to plead my case: The Spanish verb *proponer* means "to present arguments pro and con"; SJ is setting up the patterns of a formal legal defense. See Introduction, above, and Perelmuter Pérez.

l. 119 insinuation: The Spanish *insinuación* exemplifies the interplay of meanings that SJ's contemporaries would have apprehended. The Spanish and English words share these etymologically associated meanings. These include classical and late Latin definitions, forensic (legal) and rhetorical terms, and general usage. In Spanish and English, *insinuación*/insinuation possess primary meanings of "covert suggestion" and "ingratiation." Secondary uses come from law and rhetoric. The late Latin *insinuatio*, which meant "notification" or (significantly) "publication," entered legal parlance in both languages: "The production or delivery of a will for official registration, as a step toward procuring probate," according to the OED. Remember that SJ's rhetorical presentation answers the accusation of a supposed friend, who without her knowledge published a writing she had done at his request, chided her in print, and signed his chastisement as a nun. Sor Juana's language itself gives us the key to her multivalenced stance: covertly, etymologically, Sor Juana reveals the bishop's publication of her text.

ll. 120–121 that very Letter: The "Letter Worthy of Athena" the bishop had published. In the next sentence SJ claims it should make up for her nonreligious writing (leaving unmentioned the many religious *villancicos* she has authored). Then, while explicitly attributing the paucity of "sacred letters" among her writings to reverence, awe, fear, and insufficient wisdom, she implicitly censures most theological writing as arrogant and ignorant.

ll. 135–36 "Why dost thou . . . ": Psalms 49:16.

l. 137 Song of Songs: Called Canticle of Canticles in the Douay Version, it is also known as the Song of Solomon. **Genesis:** first book of the Old Testament.

l. 141 St. Jerome: c. 347–420? Jerome is SJ's "father" because he is a father of the church (as one of the four great doctors) and because SJ belongs to the Jeronymite (also Hieronymite) Order. Trained as a classical (i.e., pagan, Greek, and Latin) grammarian, Jerome became a Christian ascetic and scholar, learning Hebrew to translate the Bible into Latin (which became the Vulgate, the official Roman Catholic version). Indeed, Jerome had a vision in which angels whipped him for loving the classics more than the "barbarous tongue" of the Old Testament prophets (DCLL). Subsequently made a saint, he is a powerful "defense" for SJ against the bishop's accusation of her excessive attention to the classics. Jerome wrote exegetical works, tracts, lives of writers, and letters, and he was buried in Bethlehem, near the graves of his two close associates, St. Paula and her daughter St. Eustochium.

ll. 143–46 Then at last . . . in fleshly language": St. Jerome wrote to the Roman Christian woman Laeta, giving careful instructions on the education of her daughter Paula (a.k.a. Paula the Younger). In citing this letter, SJ counters those who believe that women should remain uneducated by showing that education for women is part of a great tradition and that a pattern set for women can be applied to men. The daughter Paula was sent to Bethlehem, as Paul instructed, to be educated by her grandmother Paula and her aunt Eustochium, eventually succeeding the latter as head of the nunnery there. *Select Letters of St. Jerome,* Wright trans., p. 365.

l. 146 Seneca: c. 3 B.C.–A.D. c. 65. A Roman philosopher, dramatist, and statesman whose moral wisdom was influential during the Renaissance. Accused by the bishop of loving pagan authors (as did St. Jerome), SJ proudly accepts the parallel drawn by the bishop and quotes several pre-Christian writers throughout the *Answer.*

ll. 146–47 "In early years . . . manifest": Although Salceda and Trueblood, following marginalia in the early editions, attribute this quote to Seneca's *De beneficiis (On Public Honors),* it appears in Seneca's *Octavia,* 1. 538. (The wording differs slightly from that given by SJ; the line reads: *"Teneris in annis haud satis clara est fides."* See *Seneca's Tragedies,* trans. Miller, vol. 2, pp. 452–53.) The suggestiveness of the play *Octavia* differs markedly from the moral essay to which textual notes attribute this quote.

l. 153 Holy Office: The Inquisition of the Holy Office, though popularly associated with the Spanish church, was actually founded by the papacy in the thirteenth century to root out a heresy that threatened Christian unity and the nascent French monarchy. At the end of the fifteenth century, it was revived by the monarchs Ferdinand and Isabella to unify their territories by expelling Muslims and Jews from Spain. For the next four centuries it was used almost exclusively against those who impugned Catholic dogma or orthodoxy; SJ thus takes care to point out that nothing she has written has done this.

ll. 154–55 "just . . . feared": We have not yet found a source for this Latin quotation.

ll. 161–62 "no one . . . impossible": Source not yet found.

ll. 169–70 four profundities of a superficial scholar / cuatro bachillerías superficiales: SJ refers, with ironic disparagement, to her studies. Self-taught, she has been excluded from the *bachiller* (roughly equivalent to a bachelor's degree) from which the term *bachillería* (prattle or unfounded statements) derives. See SJ's comedy *The Trials of a Household* (probably 1683) where a servant speaks to his enamored master about the protagonist, Leonor (OC 4.47:648–50 and 654–56).

Castaño (aside, to Don Carlos):
My lord, what a wealthy house this is,
and what an elegant lady!

Could you not have given your heart . . .
. . . to this one, and not that pitiful
Leonor, whose entire fortune
is the profundity of a superficial scholar?

[. . . aquella pobrecita
de Leonor, cuyo caudal
son cuatro bachillerías?]

(See also OC 3.303:276.) One of Sor Juana's most popular works, the play shows her early development of themes that will later be central to the *Answer*. It is an "answer" to plays by Lope de Vega and Calderón de la Barca and has one of the few male characters in Hispanic theater who dresses up as female and thus mocks with pointed hilarity the characteristic makeup, apparel, and behavior of "femininity."

(6) SJ has thus far been constrained and self-consciously defensive in speaking directly to "Sor Filotea." Here, speaking of her in-born inclination to letters and her relationship with God, she becomes free (both sincerely and calculatedly) in her expression. As a legal defense, with this paragraph the *exordium* (beginning or introduction) ends and the *narratio* (statement of relative or essential facts) begins.

ll. 178–79 My writing has never . . . beyond me: The majority of writings by nuns entailed obedience to a command. For SJ, commands came both from religious and from secular sources; in part, she may be highlighting the difficulty of having to defend herself from potential charges of unorthodoxy.

ll. 179–80 I can in truth say . . . "compelled me": 2 Corinthians 12:11. The same chapter of 2 Corinthians is cited in par. 4, above. Here SJ likens herself, reproached, to St. Paul, who (in verses immediately preceding these) "take[s] pleasure . . . in reproaches, in necessities, in persecutions, in distresses for Christ's sake: for when I am weak, then am I strong. I am become a fool in glorying; ye have compelled me: for I ought to have been commended of you: for in nothing am I behind the very chiefest apostles, though I be nothing" (2 Corinthians 12:9–11; see also 7–8). Implicitly, SJ excuses her "boasting" (about her talents), shows herself bowing to God's will, and appeals to such authorities as Aguiar y Seijas (the highest officer of the church in Mexico), to Núñez (the confessor from whom she had distanced herself), and to the bishop of Puebla (Sor Filotea) – all of whom believed in "holy ignorance" for women – for more tolerant understanding of her God-given intellectual and poetic gifts.

ll. 205–6 save to that one to whom they must be said: I.e., Antonio Núñez de Miranda, her confessor at the time.

(7) This charming narrative (pars. 7–10), based on biographical detail, is frequently cited as "the truth" about SJ's life – perhaps a measure of

the success of her highly structured and convincing rhetorical method (see Luciani, "Sor Juana: Dressing the Part"). Note the continuing parallel to the nuns' *Lives*: where they cite an insurmountable spiritual vocation, SJ claims an intellectual one (see Myers, "Sor Juana's *Respuesta*").

l. 210 To go on with: The Spanish *Prosiguiendo en* is a key phrase, emphasizing connections with both the colloquial narrative tradition of nuns' Lives and the classical rhetoric for legal defenses. There are simultaneous elements of earnestness and complex parody in both connections. Concurrent with her "straight" use of these sources, SJ makes fun of herself, juridical formalities, and the popular adaptation of those formalities in spiritual writings by nuns. The nuns wrote spiritual histories; SJ at once historicizes and fictionalizes her intellectual life as "confession," noting sufferings for learning (rather than for God) that are somewhat tongue-in-cheek.

l. 214 Amigas: Schools improvised by cultured women in their homes for the education of girls from relatively privileged families. Also *Amiga*.

(8) ll. 236–40 As soon as . . . study: Frederick Luciani has shown the parallels between this wish to dress as a man in order to be able to attend the university and the same deed undertaken by a character named "Juana" in a play by Francisco de Rojas Zorrilla, which SJ may well have read (see Luciani, "Sor Juana: Dressing the Part"). The successful novelist María de Zayas y Sotomayor, some of whose female characters disguised themselves as men, may also have been read by SJ, although it was officially illegal for novels to be imported or printed in the Spanish colonies at the time. Historically as well as literarily, cross-dressing for purposes of study and of wage earning was not unprecedented in the early modern period (see Dugaw, *Warrior Women and Popular Balladry*).

(9) ll. 247–48 I began to study . . . twenty lessons: In Europe and subsequently in its colonies, throughout the medieval period and continuing into the Renaissance and the Baroque, Latin was the primary language of scholarship, the university, and many areas of intellectual life. Most women, with the exception of a few in the upper classes, were excluded from the opportunity to learn Latin. In emphasizing the brevity of her Latin training, SJ not only boasts of her proficiency but underscores the commitment to learning that led her onto paths few women were able to follow.

l. 261 quite opposed to my character / repugnantes a mi genio: Here (as in *Carta atenagórica*) SJ employs the adjective *repugnante*, a Thomistic term used to explain what goes against one's nature (see Montross, p. 6). *Genio* and *ingenio* are complex terms in Sor Juana's period and important concepts in her self-defense, yet they defy direct translation or parallel today. In part, SJ distinguishes what we might call "innate" traits from those developed through application (see note on Gracián's essay, par. 26, below). These terms recur throughout the *Answer.* We echo Christopher Maurer's translation as "character" and "intelligence," respectively.

ll. 262–63 my absolute unwillingness to enter into marriage: The theme of the convent as a refuge in cases of unhappy love (a convention of the time) appears in *The Trials of a Household* (OC 4.128:87–92), where Leonor says:

> . . . I mean, good friend, to quit this place
> and seek a little cell
> to serve me as a quiet tomb
> where I'll bemoan my fate
> and weep for all my tragedies
> as long as I may live . . .

Critics have cited this to indicate a similar experience for SJ. A stronger convention appears in religious literature, especially nuns' *Lives*: the theme of rejecting the sacrament of earthly marriage in order to embrace the holier choice of divine nuptials. A life of celibacy in the monastery allowed certain women a degree of autonomy (see Arenal, "The Convent as Catalyst for Autonomy"). Later on, SJ implicitly compares herself to Teresa of Avila, referring (in another context) to the saint's rejection of men in favor of Christ (see par. 20).

ll. 263–65 the least unfitting . . . my salvation: This echoes, and may reflect SJ's familiarity with, a passage in St. Teresa's *Life*: "and though, even then, I could not incline my will to being a nun, I saw that this was the best and safest state, and so, little by little, I determined to force myself to embrace it." This decision, then, to enter the religious life seems to have been inspired more by fear than by love. *Complete Works of Saint Teresa of Jesus,* Peers trans., 1:19.

ll. 279 "privation . . . appetite": We have not yet found a source for this Latin quotation.

(10) ll. 291–92 the goal . . . Theology: SJ will continue to advance her argument for a humanist study of classical sources and the natural world as well as of explicitly Christian texts. Again, her important intellectual authorities here include Thomas Aquinas. "For Thomas there was no need to reject or despise whatever pagan reason had discovered of the truth; just as grace does not destroy nature but perfects it, so sacred doctrine presupposes, uses, and perfects natural knowledge (*Summa Theol.* 1a, 1.8ad2). Some truths about God exceed the ability of reason. But there are other truths that the natural reason of man is able to reach" (NCE).

l. 297 St. Paula: A wealthy Roman noblewoman (d. 414), Paula followed St. Jerome, with her daughters Blessilla and Eustochium, to Bethlehem. There she built and led the first nunneries of the Jeronymite Order. SJ's convent in Mexico City was named after St. Paula (Convento de Santa Paula de la Orden de San Jerónimo). See note to par. 5, above.

(11) Here SJ answers the central tenet of the bishop's / Sor Filotea's letter to her: all but divine knowledge should be abhorred (see "The Issues at Stake" in Introduction, above).

l. 311 **Physics or Natural Science:** In Spanish, *Física* is the Aristotelian term for what would in the Enlightenment be termed Natural Science or Natural Philosophy; because today's "physics" has such a different meaning, "Natural Science" has been added for clarity.

l. 337 **Historical Books:** Those sections of the Old Testament that recount history rather than laws or prophecy.

l. 339 **two branches of Law:** Canon and civil law; i.e., the compiled legal codes of church and state.

l. 340 **Books of Law:** The corresponding books of the Old Testament that give laws rather than history or prophecy.

l. 350 **the Cities:** Sodom and Gomorrah (see next note).

ll. 351–61 **And the number fifty . . . knowledge of Music?:** SJ likens the intervals of classical musical theory, as known in her day through Pietro Cerone's *The Musicmaker and Master: A Treatise on Theoretical and Practical Music* (Naples, 1613), to Abraham's plea for the righteous of Sodom and Gomorrah (Genesis 18:23–32). SJ's copy of Cerone's book, with annotations in her own hand, still exists; she considered herself a disciple of Cerone and refers to a treatise on musical theory she had composed, *El caracol* [The Snail], now lost (OC 1.6:13 and note, p. 387).

ll. 361–65 **Shalt thou . . . of the earth?":** Job 38:31-32. The Pleiades are a star cluster in the constellation Taurus consisting of several hundred stars, of which six are visible to the naked eye (a seventh was traditionally thought to be visible to those with keen sight). In Greek mythology, the Pleiades are seven of the daughters of Atlas (Maia, Electra, Calaeno, Taygeta, Merope, Alcyone, and Sterope) who were metamorphosed as stars after death. Arcturus is a star near the tail of the constellation Great Bear; its rising and setting were supposed to foretell tempests (LCD). The day star (or morning star) is a planet locally visible in the east just before sunrise, especially Venus. The evening star is any planet that crosses the local meridian before midnight, especially Mercury or Venus. With these examples from astronomy, SJ again cites the necessity of classical and scientific learning in the pursuit of biblical studies.

l. 368 **this Book:** The Bible.

l. 369 **this Science:** Theology (*Teología*, a feminine noun; thus the pronoun "She").

(12) ll. 377–80 At the difficult . . . from God: Roman Breviary, Office of the Feast of St. Thomas, March 7, Fifth Lesson (*Brevarium Romanum*, I, p. 780).

l. 400 and likewise with all things: Source not yet found.

ll. 410–11 chain . . . of Jupiter: For antecedents of this image, Salceda (OC 4) refers to Homer's *Iliad*, bk. VIII, and Lucian's *Dialogue of Ares and Hermes*; Trueblood *(A Sor Juana Anthology)* cites Paz in saying the image originated with Nicholas of Cusa (1440), who saw God as both center and circumference of the universe. SJ enjoyed exploring mathematical and geometric conceptualizations like this "chain," which in its abstraction is less (male)-gendered than many other figurative representations of knowledge. (See Paz, *Sor Juana*, chaps. 21 and 24.)

l. 413 Athanasius Kircher: 1602–80. This German Jesuit philosopher has been described as "an infatigable [sic] retriever of information in the service of the Church" (Franco, "Sor Juana Explores Space," p. 202, n. 29). SJ greatly admired him and drew ideas and facts from his books, which appear on shelves behind her in the famous early eighteenth-century portraits. Her reference condenses Kircher's title, which on the frontispiece of one version reads *Regnum Naturae magneticum in triplici magnete . . .* [Nature's Magnetic Realm . . .] (Rome, 1667); another title is *Magnes, sive de arte magnetica* [Magnet; or, On the Art of the Magnet] (Rome, 1641). The "chain of Jupiter" image also appears on the frontispiece of another book by Kircher (see Paz, *Sor Juana*, chap. 24).

(13) ll. 427–28 Expositors, Scholastics: SJ's "metaphorical example" here refers to two essential features of the Scholastic method (procedures for university study of medieval Christian philosophy): "exposition" (Latin *lectio*) and "'disputation" *(disputatio)*. Exposition was the foundation for disputation, but disputation was "the more original and characteristic feature" of Scholastic method (NCE); thus, those engaging in disputation are termed "the Scholastics." In the medieval university, the "master" presented analytical explanation of a text, grappling with problems presented by the author; disputation of a specific question took place at a regular time later in the academic day.

l. 434 lacking . . . a teacher: SJ expressed the same thought in her 1681/82 letter to her confessor, in the prologue to *Segundo volumen de las obras* (1692/93; OC 4.411), and in poem 51 (OC 1.159:33–36 and 41–44):

A woman ignorant and unschooled,
who has been snatching studies
in thievery, when time allowed,
from all her proper duties; . . .

An education rough and rude,
for in her early girlhood
naught but her cogitations served
to take the place of tutor . . .

(14) ll. 462–66 "What efforts . . . living with me": *Select Letters of
St. Jerome,* Wright trans., p. 419 (letter 125: "To Rusticus"). She repeats
this quotation, through "experience," in the prologue to *Segundo volumen
de las obras* (1692/93; OC 4.411).

(15) ll. 477–78 to find recreation . . . conversation: "Recreation"
was valued in many convents (and was emphasized in the Teresian rule);
indeed, in a daily period set aside for that purpose, nuns gathered for
handiwork and edifying talk. The humorous tone and detailed content
of this passage bear a marked similarity to the work of María de San José
(1549–1626), an educated Spanish disciple of St. Teresa of Avila (1515–82),
who expressed feminist sentiments in both prose and verse. SJ may well
have known the dialogues of her *Libro de las recreaciones* [Book of Recre-
ations] (1585); SJ spent a few months in a Carmelite convent in Mexico
City, where manuscripts by Spanish Carmelite nuns may have circulated, before she joined the Hieronymite Order. SJ's comfortable cloister,
however, was a far cry from those of the early reformed Carmelites, who
lived in community and closely followed vows of poverty and obedience.
(María de San José writes of her attraction to the intelligent conversation that took place among Teresa's followers. Both in the letter to Núñez
and in the *Answer,* SJ indicates that at times she felt resentment against
and isolation from her nonintellectual Sisters.)

(16) Throughout this section, note SJ's ambivalent or polyvalent concept of the "inclination," which is at once dangerous temptation/pas-
sion/appetite and worthy strength/blessing/gift.
ll. 499–500 hearing such widespread applause: SJ wrote about the
vicissitudes of this acclaim in the epistolary ballad "Apollo help you, as
you're a man!" (see Selected Poems, below) and in *The Trials of a Household* (OC 4.37:291–94 and 316–20), where Leonor says:

. . . for if I say I was from the first
applauded as a miracle
of intelligence, I am belied
by the foolishness of saying so . . .

. . . I was the admired target
of the attentions of all people,
so that all, at last,

worshipped as innate what were
merely acquired laurels.

l. 507 those persons . . . desiring my good: This refers to all those
in her intimate circles – other nuns, men and women of the viceroyalty,
clerics – who misguidedly believe her (and any woman's) dedication to
learning censurable: including, of course, and perhaps most specifically, her former confessor and the bishop/Filotea (see next note).

ll. 510–12 All this study . . . wit and cleverness: This reformula-
tion of hearsay refers to the bishop's/Filotea's letter to SJ (which cautioned
that women could study if it did "not remove women from a position
of obedience" and urged that SJ improve her "natural predisposition . . .
by sometimes reading the book of Jesus Christ" in addition to classical
authors [Trueblood trans., pp. 200–201]). SJ also seems to recall the words
of Núñez, whom she contested in her letter of 1681/82 (e.g.: "Is not God,
who is supreme goodness, also supreme wisdom? Then why would He
find ignorance more acceptable than knowledge? That St. Anthony was
saved in his holy ignorance is well and good. St. Augustine chose the
other path, and neither of them went astray" [Peden trans., in Paz, *Sor
Juana*, p. 500]). See "The Issues at Stake" in Pt. II of the Introduction, above.

l. 514 my own executioner!: In veiled manner, here and elsewhere,
SJ announces a coming decision to silence herself (see "A Different
World–View, a Different Law," in Pt. II of the Introduction, above).

(17) l. 515–16 doubly unfortunate: An ironic and critical reference
to the social attitudes about writing by women and nuns (see Ludmer,
"Tricks of the Weak"; Moraña, "Orden dogmático").

l. 519 significance: SJ threads together complex ideas and analogies
(see "Sor Juana's Art and Argument" in Pt. II of the Introduction, above,
and note to par. 21, below).

(18) l. 530 impious [Niccolo] Machiavelli: 1469–1527. The Italian
political philosopher, statesman, and author of *The Prince*, which earned
him a reputation for calculating ruthlessness.

(19) SJ here employs the tone and style of sermons (which were favorite
reading material for many literate people as well as part of almost everyone's daily oral fare). SJ offers an emotionally stirring but rational counterpart to, and theological commentary on, St. Teresa of Avila's
meditations on the same subject. That SJ has Teresa in mind will be evi-
dent in the next paragraph. Admiration for the beauty of Christ's face
and body was the only licit terrain for women (especially nuns) to express such amorous sentiments. SJ employs this female tradition in her

strategy of gender-attitude reversal and counterbalancing seen throughout the *Answer*.

l. 535 **Christ's bodily form:** The Spanish *su presencia* has a more strongly embodied sense than the English cognate "presence"; the emphasis on Christ's *presencia* / bodily form here evokes the Thomistic-Aristotelian focus on the Incarnation.

ll. 546–47 **the face of Moses . . . became intolerable:** In the passage SJ cites here, the Douay Version follows a Renaissance misreading, translating literally the phrase in Exodus 34:29–30 (from Latin *cornuta facies*) as "the face of Moses horned." BAC explains that the phrase should be understood metaphorically: Moses' face was framed by rays of light and glory. This is in keeping with SJ's points about divine beauty and her linking of the Old and New Testaments.

(20) l. 556 **Our Holy Mother, my own mother Teresa:** Repeated mention of the saint allows SJ to pull her antagonists into a first-person-plural viewpoint and to shield her own berating of male stupidity from direct accusation. She continues her role as exegete (commentator) on the work of this one – of only two – women doctors of the church. The other is St. Catherine of Siena, also designated such in 1970. Although the title was not official until so recently, even in the sixteenth century it was commonly used by writing nuns to praise Teresa's learning and piety.

(21) ll. 569–70 **"What do we . . . many miracles?":** John 11:47. SJ here continues subtle and meaningful wordplay, harking back through the Spanish *seña* to its Latin root *signa,* plural of *signum* (with related meanings including "sign," "miracle," "significance"). In all her writing SJ relies upon the realization, first, that human words are *signs* and not the "things" they point to (an intellectual perception explored in the Baroque and recovered in our own day); and, second, that the divine Word became flesh and worked "Signs," or miracles. For this, Christ was condemned by learned hypocrites. SJ, known as a "miracle of intelligence" (see her play *The Trials of a Household*), suffers condemnation which she likens to his in the tradition of the *imitatio Christi,* or "imitation of Christ," to which all Christians and especially members of religious orders were enjoined.

l. 585 **"root . . . the people":** Isaiah 11:10 (Douay Version). An example of the multiplicity of connotations SJ was managing can be given here. "A root of Jesse" literally means "of the family of David" and is an Old Testament prophetic phrase taken to designate Jesus (Jesse was David's father). David is a symbol for SJ of poetry and the humanities in service of the sacred. Here she cites from the section of Isaiah known as the Book of Emmanuel, which announces the virgin birth of the Messiah. (In another work SJ had traced the Virgin's lineage, and in another cited the medieval claim that "Eve" had become "Ave" [Mary], cleansed of the sins for which Adam was responsible.) Immediately preceding the verse cited here is the famous peaceable kingdom passage, in which the wolf lies down with the lamb and the lion with the kid (Isaiah 11:6–7), followed by the less well known "The suckling child shall play over the hole of the asp, and the weaned child shall put his hand on the adder's den." A few lines earlier we find a call from God for women to use their voices, a theme SJ is about to take up: "Cry aloud O daughter of Gallim!" (10:30). St. Jerome, SJ's spiritual father, had especially praised the spirituality of Isaiah and, along with others, valorized its great literary merit.

l. 586 "for a sign . . . contradicted": Luke 2:34. The preceding verse reads, "And his father and mother were wondering [marveled] at those things which were spoken concerning him." SJ selects a passage that emphasizes both parents' response. Simeon (the "just"), who speaks these words, goes on to address Mary. BAC underscores a notable parallel between the son and the mother in the next two verses: "Behold, this child is set for the fall, and for the resurrection of many in Israel, and for a sign which shall be contradicted; and thy own soul a sword shall pierce, that, out of many hearts, thoughts may be revealed." Subsequent verses tell of the aged prophet Anna, who voiced thanksgiving to God and spoke to those who sought the redemption of Jerusalem. That is, SJ selects quotations from texts that echo her main arguments in order to urge the correction of misunderstandings and show precedents for women's exercise of interpretive power and active participation in the constitution of what is considered sacred.

(22) Here SJ recounts the afflictions of elaborate figures vis-à-vis themes already introduced: humiliation, betrayal, and defenselessness. SJ's syntax in the original stresses the feminine gender of the *figura* placed vulnerably on high.

l. 605 [Baltasar] Gracián. 1601–58. The work of this Spanish Jesuit – priest and author, stylist, moralist, and satirist – was influential for SJ. She may possibly have known of his troubles with the Jesuit Order, which unsuccessfully prohibited him from publishing what he wrote "so brilliantly on worldly wisdom and on political behavior" (*The Art of Worldly Wisdom*, Maurer trans., p. xiv).

ll. 605–606 "The advantages of intelligence are advantages of being": This quote is from *El discreto* ["The Worldly Wit"] (1646), the first essay in the treatise *Genio e ingenio* [Character and Intelligence]. Gracián, *Obras completas*, p. 80.

ll. 614–15 "It is . . . greater intelligence": Martial (Marcus Valerius Martialis, A.D. c. 40–c. 104), the Roman-Spanish satirist and poet. Verse cited: "A friend will often cede his gold, his treasures, his fields; / one willing to concede intelligence is rare" (*Epigrams* VIII.18). Gracián paraphrases this in his *Art of Worldly Wisdom*: "Most people do not mind being surpassed in good fortune, character, or temperament, but no one, especially not a sovereign, likes to be surpassed in intelligence" (Maurer trans., p. 4). Martial's verses, characterized by original meter and form and by a twist of wit ending each thought, became models for the modern epigram. During the Renaissance, in Europe, he was considered too crude for women to quote; SJ cites an off-color passage in par. 38, below.

(23) Throughout this paragraph, SJ continues entwining classical with Old and New Testament worlds and wisdom, a characteristic of humanists and some Christian scholars of the early period and of Renaissance writers. But her summoning of classical sources disobeys the bishop's exhortation.

l. 636 Pliny: Probably Pliny the Younger (A.D. 62–c. 114), author of *Letters* and *Panegyricus* (a panegyric to Trajan).

l. 637 Aulus Gellius: A.D. c. 123–c. 165). This classical writer preserved excerpts from Greek and Latin writings in his *Attic Nights*, a literary storehouse of notes on philosophy, criticism, jurisprudence, and other matters (BLQ).

ll. 645–46 "I have gone . . . through it": Job 1:7.

ll. 647–48 "Your adversary . . . devour": 1 Peter 5:8.

l. 649 "Now shall . . . cast out": John 12:31.

ll. 652–53 "Thorns and thistles . . . to thee": Genesis 3:18.

l. 654 "His Mother the Synagogue: This notable reference parallels the later "Holy Mother Church," so that the central Judaic and Christian institutions are seen as female (in an instance of SJ's ecumenical range). SJ recurrently associates motherhood with creativity and wisdom. (See note to par. 40, below.)

ll. 655–56 daughters of Zion . . . triumph: Luke 23:28. Jesus tells the women to weep not over him but for themselves. The women following the cross in verses 27–29 is an important image for SJ's purposes.

(24) **l. 663 Our very Life . . . give new life to dead Lazarus:** Another "incarnational" Thomistic-Aristotelian image; by implication, one of Christ's chief miracles is "womanly," the giving of life.

ll. 665–67 "Rabbi . . . thither again?"; "Are there . . . the day?": John 11:8, 9. A double comparison is put forth: just as there are twelve hours in a day, so Jesus' days are fixed; and there is time and dark enough to go without danger to Judea (BAC). SJ contests the bishop's claim (early in his letter to her) that Christ's parables were not understood and therefore not considered to be miracles.

l. 676 "Let us also . . . with Him": John 11:16.

l. 680 The Jews themselves . . .: In this condemnation, SJ reads as a Christian of her culture: the Jews are to blame for Christ's death. In other instances, citing the Old Testament, SJ praises Jews for their virtue, wisdom, leadership, and poetry.

ll. 682–84 "Many good works . . . stone me"; "For a good work . . . for blasphemy": John 10:32–33.

ll. 697–701 In all that I have said . . . the other: SJ here rebukes such men as Vieira, Aguiar y Seijas, Núñez, and the bishop, summarizing the reproach that runs through the *Answer*. She ends her exegesis or *explication de texte* (a vying with the bishop in his own field, since he spent years and thousands of pages writing clarifications of disputed passages of Scripture) by drawing a comparison between the persecution of Christ and her own. Her audacity was perhaps less striking in her own time, when everyone was encouraged to imitate the Passion (suffering) of Christ, especially nuns and monks, and when hyperbolic comparisons were the common currency of expression.

(25) ll. 703–4 "But . . . afar off": Luke 22:54.

ll. 704–5 "not knowing . . . said": Luke 9:33.

ll. 708–9 "Woman, I know not . . . I am not": SJ "misremembers" the gender of persons addressed here, in quoting Luke 22:60 and 58. The Bible has: "Man, I know not what thou sayest. O Man, I am not . . ." (Salceda's notes [OC] correct her slip without mentioning it; Trueblood does not comment.) In the verse immediately preceding (22:57), Peter does address a woman. However, it is interesting that SJ's errors linguistically "dress" or "disguise" two men as women.

l. 712 "This man . . . with him": Luke 22:56.

ll. 716–18 The soldier . . . maidservant . . . trouble him: SJ again parallels her own situation, with ecclesiastic "soldiers" accosting her from without and convent "maidservants" (of whom the mother superior mentioned in the next paragraph is emblematic) from within.

ll. 718–22 I confess . . . from study: SJ ends the paragraph with a comparison – her love of knowledge has been like Peter's – intensifying the references to torture and introducing a personal anecdote of "prohibition from study."

(26) ll. 723–25 a very saintly . . . should not read: In presenting the spectre of the Inquisition, which investigated possible heresy, SJ gives a striking parallel with a passage in María de San José's *Book of Recreations,* First Recreation: ". . . for there have been many [women] who have been equal and even superior in learning to a great many men. . . . [M]any servants of God came to confess us, among them one . . . [who] grew angry when he saw us crossing ourselves in Latin, as if we were uttering heresies. And quite deliberately he set about scolding us, and told us that women should on no account meddle in all sorts of erudite babble and deep waters. . . . [H]e must have been a bit simple, that servant of God" (Powell trans., in Arenal and Schlau, *Untold Sisters*, pp. 94–95).

ll. 730–31 for my book all the the intricate structures of this world: Anne Bradstreet, SJ's New England contemporary, also wrote of studying the book of the world; this is a classical and medieval trope that has appealed to poets up to our day.

l. 739 character and intelligence: SJ's phrase, *genios e ingenios*, echoes Baltasar Gracián's treatise *Genio e ingenio* (see note to par. 22, above). Our phrase follows Christopher Maurer's translation of Gracián's *Art of Worldly Wisdom*. No two English words convey the full range of meaning. *Genio* includes "temperament" or "personality" as well as "genius"; *ingenio* includes "wit," "cleverness," "ability."

(27) l. 759 whether a matter of nature or custom: SJ here appears to vacillate as to whether this aspect of her "inclination" is inborn or self-developed.

ll. 762–63 this madness of mine / esta mi locura: a colloquial, calculated, "trivializing" or jocular reference to SJ's obsession, passion, and irrepressible curiosity. (Perhaps SJ, like Saul, is "cured" by music and, by extension, the humanities – see reference to the curative harp at the end of this paragraph.)

l. 775 Solomon's mysterious ring: SJ may conflate Solomon's ring with his legendary seal, seen as uniting heavenly and earthly principles by occult sources. Some sources do distinguish ring and seal. Walker, *Women's Dictionary of Symbols and Sacred Objects,* mentions rings (p. 12) and seal (pp. 69, 72) and echoes SJ's description with "various forms" of hexagram and pentacle; see also Walker, *Women's Encyclopedia of Myths and Secrets,* pp. 946–50. In the Bible, Solomon worshipped the goddess (3 Kings 11:5). This phrase indicates sources of women's traditions in the books SJ read, possibly illicit readings.

(28) l. 789 inanities / frialdades: Ironic (*frialdad* literally refers to "lack of heat," doubly ironic in the context of a discussion of cooking; as English "inanity" does to "lack of content or substance"). SJ "innocently" shows how she practices science; having been "prohibited" her books, she explored alternative routes to knowledge ("women's ways of knowing"). The domestic sphere is not to be disdained as a source of wisdom. SJ prepares the ground for her "jest" about the incongruity of Aristotle at the stove by mentioning another male writer as an authority (see next note).

l. 792 Lupercio Leonardo: Should be his brother *Bernardo* Leonardo de Argensola (1562–1631), a Spanish poet and satirist; in "First Satire," ll. 143–44.

l. 794 Aristotle: A Greek philosopher (384–122 B.C.) who studied with Plato, taught Alexander the Great, and wrote on logic, natural science, ethics, politics, and poetics. His familiar and domestic presence underscores SJ's familiarity with Thomistic-Aristotelian thought.

l. 796 cogitations / cogitaciones: An example of SJ's use of a distinctly Latinate vocabulary. Salceda defines the word, which is from the Latin for "act of thinking," in notes to OC; the cognate is more familiar in English than in Spanish.

l. 804 not even my sleep has [or, my dreams have] been free: "Sleep" and "dream" share the word *sueño* in Spanish. Sor Juana used this double sense as a setting for her philosophical poem *First Dream*, mentioned as *Dream* in par. 43.

l. 811 in order not to weary you: A commonplace phrase in epistolary rhetoric (Perelmuter Pérez, "La estructura retórica"). This ends the "narration" and moves into the "proof."

(29) ll. 816–19 If studies . . . of mine: While insisting that she has no control over her studious "inclination," SJ echoes parts of her 1681/82 letter to her confessor contesting the idea that men should be praised but women condemned for using their minds.

ll. 821–23 And so I entrust . . . or reluctance: In the 1681/82 letter to Núñez, ten years earlier, SJ had resisted his judgment; here, writing publicly, and perhaps because she was deciding to desist from study and was facing changed circumstances, she closes the first part of her defense with the language of jurisprudence as well as of religious obedience (see "Rhetorical Forms" and "Letter to Her Confessor" in Pt. II of the Introduction, above).

(30) This paragraph begins the "proof"; conventionally, the "most highly structured" section of rhetorical argument (Perelmuter Pérez, "La estructura retórica"). Earlier in the text, SJ has spoken of and for herself; now she establishes precedents among outstanding women. Mention of men in this and the next two paragraphs in part reflects SJ's concerted effort to equalize genders – to make women peers, if not superiors. If SJ did not know Christine de Pizan's *Book of the City of Ladies* (we suspect she may have), she did share a personal interest in refuting misogyny and a female writer's stake in an authorizing female tradition. Both authors address themselves explicitly to feminist concerns. Boccaccio's *De mulieribus claris* [Concerning Famous Women] was in any case a source for both the French and the Mexican writer.

l. 826 exemplars: SJ is playing on multiple meanings (true in English as in Spanish) of the word "exemplar" *(ejemplar)*: a person or thing that serves as a model for imitation, an example; also, a copy of a book, manuscript, etc. Above, SJ has stated that her inclination to study is so strong that she needs neither teacher nor books to pursue it. Here, she will list women – models of intelligence and behavior – whom she has "seen" because she has "read" them: they are both "models," or patterns for imitation, and "texts," copies, volumes.

ll. 828–37 Deborah: In Judges 4 and 5, Deborah exercised religious authority through legal duties, military leadership, and prophecy; known for her gifts of discernment, she is one of the most powerful biblical women. **Queen of Sheba:** In 1 Kings 10:3, and 2 Chronicles 9, the queen visited Solomon to verify for herself the reports of his wisdom; a woman of legendary wealth, she sent him gifts and is said to have inspired the Song of Songs. **Abigail:** In 1 Samuel 25, Abigail is a seer and prophet whose beauty and intelligence won over David, who married her. **Esther:** See second note to par. 5, above. **Rahab:** In Joshua 2 and St. Paul's Epistle to the Hebrews 11:31, Rahab is the harlot (prostitute) whose piety led her to hide Joshua's spies. **Anna [Hannah]:** In 1 Samuel, she became mother of Samuel at an advanced age, after years of awaiting pregnancy. Of the six only Abigail and Rahab are absent from Christine de Pizan's *Book of the City of Ladies.*

(31) l. 839 Sibyls: Mythological female seers and prophets of antiquity (varying in number, in later times reported as ten), often painted and sculpted by the artists of the Renaissance. In seeing them as prophets of the Incarnation of Christ, SJ follows St. Isidore of Seville (c. 560–636), in his encyclopedic *Etymologies,* and Boccaccio (1313-75). She refers to some of them by name in her poem 38. Christine de Pizan opens the second part of *The Book of the City of Ladies* with a chapter on the ten Sibyls: "They even spoke more clearly and farther of the coming of Jesus Christ . . . than all the prophets did . . . " (II.1.3, 100).

l. 841 stupefy the imagination / suspenden la admiración: The Spanish phrase was originally probably a hyperbolic redundancy; became idiomatic.

l. 842 Minerva: The name is related etymologically to the Sanskrit for "full of mind or sense" which passed to the Latin root for "mind." This Roman goddess of wisdom is traditionally identified with the Greek Athena (to whom SJ was compared by the bishop in titling her critique of Vieira "Letter Worthy of Athena"). Also a name for Isis, the "great mother goddess," about whom SJ wrote in many of her works and who appears in an engraving in a book by A. Kircher (note to par. 12, above) that SJ used.

l. 844 Polla Argentaria: First century A.D. Wife of the Spanish-born poet Lucan (A.D. 39–65). We find no source for her collaboration with him on the *Battle of Pharsalia;* the Latin title of this unfinished epic poem on the civil war between Caesar and Pompey, the sole extant work by Lucan, is *Bellum civile,* also referred to simply as *Pharsalia* in BLQ. Statius' poem about her (*Silvae* 2.7) calls her a patron of literature; she cultivated her husband's memory after his death and was celebrated for it.

l. 846 the divine Tiresias: In Greek mythology a seer; the son of a nymph, he knew sexuality both as a male and as a female; he was blinded by one god for seeing Athena naked, cured by another. SJ's use of the word "divine" indicates that she knew the stories related to Tiresias; if the father was "divine," the daughter Manto might inherit some of that divinity (see Ovid, *Metamorphoses* 6.7). Ovid and Boccaccio both mention Manto as a seer. One of the passages from the 1403 edition of *The Book of the City of Ladies* that strongly suggests to us that SJ was acquainted with Christine de Pizan's work is the following, on Manto:

> If women are able to apprehend and fit to learn literary and scientific subjects, I want you to know for certain that the arts likewise are not forbidden to women, just as you will hear. . . . The supreme mistress of the art [of divining] was a maiden, the daughter of Tiresias, who was the high priest of the city of Thebes (or what we would call the bishop, for in other religions priests could marry). This woman, who was named Manto . . . possessed such a brilliant and wide-ranging mind . . . (I.31.1, 68–69).

l. 847 Zenobia: Zenobia Septimia, matriarchal warrior queen and ruler of Palmyra (A.D. c. 266–72); extended her Syrian kingdom into Egypt and Asia Minor. Facing the emperor Aurelian in battle, she "bore the labors of the field like the meanest of her soldiers, and walked on foot fearless of danger" (LCD). Admired for her literary talents, she was trained in history, philosophy, and several languages. (Cited in *The Book of the City of Ladies,* I.20.1, 52–54).

l. 848 Arete: Literally "virtue, valor." Founder of a school of philosophy (fourth century B.C.), Arete was instructed by her father, Aristippus, and was tutor of her son, A. the Younger (mockingly called *mater-didactus,* or "mother-taught"), and of others. (Appears in Diogenes Laertius, *Second History of Philosophy,* chaps. 72, 84–86.)

l. 849 Nicostrata: Carmenta in Latin; she was a healer, teacher, expert in Greek literature (adapted Greek characters to form the Italic alphabet), and mythical Greek prophet. She begat Evander, early founder of Rome, with Hermes. Christine de Pizan says: "she worked and studied so hard that she invented her own letters, which were completely different from those of other nations. . . . [F]or [the Italians] this discovery was so fantastic that they not only deemed this woman to be greater than any man, but they also considered her a goddess and even honored her during her lifetime with divine honors" (*The Book of the City of Ladies* I.33.2 [Richards trans., p. 72]; also see I.37.1, I.38.4, II.5.1).

l. 850 Aspasia Miletia: c. 450 B.C. Reputed teacher of eloquence in Athens, likely had a salon; she exercised influence on writers and philosophers and is mentioned in Plato's dialogue *Menexenus.* Plutarch writes: ". . . some say, was courted and caressed by Pericles on account of her knowledge and skill in politics. Socrates himself would sometimes go and visit her" (*Life of Pericles* 200).

l. 851 Pericles: c. 490–429 B.C. Not a philosopher as SJ says, but an Athenian statesman.

l. 851 Hypatia: d. A.D. 415. This Alexandrian philosopher, mathematician, and astronomer occupied the chair of Platonic philosophy (Scott, " 'La gran turba' "). She was persecuted and died at the hands of fanatic monks; Trueblood and Paz speculate on SJ's interest in a possible parallel with her own situation. Following Paz's interpretation, Willis Barnstone observes, "The philosopher Hypatia has traditionally been evoked as a symbol of surviving Greek intellectual civilization in its last distinguished manifestation before succumbing to the brute barbarism of Christian bigotry and iconoclastic violence" (*Six Masters of the Spanish Sonnet,* p. 82).

l. 853 Leontium: Fourth and third centuries B.C. Says Christine de Pizan: ". . . such a great philosopher that she dared, for impartial and serious reasons, to correct and attack the philosopher Theophrastus" (*The Book of the City of Ladies* I.30.3, 68). She was a hetaera, a sexual and intellectual companion of upper-class men; in the fourth century such people attracted public attention and admiration. Her style was praised by Cicero in *De natura Diorum* 133 (though he finds it shameful to have a woman of her social status meddling in writing; Romans were stricter than Greeks in excluding women's cultural participation).

l. 854 Julia: Second and third centuries A.D. SJ's "Jucia" is probably a typographical error. The reference is to Julia Domna, a Syrian who married Emperor Septimius Severus; she was learned in philosophy and geometry, influential in politics (Lefkowitz, *Women in Greece and Rome;* Scott, " 'La gran turba' ").

l. 854 Corinna: Fifth century B.C. A Greek poet from Boeotia, among whose writings are narrative choral lyrics for an audience of women; she was insulted by Pindar for rivalry with him (Barnstone; Lefkowitz). Recently papyruses of her work have been found; see Snyder, *The Woman and the Lyre.*

l. 854 Cornelia: Second century A.D. Celebrated as the ideal of Roman motherhood; praised by Seneca; well educated and admired for her letter-writing style by Cicero (Lefkowitz, *Women in Greece and Rome;* Scott, " 'La gran turba.' "

Annotations to La Respuesta / The Answer   127

l. 856 Muses: In Greek mythology, nine patron goddesses of the arts (daughters of Zeus and the Titan Mnemosyne, who personified memory): Calliope (epic poetry); Euterpe (music and lyric poetry); Erato (love poetry); Polyhymnia (oratory or sacred poetry); Clio (history); Melpomene (tragedy); Thalia (comedy); Terpsichore (dance); and Urania (astronomy).

l. 856 Pythonesses: Soothsayers, diviners; priestesses of Apollo who delivered oracles at Delphi.

l. 860 Egyptian Catherine: I.e., St. Catherine of Alexandria, third century A.D. Christine de Pizan tells in detail the story of the saint's great gifts, of her examination by fifty philosophers from far and wide who were so impressed that they converted to Christianity, of the martyrdom of those she caused to convert, of her own martydom on spiked wheels, and of her beheading (*The Book of the City of Ladies* III.3.1-2, 219-22). Traditional patron of philosophers and specifically of the Mexican university of SJ's day (the Real y Pontificia, or "Royal and Papal," University), Catherine was SJ's favorite saint. For Catherine's festivities SJ was commissioned in 1691 by the Cathedral of Antequera (Oaxaca) to write *villancicos* (See Selected Poems, below). At several points in history, however, the church questioned this St. Catherine's authenticity and prohibited her veneration. She was definitively declared fictitious and barred from the saintly pantheon recently. The Norwegian theologian Kari Vogt suggests the possibility that Catherine was a compensatory projection of the murdered fourth-century philosopher Hypatia (*Image of God*, p. 143).

l. 861 Gertrude: Saint Gertrude the Great (1256-1302/03). This German Benedictine (one of many learned nuns at Helfta in Saxony) was a mystic visionary and theologian.

l. 863 Paula: Saint Paula the Elder. See note to par. 10, above.

ll. 864-65 expert . . . Scriptures: Shows SJ was well aware of women's "struggles for interpretive power" (in Jean Franco's phrase); here located with Paula, hierarchically SJ's strongest female forebear – thus, strong justification of SJ's right to interpret Scripture.

l. 866 unequaled Jerome, the Saint: See note to par. 5, above.

ll. 869-70 "If all . . . of Paula": SJ refers to a letter written by Jerome to Eustochium, one of Paula's daughters, after Paula's death. (Here SJ cites Jerome in Spanish, not Latin.)

ll. 870-74 Blessilla, Eustochium, Fabiola: These women belonged to the circle of St. Jerome, whose writing they stimulated by encouragement, questioning, discussion, etc. Blessilla and Eustochium were daughters of Paula. Jerome's letter to Eustochium served as model for SJ's *villancicos* for the feast of San Pedro Apóstol.

l. 875 Proba Falconia: Fourth century A.D. Christine de Pizan says of the author of the *Cento:* "she would take several entire verses unchanged and in another borrow small snatches of verse and, through marvelous craftsmanship and conceptual subtlety . . . [follow] all the stories of the Old and New Testament. . . . Someone who only knew this work would have thought that Vergil had been both a prophet and evangelist. . . . Boccaccio himself says that this woman merits great recognition and praise, for it is obvious that she possessed a sound and exhaustive knowledge of . . . Holy Scripture" (*Book of the City of Ladies* I.29.1, 66).

l. 877 Queen Isabella: This reference is unclear and disputed. Violante of Aragon, not Isabella, was the wife of Alfonso X "the Wise" (1221–84) and was said to have collaborated on his *Books of Astronomical Knowledge.* Alfonso's grandmother, Berenjuela de Castilla "la Grande" is said to have inspired his love of culture. SJ may have been thinking of Isabella the Catholic, queen of Castile (wife of Ferdinand), who studied Latin with Beatriz Galindo and had many intellectual interests.

ll. 881–82 Christina Alexandra, Queen of Sweden: 1626–89. A woman SJ could not but have admired: for rejecting her father's and her country's Protestantism and converting to Catholicism; for her learning and her patronage of the arts; for bringing the philosopher and mathematician Descartes ("I think, therefore I am") to her court; for refusing to marry; for abdicating her throne; for turning her Italian palace-in-exile into a center of Roman intellectual life; for dressing, when she pleased, as a man. It is not unlikely that, through the aristocratic gossip to which she was privy, SJ knew of her passion for one of the ladies at court and of her long-term relationship with a cardinal (Scott, " 'La gran turba' "). She was buried in St. Peter's in Rome. SJ's reference to this extraordinary figure points up that when faith was unquestioned, the highest levels of the Catholic church admitted all manner of behavior (especially among the rich and powerful) otherwise – and now – considered socially censurable.

l. 883 Duchess of Aveyro: (Portuguese Abeiro), María Guadalupe de Lancaster [Alencastre, *sic*] y Cárdenas (1630–1715), descended from the royal house of Portugal and a relative of SJ's patron and friend the Countess of Paredes. A favorite at court in Madrid, where she is said to have been consulted on matters of state, a frequent visitor to the royal convents of the Encarnación and Descalzas Reales, she knew Greek, Latin, Italian, and French in addition to Spanish and Portuguese; well versed in Scripture, she recited the Psalms by heart (Barbeito C., "Escritoras madrileñas"). Called "Mother of the Missions" for her support of the Jesuit missions in Mexico, she was a friend of the Jesuit astronomer Father Eusebio Francisco Kino (1645–1711), to whom SJ wrote a poem. SJ calls her "Great Minerva of Portugal" and "Shining Spanish Sybil" (perhaps she parodied the hyperbolic epithets she was accustomed to hearing about herself, or indulged courtly ingratiation or ironic emulation). In the poem dedicated to the countess (poem 37), she takes this fashionable name-game to the limit, suggesting that two women, both writers, might consider it sport to caricature the poetic (mostly male) fashions of their own time (Correspondence with Barbeito C.).

l. 884 Countess of Villaumbrosa: Little is known of her. She was patron of an Andalusian Dominican nun (Sor María de la Santísima Trinidad), whom she helped found a convent about 1670. The nun dying soon thereafter, her biographer dedicated his account to the Count and Countess of Villaumbrosa in 1671 (Correspondence with Isabel Poutrin).

(32) l. 885 The venerable Dr. Arce: Juan Díaz de Arce (d. 1653), Mexican theologian and professor of philosophy and Holy Scripture. Trueblood (*A Sor Juana Anthology*) renders the full title of his work in English as *Fourth Book of Expository Questions for the Fuller Understanding of the Holy Bible; or, For the Bible Student* (1648). The first three books were published together in 1647.

ll. 887–88 "Is it permissible . . . Holy Bible?": SJ cannily introduces this theme via Arce and raises the negative responses first, following the bishop's game (Fernández de Santa Cruz had stated support for women's education and then seemed to retract it).

ll. 890–91 "Let women . . .": 1 Corinthians 14:34–35 –"Let women keep silence in the churches: for it is not permitted them to speak, but to be subject, as also the law saith. But if they would learn anything, let them ask their husbands at home. For it is a shame for a woman to speak in the church." Using logic and syllogisms, SJ here begins in Aristotelian-Scholastic manner to pursue her central argument: viz., the Bible does not sentence women to silence. Rather, Pauline epistles have been distorted and misunderstood: Paul meant there should be silence in church so that the sermon might be heard; older women who taught others, and women who customarily discussed theology with each other, were not to interrupt services.

ll. 893–94 "The aged . . . well": Titus 2:3–4 –"The aged women, in like manner, in holy attire, not false accusers, not given to much wine, teaching well: That they may teach the young women to be wise, to love their husbands, to love their children . . ." Surrounding text also exhorts old and young men to be sober.

l. 899 beneficial . . . to them: SJ bolsters her argument in favor of women's education with a moral dimension – defending not only her own rights, but what should "Christianly" occur with all "gifted" nuns and other women. This is a powerful moment, especially in the context of her attack, immediately following, on male heretics.

l. 915 such men as these: SJ targets male heretics, as the church concerned itself with (potential or actual) female heresy. She is radical in her insistence that women and men alike may be singularly fit, or temperamentally unfit, to pursue learning.

ll. 915–16 "For wisdom . . .": Wisdom 1:4 – "For wisdom will not enter into a malicious soul, nor dwell in a body subject to sins."

(33) l. 926 madman: Trueblood (*A Sor Juana Anthology*) states that SJ was thinking of the widely reproduced emblem, *Insani gladius* [The Sword in the Hands of the Madman] by Andrea Alciato (1492–1550), pioneer of Renaissance emblem literature.

l. 929 Pelagius: c. 360–c. 420. This theologian, born in what are now the British Isles, was combatted by Jerome and Augustine because of his view that the will was always free to choose good or evil (thus limiting the roles of grace and original sin). SJ might have found the Pelagian position sympathetic; she is proving her orthodoxy here.

l. 930 Arius: 256–336. A priest of Alexandria, he advanced a doctrine that opposed the concept of the Trinity and that was declared a heresy for considering the Son subordinate to the Father; this view – the Arian heresy – was defeated at the Council of Nicea in 325 (DCLL).

l. 931 Dr. Cazalla: I.e., Agustín Cazalla (1510–1559), a chaplain to the king and canon of Salamanca Cathedral who became a follower of Martin Luther (1483–1546, founder of the Protestant Reformation which divided Christian faith and was stringently opposed by Catholics). Cazalla was burned to death by the Inquisition. Histories (e.g., Tuñón de Lara, ed., *Historia de España*, vol. 5) and popular tales always mention his sister María, the Protestant leader of the Cazalla family (a group of siblings who had converted). Women were officially seen by the church as prone to heretical sectarianism; SJ here is being deliberately selective in naming Agustín, in order to strengthen her argument.

ll. 940–43 "For I say . . . of faith": Romans 12:3.

ll. 944–45 not to women but to men . . . not only for women: Here and at the beginning of the next paragraph SJ suggests a generic feminine, by the same logic as the generic masculine: St. Paul in speaking to "men" was speaking also to women, and vice versa.

(34) ll. 952–53 all men . . . first of all: SJ points up the false inclusiveness of the generic masculine and makes fun of its exclusions in this phrase.

ll. 965–67 "The just man . . . my head": Psalms 140:5. BAC titles this "Prayer of the just against the Aspersions of Enemies." Verse 5 of the psalm immediately preceding reads: "Keep me, O Lord, from the hand of the wicked: and from unjust men deliver me. Who have proposed to supplant my steps: the proud have hidden a net for me." Righteously vengeful, this passage strengthens a reading of the *Answer* as a declaration against persecution.

(35) l. 970 To Leta . . . Her Daughter / ad Laetam, de institutione filiae: Letter by Jerome to Leta (daughter-in-law of St. Paula) regarding the education of the child who was named after the saint, her grandmother; little Paula grew up in the convent, remained a virgin, and became Jerome's companion in his old age. Scott ("Let Your Women Keep Silence") points to SJ's manipulation of Jerome's text to forward her advocacy of education for girls: SJ uses Arce's reasoned authority to counter the anti-intellectual sympathies of her antagonists regarding women's education (among whom one could count some women, including St. Teresa). St. Paul's phrase, she asserts, does not insist that women remain ignorant; via Arce, SJ reinforces Paul's reference to older women as "teaching well." (See note to par. 32, above.)

ll. 970–79 "[Her] childish . . . fixed task": Jerome, *Select Letters* (Wright trans.), pp. 345–47.

ll. 982–83 Marcella: Jerome dedicated many of his biblical studies to his disciple Marcella, a patrician Roman widow about whom it is said: "eager for information [she] would not accept any doubtful explanation, so that Jerome found himself in the presence of a judge rather than a disciple. At times she took her teacher to task for his severity and quarrelsomeness" (Smith and Wace, eds., *Dictionary of Christian Biography,* 3:803). Salceda mentions sixteen letters Jerome addressed to her and an homage written after her death in a letter to Principia. Actually the "letters" were treatises to explain philological and exegetical questions of Scripture (Scott, " 'La gran turba,' " p. 33). Jerome underscores Marcella's own learning in the letter written after her death.

l. 983 Pacatula: Consecrated to a celibate life from birth. Jerome wrote a letter of instruction to her (i.e., to her father) regarding her training (*Select Letters of St. Jerome,* no. 128).

l. 987 "teaching well": See note to par. 32, above.

ll. 987–88 "let her repeat the task to you": Jerome, *Select Letters,* Wright trans., no. 128.

(36) This paragraph strongly paraphrases Jerome's letter no. 128, to the child Pacatula (mentioned immediately above), in his concern that "females should only mix with their own sex" and in advice that she should "let her teacher be her companion, her attendant, her guardian . . . sober, grave, skilled in spinning, saying only such words as will train a girl's mind in virtue" (Wright trans.; see esp. par. 4, pp. 474–79). Jerome, too, echoes Paul, 1 Timothy 5:13; SJ continues her appropriation of these two renowned misogynist authorities in support of women's learning.

ll. 993–94 for lack . . . poor women: Like Mary Wollstonecraft (see Preface, above) and others, SJ attributes women's "feebleness" to their lack of education.

ll. 1007–8 just as is done with sewing: Opposition of needle and pen was a common literary trope in the Renaissance; not uncommonly used by women to express resentment at limitations, and by men and some women to praise females who employed both instruments. A seventeenth-century engraving of a nun who was a prolific writer, the Madre Rocaberti (Sor Hipólita de Jesús, 1549–1624), in the Escorial Library, Spain, shows her, quill in hand and pincushion strapped to her wrist.

(37) ll. 1024–25 repeated handling . . . contact / el manoseo de la inmediación: This phrase emphasizes "spoilage" caused by repeated close contact – *manoseo* is an arrestingly physical and popular term in this context. While speaking of women's vulnerability to abuse, SJ gives it an entirely different focus from the oft-quoted remark in which her first biographer, Diego Calleja, spoke of the beautiful (but not wealthy) woman as a white wall inviting men to besmirch her. For SJ, men endanger women, not women men. However, neither sex is turned into a passive object; SJ speaks of activities in daily life and social interaction. SJ has moved from biblical to social commentary; she voices strong opinions on issues that affected everyday life and the interactions between the sexes outside the convent.

ll. 1029–1030 "Let women keep silence in the churches": In countering what was considered St. Paul's "prohibition" (1 Corinthians 14:34–37; echoed in 1 Timothy 2:9–12 and Titus 2:3–5) SJ concurs with and continues some of St. Teresa's arguments on the matter of women's active participation in the church and women teaching other women. Their exegesis on this passage is in precise agreement. By employing the word *atados* (tied) in reference to the authorities' dogged insistence, SJ may well have wanted – jestingly but pointedly – to remind the bishop of the following passage from the Teresa's *Spiritual Testimonies (Cuentas de conciencia* 16): "The Lord said to me: 'Tell them [those who opposed her activities] they shouldn't follow just one part of Scripture but that they should look at other parts, and ask them if they can by chance tie my hands' " (Weber trans., p. 39). (See also *The Way of Perfection* 15.6.)

l. 1032 "teaching well": See note to par. 32, above.

l. 1033 Eusebius: c. 260–c. 340, bishop of Caesarea; called the father of church history for his *Historia ecclesiastica.* This citation is a justifying introduction to the next paragraph, where SJ will continue to do as Eusebius did: present material from earlier work and present the results of her own research.

(38) ll. 1039–40 many passages: I.e., of Scripture.

ll. 1040–43 one must know a great deal . . . divine letters: Here, SJ seems to say, "as I do and have just demonstrated regarding the *taceant* [admonition to keep silence], and I could only know such things through study, you dolts!"–wonderful turn in SJ's argument, continuing in par. 39 and referring back to 37. SJ directly answers the bishop and explains her opposition to his urging that she ignore all earthly matters.

ll. 1043–44 "Rend your hearts . . . garments": Joel 2:13.

ll. 1045–46 as was . . . blasphemed: Matthew 26:65-66–"Then the high priest rent his garments, saying: He hath blasphemed; what further need have we of witnesses? . . . What think you? But they answering, said: He is guilty of death." SJ is defending herself against a charge akin to blasphemy; reference to the "evil high priest" perhaps suggests the power of her addressee. SJ again picks up the parallel she had made between herself and Christ as a defense against the accusation of blasphemy.

l. 1047–48 on the aid and comfort of widows: See, for example, 1 Timothy 5:3-16. This shows SJ's close attention to biblical treatment of women and her particular concern with Paul's authority in the Epistles.

l. 1049 strong woman: The entire chapter of Proverbs from which this citation comes illustrates the importance of teaching by mothers and older women. Thus, in 31:1, Lemuel learned prophecy from his mother. Debate and contestation follows: "Who shall find a valiant woman?" (31:10). Affirmation continues throughout this last chapter of Proverbs.

l. 1049–1050 "Her husband . . . gates": Proverbs 31:23.

l. 1051 "Give land to God": Refers to the Old Testament custom of returning land every fifty years to its original owner (God) for one fallow year. This symbolic ritual formed part of the Jubilee. (It is possible to see here, also, an implicit critique of the Spanish conquest of Indian lands.)

l. 1052 hiemantes: Luke 7:44-45. The early Christian church had four successive categories of public penance consisting of exclusion from full participation in communal observances. *Hiemantes* (from *hiems,* "winter"; those who suffer inclemencies of weather) was a term applied to the first group. They were required to stand outside the church porch or entrance, entreating the prayers of the congregation and intercession with the bishop: that they might be allowed to pass to the second category and stand with those who were permitted to enter the outermost part of the church but not to interact with the congregation, and so on. (See Salceda's note, OC4, 658, for detailed discussion.) This and the following passage deal with sin, penitence, and forgiveness. SJ's 1681/82 letter to Núñez criticizes the application of overly harsh penance, speaking of not being forced to do penance but of making her own decision to do it.

ll. 1054–56 complaint . . . washing of feet: Luke 7:44-45. In this passage, Jesus "complains" to Simon the Pharisee, concerning Simon's negligence in failing to wash the feet of his guest (a Hebrew custom), whereas a "woman who was a sinner" has washed Jesus' feet with tears and wiped them with her hair. Precisely because her sins were greater, Jesus stresses, she has been forgiven more and will therefore love him more strongly. (This woman has been traditionally identified with Mary Magdalene.) In giving this example, SJ tacitly recalls the occasion of Vieira's sermon, which had prompted her critique: Maundy Thursday is the day Christ washed the feet of his disciples.

l. 1057 humane letters: SJ is giving an example throughout this paragraph of what it means to engage in humanist scholarship.

ll. 1058–59 "Honor the purple" [or that which is clad in purple]; "to put a hand to him" / "manumittere eum": SJ follows a popular, probably erroneous etymology here; *manu emittere* signifies "to release [a slave] from one's hand," not "to strike with the hand"). To present-day readers, both phrases may suggest pointed examples of SJ's struggle with authority. (We should bear in mind that SJ herself was a slaveowner.) They can be read, however, less directly. SJ may have had in mind theological texts, exegeses, and sermons that were discussed and debated by the bishop, St. Teresa, and others of the period. On a political level, she may have been alluding to her close contacts with the Spanish crown through the viceroys.

ll. 1061–62 "The heavens thundered": Virgil (Publius Vergilius Maro, 70–19 B.C.), the Roman poet whose *Aeneid* is considered one of the great epic poems in world literature. SJ's reference to favorable omens appears twice (*Aeneid* II.693, IX.631). Trueblood (*A Sor Juana Anthology*) suggests it is an erratum for "it thundered on the left." SJ may, however, have been using an alternative version of commonly noted signs of good or bad luck.

ll. 1063–64 "You never ate hare": From Martial (see note to par. 22, above). Continuing her reversals of gender stereotypes, SJ cites V.29 (woman tells man he will be beautiful if he eats hare): "If at any time you send me a hare, you say Gellia: 'Marcus, you will be comely for seven days.' If you are not laughing at me, if you speak truly, my love, you, Gellia, have never eaten a hare" (Ker trans., 1:319).

ll. 1067–68 ". . . things of home"; promontory of Laconia: "An allusion to the difficulty of sailing around this promontory in the southeastern Peloponnese" (Trueblood, *A Sor Juana Anthology*, p. 234). Salceda (OC) mentions as sources St. Isidore, *Etymologies* XIV.7, and the *Odyssey* II. 287, IV.514, IX.80, XIX.187. This suggests a reference to SJ's own perilous position.

ll. 1069–74 "No doorframes . . . nor shall the priest give his blessing": SJ unites the biblical-historical sphere with social, contemporary, and biographical reality. General readers would understand the analogy; those close to her would be reminded of her rejection of the confessor Núñez.

ll. 1077–78 putting the plural in place of the singular: In lines not included in this volume from her comical (but critical) poem "Apollo help you . . . ," SJ says: "and because the rule says: / the plural standing for the singular" (ll. 87–88), referring to the ancient rhetorical figure of synecdoche (which represents a more inclusive term by a less inclusive term or vice versa). The same stanza, however, jokes about using a plural, *refranes* ("proverbs"), because the syllable count calls for it. SJ has quoted the commonly expressed mother's regret at giving birth to a daughter. The citing of rhetoric and grammar as a metaphor for physical and social gender is receiving attention from Renaissance scholars. This paragraph offers several examples of such uses.

ll. 1078–79 moving from second to third person: Corrected in some Bibles, the grammatical disjunction was discussed by many scholars. As is characteristic of some medieval and Renaissance authors, SJ uses grammar both literally and figuratively (see Alford, "The Grammatical Metaphor"; Shepherd, *Women's Sharp Revenge*, pp. 166–67). St. Teresa, in a work on the Song of Songs that she was forced to burn, mentions that the passage cited had attracted much comment and speculation; she describes the matter concretely, rather than abstractly as SJ does ("Conceptos del amor de Dios," in *Escritos de Santa Teresa*, pp. 389–404). A copy of Teresa's commentary was hidden, then circulated in manuscript form and printed in Brussels after her death. It is not unlikely that SJ knew the Brussels edition with its prologue by Jerónimo Gracián, spiritual director and friend of María de San José (Gracián states that fear of the Lutheran heresy had caused suppression of the commentary). Daniel de Pablo Maroto: "at the time she wrote it the Lutheran heresy was causing harm, because it opened the doors for women and stupid men to read and comment on holy scripture" ("Meditaciones," p. 390). SJ seems to be in dialogue both with Gracián and St. Teresa. Possible sources for SJ's obtaining the book could have been the Duchess of Abeiro (Aveyro), a relative of María Luisa, the vicereine; or the Carmelite convent where SJ spent a few months before becoming a Jeronymite.

ll. 1079–80 "Let him kiss . . . better than wine": Song of Songs (in Douay Version "Canticle of Canticles") 1:1. SJ returns to the Canticles, commenting as St. Teresa had before her on its most erotic verses (Weber, *Teresa of Avila,* p. 115).

ll. 1081–82 the genitive case, instead of the accusative: Another example of the use of the grammatical metaphor. Just as SJ was interested in music theory, so was she fascinated by the theoretical and symbolic aspects of grammar. In Elio Antonio de Nebrija's Spanish grammar (the first published, in 1492) the explanations of the cases acknowledge the significance of the words that describe them. SJ, in preferring the genitive to the accusative, implies rejection of the "accusatory" stance taken against her (and other women) and support for a stance that is "life-giving" ("genitive").

l. 1082 **"I will take the chalice of salvation":** Psalm 115:4/13 ("cup of health" in the King James Version). A few lines down (9/18) we find a possible foreshadowing: "I will pay my vows to the Lord in the sight of all his people." Both the grammatical example with which SJ introduces her citation (see our interpretation, preceding note) and the meaning of this psalm of gratitude and appeal to God reflect SJ's resistance to hostility in her milieu, her insistence that salvation will come from God and not from misguided clerics, and her impending decision to desist from further writing.

ll. 1083–84 **in place of the masculine . . . adultery:** SJ continues to play with substitutions, reversals, and extensions, commenting both on Scripture and on social practice. Precisely through the rhetoric she uses to argue her points, she exemplifies them.

(39) l. 1087 the principles of logic: SJ refers in conventionally abbreviated form to a twelfth-century treatise on formal logic by Petrus Hispanus that became widely known as a summary of the elemental principles of formal logic. Here SJ parallels the clichéd accusation against women who have *cuatro bachillerías* (par. 5, above: "four profundities of a superficial scholar") with a jibe against men who know four terms of logic.

l. 1088 **"Let women keep silence in the churches":** 1 Corinthians 14:34 (see pars. 32 and 37, above).

l. 1090 **"Let the woman learn in silence":** 1 Timothy 2:11. SJ omits the next phrase: "with all subjection," an example of what Scott identifies as SJ's "manipulation" of misogynist texts to serve her argument (see " 'La gran turba' ").

l. 1092 **must needs keep quiet:** SJ gives *her* interpretation of the biblical passage that had been used for centuries to silence women and on which the entire *Answer* centers. The paragraph brings to a climax her defense of personalized education accessible to those suited for it by talent, and not exclusive to a particular gender or class.

l. 1093 **"Hear . . . be silent / Audi Israel, et tace":** SJ seems to cite imprecisely Job 33:31, *Attende, Job et audi me, et tace,* and 33:33, *audi me, tace* ("Attend, Job, and hearken to me: and hold thy peace, whilst I speak. . . . hear me: hold thy peace").

ll. 1108–9 **Gertrude:** 1256–1302. See note to par. 31, above; with the second mention of this figure SJ reasserts her acquaintance with the long intellectual, monastic tradition of women. **Teresa:** 1515–82. Santa Teresa de Jesús de Avila (St. Teresa of Avila), the third of four explicit references to her. **Brigid:** 1303–73. Well educated in theology, she was the first woman to author a monastic rule. Never actualized according to her original plan, it was the blueprint for a gynocentric double order of men and women (conversation with Kari Elisabeth Børresen). Adviser to royalty, critic of the pope in Rome, she became a widow on return from a pilgrimage to Santiago de Compostela. She was founder of the Bridgettines in Sweden; the original convent at Vadstena was an intellectual center (Scott, " 'La gran turba' "). **nun of Agreda:** María de Jesús (1602–65), author of a voluminous life of the Virgin Mary, *La mistica ciudad de Dios,* with which SJ was acquainted.

ll. 1114–15 Martha and Mary: Luke 10:38–42; John 11:5, 12:7–8. Conventionally associated with two opposing types of woman: Martha, active tender of the hearth, is contrasted with Mary, contemplative follower of Christ's mission. Elisabeth Schüssler Fiorenza and other feminist religious scholars reinterpret these and other biblical figures, abandoning the traditional simplifications of misogynist exegesis and ascribing to women much more active roles in the formation of early Christianity. **Marcella:** See note to par. 35, above. **Mary the mother of Jacob** (according to Scott, SJ possibly means James instead of Jacob here) and **Salome** (Mark 15:40–41) were witnesses of the Crucifixion, two of the three women to whom the risen Christ first appeared.

l. 1119 María de la Antigua: 1566–1617. A Spanish nun, widely known to her and SJ's contemporaries as author of religious treatises and poems collected and published posthumously (*Desengaño de religiosos,* 1678).

l. 1127 St. Cyprian: Late third century. Both he and St. Augustine exemplify the rational, intellectual Catholicism with which SJ identifies herself. Cyprian had been Christianized by Justina of Antioch, his partner in life and in martyrdom – they were beheaded together (DCLL). Another theme mentioned in the annals concerns attempted attacks against Justina's chastity (by another man and by the saint himself, before conversion).

l. 1127 "That which . . . deliberation": Source not found.

l. 1129 St. Augustine: 354–430. One of the four principal Latin doctors of the church (SJ mentions all four; the others are Sts. Ambrose, Gregory the Great, and Jerome). He is looked upon as the enormously influential founder of Christian theology and the systematizer of Christian doctrine; best known through his autobiographical *Confessions.*

ll. 1131–32 "We learn . . . do them": Source not found.

l. 1132 where is my transgression: Having proven that the church allows women to write (even those who are not saints), SJ will focus on the immediate cause of her condemnation. She underscores the legal rhetorical form by citing Quintilian (see note to par. 1, above) and by employing such words as "transgression" and, in the following paragraph, "crime."

ll. 1135–36 "Let each . . . own nature": *Institutio oratoria.* (Not found in the place cited by Trueblood, *A Sor Juana Anthology;* Salceda, OC, gives no source).

(40) l. 1139 **Holy Mother Church:** SJ pointedly uses this common turn of phrase (church is feminine, in Latin as in Spanish, and referred to as "mother"). Earlier SJ referred to the synagogue also as mother (see note to par. 23, above). SJ frequently explored the idea of the female origins of culture.

ll. 1144–45 **Is his opinion . . . Holy Faith made manifest:** This insistence resembles the sarcasm SJ earlier expressed to her confessor Núñez in her letter of 1681/82 (see Introduction, above).

l. 1148 **Titus Lucius / Tito Lucio:** Several bishops named Titus might be referred to; one wrote a commentary on Luke.

l. 1149 **"Respect befits the arts" / "Artes committatur decor":** Possible readings also include "Comeliness/beauty befits/accompanies the arts."

l. 1150 **blessed Society [of Jesus]:** The Jesuit order, to which both her ex-confessor Núñez and Archbishop of Mexico Aguiar y Seijas belonged. The latter's admiration for Vieira was well known.

l. 1151 **Pliny:** See note to par. 23, above.

ll. 1151–53 **"The situation . . . by name":** We have not found a source for this citation from Pliny.

l. 1155 **as the critic says:** The anonymous critic has never been identified.

l. 1160 **rabbit's laughter:** Considered a reflex at the time of a rabbit's death; thus applied to one who laughs unwillingly or insincerely (DRA).

(41) ll. 1169–70 **two nuns in this City:** Key to SJ's argument and perspective. SJ reverts once more to Dr. Arce's authority. SJ tacitly criticizes the religious-theological training common in Mexico for men (even that was rarely available to women), and she defends her own intellectual history. Explicitly SJ reopens or holds open the polemic that had led St. Teresa to burn her manuscript concerning the Song of Songs. Cleverly SJ likens the bishop to Arce, and herself to the ideal he presents, particularly regarding how intelligent nuns should spend their time.

ll. 1176–77 **"I thought . . . in Spanish":** Citation in Arce not found.

(42) Throughout this paragraph, SJ cites both female and male figures as authorities defending the use of poetry.

l. 1190 **"Whatever . . . in verse":** Ovid, *Tristia* 4.10.26. SJ's poem 33 refers to the innate gift thus: "I was born so much a poet / that, like Ovid, when whipped / I let out cries in rhyme and meter."

l. 1194 **Sibyls:** See note to par. 31, above.

l. 1195 **King David:** The second king of Judah and Israel (1010?–970? B.C.), he was the father of King Solomon and reputed author of many of the Psalms.

ll. 1195–96 great . . . beloved Father: St. Jerome, as scholar and commentator.

ll. 1196–99 "In the style of . . . slowly forward": Iambics, alcaics, sapphics, and half-feet are verse forms used in Greek and Latin poetry (sapphics are named after the poet Sappho). SJ quotes Jerome ("beloved Father") in his preface to the second book of the *Chronicle* of Eusebius Pamphilus. Jerome praised classical authors, comparing them to David, the great biblical poet. SJ cites this praise, thus contesting the bishop who had warned her about such pagan preferences in his letter/preface to the "Letter Worthy of Athena," reminding her of the legendary censorship of the saint's weakness for the writers of antiquity. SJ defends the saint as well as defending the usefulness of his knowledge for the appreciation of Scripture; implicitly, SJ is again defending the usefulness of humanist knowledge for appreciating Scripture.

l. 1197 Horace: Quintus Horatius Flaccus, 65–8 B.C., the Latin poet recognized as among the greatest of lyric poets.

l. 1197 Pindar: 518?–c. 438 B.C. Generally regarded as the greatest Greek lyric poet.

l. 1200 Canticle of Moses: A portion of the Divine office, with words from the Bible; based on tradition that held Moses to be the author of the Pentateuch (five books containing the Law) – a way of sacralizing and preventing tampering with the text.

l. 1200 most of Job: This refers to the Book of Job in the Old Testament (also cited in par. 11, above), a work ascribed by some to Moses (DCLL). Job's fortitude in the face of extreme adversity is tested by Satan, with God's permission. His faithfulness to God is unshaken, and (in the passage surrounding the quote in SJ's par. 11) Job acknowledges the greatness of God and the limitations of his own powers and knowledge.

Salceda (OC 4. 661) cites a modern Spanish translation of the passage to which SJ refers (S. Isidoro, *Etimologias*, VI, 2, trans. L. Cortes, BAC): "The beginning and the end of the Book of Job are written in prose; but from the middle of the book, at the passage beginning *'Pereat dies in qua natus sum'* ('Let the day perish wherein I was born'; 3:3), to the passage where Job says *'Idcirco ego me reprehendo et ago poenitentiam'* ('Therefore I reprehend myself and do penance in dust and ashes'; 42:6), it is written in *heroic verse*" (English trans. of Cortes by Powell; biblical verses Douay).

l. 1201 St. Isidore: Biship of Seville (c. 560–636) who organized the Catholic religion in Spain; his encyclopedic writings influenced medieval literature and art.

l. 1202 Epithalamia: These are wedding songs. Here we have the third reference in the *Answer* to the Song of Songs. Such repetition asserts the appropriateness of praising poetry and the right of women to express such praise; beyond that, indirectly, it asserts the right of all intellectuals to appreciate Scripture and perform exegesis.

l. 1202 Jeremiah: A Hebrew prophet (c. 650–c. 585 B.C.) whose Old Testament book bears his name (in the Douay Version, *The Prophecy of Jeremias*) and to whom the subsequent book. *Lamentations,* is ascribed.

l. 1203 Cassiodorus: c. 490–c. 585. He founded a monastery devoted to the preservation and transmission of knowledge, both sacred and profane. SJ's quotation has not been found in Cassiodorus.

l. 1206 St. Ambrose: 339–97. One of the four great Latin doctors of the church; statesman, theologian, eloquent preacher, his name was associated (possibly in error) with the *Te Deum,* or "Ambrosian Hymn."

l. 1206 St. Thomas: See note to par. 1, above. Not primarily known as a poet, Thomas Aquinas wrote the hymn *Pange, lingua* [Sing, My Tongue], of which the first and last verse are customarily sung during the Latin Mass. SJ's naming St. Thomas at the opening and near the close of her *Answer* underscores her awareness of Thomistic-Aristotelian thought.

l. 1207 St. Bonaventure: 1221–74. Franciscan friar and Scholastic theologian. He brought about a temporary reconciliation between the Roman Catholic and the Greek Orthodox church and in his writings reconciled Aristotle's learning with Augustinian Christianity (DCLL; CE), thus providing an early precedent for SJ's intellectual stance in favor of reconciliations and also pointing to an acknowledged tradition of dissent.

l. 1209 Aratus: Cited in Acts 17:28. One of two Greek poets St. Paul quotes and paraphrases; the other is Epimenides, whom SJ calls **Parmenides** in the next citation (Titus 1:12), in which the Cretans are called liars.

ll. 1209–10 "For in him . . . are": Acts 17:28.

l. 1211 "The Cretians [sic] . . . bellies": Titus 1:12.

l. 1212 St. Gregory of Nazianzus: c. 330–390. One of four fathers of the Greek church, he wrote poems and many theological works and is depicted holding a book, sometimes in the company of personified figures of Chastity and Wisdom (Sophia) who appeared to him as he was reading (DCLL; CE).

ll. 1219–20 the sacred translator: Refers to Jerome, as translator from Hebrew and Greek of the Vulgate (or "popular") Bible, a Latin version approved by the Council of Trent as the definitive Roman Catholic text.

(43) l. 1234 Dream: I.e., the *Primero sueño* [First Dream]. This is a self-consciously ingenuous remark – the 975-line philosophical poem was anything but a trifle (see "A Poet-Scholar" in Pt. II of the Introduction, above).

l. 1234 The letter . . . so honored: "Letter Worthy of Athena."

ll. 1268–69 I shall never . . . the pen again: Echoed some lines down with ". . . to keep still." If we connect this statement with the assertion SJ made toward the beginning (that the meaning of a silence must be explained), then we can read it as a declaration of her coming silence.

ll. 1271–72 "Honest words . . . retreat": Jerome, *Select Letters*, Wright trans., pp. 474–75.

ll. 1272–76 "It is the nature . . . to hide away"; "An accusation . . . who made it": Sources for these Latin phrases not found.

l. 1287 St. John Chrysostom: c. 347–407. Greek doctor of the church; Patriarch of Constantinople, known for his eloquence, asceticism, and charity. SJ has attempted to follow the patriarch: to convince and teach.

ll. 1288–89 "One's slanderers . . . taught": Source for this quotation from St. John Chrysostom not found.

l. 1289 St. Gregory: c. 540–604. One of the four original doctors of the church (i.e., Sts. Gregory the Great, Ambrose, Augustine, and Jerome); author of theological works and pope during a period of expansion of the Roman church. Notably, Sor Juana is backing her arguments with the highest ecclesiastical authorities here.

ll. 1289–90 "It is no less . . . defeat them": Source for this quotation from St. Gregory not found.

l. 1307 "'Beware, Romans . . . bald adulterer": Salceda and Trueblood cite Suetonius (A.D. 70–140; author also of lives of grammarians and Roman poets, known only in fragments), *The Twelve Caesars*, "Julius Caesar," 51. The passage in Suetonius is reminiscent of, but different from, the line SJ quotes; she may misremember, or she may be recalling another text or author. Important here is SJ's use of a classical source assigning the sin of adultery to men; sources following the Bible more commonly condemned women for it. See Suetonius, *De Vita Caesarum*, p. 26.

l. 1328 "Or what hast thou . . .": 1 Corinthians 4:7.

l. 1342–43 "One must believe neither . . . who reviles": Source for this quotation from St. Augustine not found.

ll. 1351–52 Exercises for the [Feast of the] Annunciation; Offerings for the [Seven] Sorrows [of the Virgin]: Two of SJ's few pieces of writing for devotional use by other nuns and the public. The Feast of the Annunciation marks the Angel Gabriel's "announcement" to the Virgin Mary of her pregnancy. Traditionally, the seven sorrowful events in the life of the Virgin focus on various sufferings of her son. SJ's claim that, of all her writing, only these texts were printed "at [her] pleasure" is strategically motivated, showing that she has written religious materials for private devotion. The Virgin Mary and the Incarnation are essential to SJ's woman-centered theology.

l. 1365 the Poet: A customary reference to Virgil. Salceda (OC) claims SJ was "distracted"; the words are Ovid's.

ll. 1366–67 "Even when strength . . . content with that" / "Ut desint vires, tamen est laudanda voluntas: / hac ego contentos, auguror esse Deos": Ovid, *Ex Ponto* [From the Black Sea] 3.4.79–80. (*Vires* is plural of *vis,* "strength" or "force.") A pun might suggest itself, based on deliberately misreading *vires* instead as a Spanish plural for *vir*/man – "Even when men are lacking, still the [good] intention must be praised" – in keeping with SJ's ironic defiance.

(44) l. 1375 "It is shameful . . . acts of kindness": Seneca, *On Public Honors* 5.2.1.

ll. 1377–79 Thus God behaved . . . worthy amends: SJ returns, in this key position in her essay, to the assertion of God's kindness to humankind, echoing the argument of the so-called *Carta atenagórica,* or "Letter Worthy of Athena," which prompted her interchange with the bishop/Sor Filotea in the first place.

(45) In this and the final paragraph, SJ expresses the formulaic humility and willingness to change anything not found proper, required in closing not only by rhetorical convention but in obedience to the dictates of monastic orders and of the Inquisition, a branch of which reviewed everything that was written for public consumption. In this sense, the rhetoric of humility is not ironic, but requisite for publication and acceptance.

ll. 1382–83 a nun of the veil . . . unveiled: The pun plays on the physicality of the gendered bodies underlying this difference in status. Here SJ plays with the bishop's double (pseudonymous) identity. The implied physicality of this reference to her addressee's "person" essentially unveils "Sor Filotea," fully acknowledging the difference in status between the writer and the bishop.

ll. 1386–87 the familiar terms of address I have employed: SJ draws attention to the second-person familiar *Vos,* a Spanish pronoun used in her day for addressing intimates and familiars (and God). She emphasizes her equality with the fictive "Sor Filotea," while she highlights her subordinate status to Bishop Manuel Fernández de Santa Cruz.

Selected Poems

Introduction

In making this brief selection of poetry we were guided on the one hand by our interest in Sor Juana's poetic elaborations on topics addressed in the *Answer* and, on the other, by our desire to offer at least a glimpse of the range of styles, themes, and tones in her repertoire.[1] Sor Juana's plays and poems incorporate many registers and styles of language. She reproduces the foreign accents of nonnative speakers of Spanish (of Portuguese, Nahua – "Indian" – African, and Basque origin) as well as the erudite cadences of clerics in the Latin church; she writes in the tradition of widely produced dramatic authors and the poetry "academies" of Madrid and Seville. Her idiomatic and elite nuances reveal both the silent pages of the enormous numbers of books she read and the turns of phrase she heard from people in every strata of Mexican society (servants, priests, enslaved laborers, aristocrats). All these elements grace her lines.

Sor Juana's intellectual development occurred in a kaleidoscopic world, at once sensual and stark, earthbound and given to flight. Baroque Mexico saw the clash and meeting of cultures, the incomplete destruction of one empire and the mimicking importation of another (the Spanish monarchy was brought across the ocean as the colonial viceroyalty). Sor Juana's poetry mirrors the

---

[1]See "Poet-Scholar: Sor Juana's Writing," in the main Introduction, for a survey of Sor Juana's range of styles. Not represented in this selection are her verse dramas, which would have to be so briefly excerpted as to distort the work. The source for all poems is OC, and the poem numbers used here come from that edition. Some of the poems have headnotes (in brackets); these are probably not Sor Juana's, but additions made by the first publisher.

richness of that world's artistic and religious visions. Her work exudes humor, irony, and wit even when expressing sorrow. Spontaneous and variegated, some poems remind us of colorful marketplaces in the central plazas of Mexican towns and of refrains in boisterous popular songs. Her verse is also sumptuous and highly crafted, like the churches where her *villancicos* were sung and the royal chambers where her plays were performed.

A Note on Meter and Rhyme

Spanish verse counts syllables, stressed and unstressed.[2] When one word ends with a vowel and the next begins with a vowel (or silent *h*), the two vowel sounds blend and count as one syllable. A convention imposing a two-beat ending governs words that do not conform – adding or subtracting an "imaginary" final syllable where necessary. Each line bears two heavier beats that vary in placement.

Spanish rhyme is of two kinds. Assonantal (*rima asonante*) repeats only the vowel sounds of final syllables: the final *a–e* of *santiguarme, triquitraques, dictamen, Extravagantes* in the first two stanzas of poem 49 (included here), for example. Consonantal (*rima consonante*) resembles what English verse considers true rhyme, repeating the entire sound of the final syllable(s): the final *-ado, -olo, -ida,* for example, of *osado, bañado, Apolo, sólo, atrevida, vida* in the last six lines of poem 149 (also included here). Popular and learned forms have persisted in Spanish poetry since the Middle Ages, often practiced by the same poet. Both types employ the common elements of versification, though popular lines are shorter – eight syllables or less.

Sonetos/*Sonnets*

The sonnet, a fourteen-line poem with an elaborate rhyme scheme, enjoyed great popularity in the seventeenth century among the poets Sor Juana admired – including, for example, Quevedo, Góngora, and Lope de Vega.[3] The Petrarchan sonnet

---

[2]A brief presentation of the principles governing verse forms can distort subtleties. An excellent source is Nelson, "Spanish," pp. 165–76.

[3]Quevedo (Francisco Gómez de Quevedo y Villegas, 1580–1645), Góngora (Luis de Góngora y Argote, 1561–1627), and Lope de Vega (Lope de Vega Carpio, 1562–1635) were three of the most famous Spanish poets of the Siglo de Oro (the Golden Age). Quevedo was known as a poet, satirist, moralist, and novelist. Góngora was known for his striking metaphors and inventive neologisms. The similarities between Sor Juana's *First Dream* and Góngora's *Soledades* have often been

form, brought from Italy to Spain in the fifteenth century, differs in structure from its Shakespearean counterpart, more familiar to readers of English. Each of the fourteen lines is eleven syllables long (called *endecasílabo*). The poem is divided into two four-line stanzas (the octet) and two three-line stanzas (the sestet).

Sor Juana must have taken pride in becoming an accomplished sonneteer, given her interest in tests of skill and ingenuity, mathematical formulas, and musical symmetry. She delighted readers with reasoned conceits on emotions such as envy, jealousy, and grief; variations on well-known lines from other poets; and clever twists in her endings. The sonnets, along with the *redondillas* of the "Philosophical Satire" (see below), are her most often anthologized and commented-upon poems.[4]

The first of the four sonnets we present is Sor Juana's most famous ("This object which you see – a painted snare," poem 145). She ends it by transforming a line from a well-known sonnet by Góngora, in which the speaker threatens his beloved with the rapid waning of her womanly beauty.[5] Sor Juana changes the prepositions of Góngora's ending: his *en tierra, en humo, en polvo, en sombra, en nada* (literally, "[changed] into earth, into smoke, into dust, into shadow, into nothing") becomes her *es cadáver, es polvo, es sombra, es nada* ("is a corpse, is dust, is shadow, and is gone"). This simple transformation emphasizes the subjectivity and indeed substance behind a female "image" thus reduced to nothing. She interrupts a masculine tradition to speak in a woman's voice. With her verbal art, the poet engages the convention by which a male poet (as active voice) describes a painted portrait of a woman (as passive image). She refuses women's idealized enshrinement in agelessness, which implies a condemnation to worthlessness as they age. Thus, she defies the "master" poet, Góngora, as well.

Critics read the ambiguities of the second sonnet in this selection ("With all the hazards of the sea in mind," poem 149) in different ways. In our reading, Sor Juana entwines and lauds irrevocable

---

debated. Lope de Vega, one of the world's leading writers for the stage, was Spain's most important and most prolific dramatist. These three figures, along with dozens of other poets (an increasing number of women, including Lope de Vega's daughter, Sor Marcela de San Félix, finally being recovered and included), revitalized Spanish verse, producing some of the most beautiful poetry of the Baroque period.

[4]Octavio Paz is among the most sensitive critics of Sor Juana's sonnets and other poetry, though problematic on questions of gender. For a recent treatment of Sor Juana's love sonnets, see Gimbernat de González, "Speaking through the Voices of Love."

[5]"Mientras por competir con tu cabello . . ." in Del Río and Agostini de del Río, *Antología general,* 1:623.

seclusion and intellectual fearlessness. Is the decision to take life-long vows an exemplary daring or a lamentable foolhardiness? Must reclusion be accompanied by active striving? Is the poet prophesying or defending her own arduous path? Some hear regret, others discern praise in the last lines. Sor Juana moves from images of seafaring, bullfighting, and horsemanship in the octet (feats associated with heroism and masculine physical prowess) to mythic risk-taking and poetic quest in the sestet. The conclusion sketches an attempt to challenge the gods – a deed she praised in her philosophical poem *First Dream* – and associates it with choosing "a way of life that must endure till death": suggesting the courage of a woman who takes monastic vows.

The two subsequent sonnets ("This afternoon, my darling, when we spoke," poem 164, and "What's this, Alcino?" poem 174), while following the conventions of courtly love poems, pointedly capture many emotions that color passionate relationships, and they excel in the clear-reasoned, aphoristic wit of their endings. In both, Sor Juana displays her penchant for joining the abstract, ideal plane with the sensorial, material world. In the first she exemplifies what she says in the final line of another sonnet (not included here): "only what I can touch do I see." She plays the distanced, philosophical mediator of a love quarrel in the second, and she displays her scientific fascination in a metaphorical conceit taken from physics (the evaporation and condensation of liquid).

Sátira filosófica/*Philosophical Satire*

Redondillas means literally "little round ones": the stanzaic form is thus known after the circularity of its rhyme scheme, *a b b a*, rhyming the inner two lines and the outer two. Four-line stanzas are composed of eight-syllable lines.

In "You foolish and unreasoning men" (poem 92) Sor Juana exposes the social position of women, revealing it as historical and ideological, crossing class lines and including not only such patrician figures as Thais[6] and Lucretia[7] but the prostitutes of New

---

[6]An Athenian hetaera (courtesan, "concubine," and intellectual companion) of the late fourth century A.D., Thais was mistress to Alexander the Great and Ptolemy. She was a traditional symbol of female libertinage, though Sor Juana's list of illustrious women in the *Answer* certainly shows the nun's capacity to admire such a woman's accomplishment.

[7]In Roman legend, Lucretia was a traitorously seduced wife who dutifully committed suicide after she was raped by a son of Tarquin the Proud; she came to represent "the virtuous wife." Her death led to the expulsion of the Tarquins and establishment of the Roman republic.

Spain as well. The poem broadens a critique explored in her farce *The Palace*, where the characters (Love, Respect, Courtliness, Favor, Hope; with their referee, a Master of Ceremonies) contend not for the favors but for the contempt of the ladies. They engage in a contest of wits, revealing women's untenable position vis-á-vis courtly mores in palace games of love.

The poem may owe its wide popularity in the Spanish-speaking world in part to the suppressed anger it reveals in women and the giddy catharsis (as a dispelling of guilt) it permits men. Sor Juana aptly and characteristically reverses gender attributions in placing the burden of representation as "the world, the devil, and the flesh" on the males rather than the females of the species.

Villancicos/*Carols*

The *villancico* combines various metrical and stanzaic forms — *redondillas, romances,* and others — in sets that originally were sung chorally by two or more voices. The poems are carols, in the sense of "song or hymn of religious joy" (OED). The *villancico* form evolved from humble origins — songs of *villanos,* or peasants — in Muslim Spain. By the seventeenth century, *villancicos* had evolved into sequences of compositions sung and performed in church services on religious feast days. With such origins, the form was considered *arte menor* (minor art) as opposed to *arte mayor* or cultured poetry. This status allowed Sor Juana to elaborate on theological topics with relative freedom, particularly as compared with the outward restrictions she encountered in writing her critique of Vieira's sermon or the internalized constraints with which she must have wrestled in framing the *Answer.*[8] Sor Juana's *villancicos* receive increasing critical attention not only for their lively and intricate treatment of religious material but also for their blending of musical, dramatic, sacred, profane, popular, and elite resources.

Sor Juana composed twelve complete sets of *villancicos* for liturgies honoring various saints and feast days. Each set is grouped into three "nocturnes" (of three poems, in various stanzaic forms), equaling nine compositions in all (or eight, with the *Te Deum* taking the place of the ninth). A breadth of linguistic modes conveys the joyful religious "lessons" of these pieces, intended to instruct but also to relieve the gravity of the solemn Latin Mass.

---

[8]Méndez Plancarte speculates that Father Diego Calleja introduced Sor Juana to *villancicos,* sending her examples of his own, written in collaboration with the most famous cultivator of this genre, León Marchante (OC 1. xxxiii and OC 2. xlvi–lxxi).

The series to Saint Catherine of Alexandria comprises the last of the twelve sets of *villancicos* Sor Juana wrote.[9] Composed in 1692, the St. Catherine series was performed eight months after the date she gives in closing the *Answer* (1691) and could be described as lyric companion-pieces or indeed as a sequel to that essay. Having written her last word in self-defense, Sor Juana abandoned restraint. For thousands of the faithful at the cathedral of Oaxaca, she prepared what is probably one of the most feminist texts ever to be performed in the context of Catholic liturgy.[10] Hagiographic superlatives fit her learned subject, the "Egyptian Catherine," in whose gifts and travails Sor Juana saw reflected her own talents and challenges. The poet "plays" musically, humorously, and hyperbolically on themes familiar to us from the *Answer*: the merits of intelligence, the irrelevance of gender in matters of reason, the lack of humility among men who consider themselves wise, the distortions caused by unthinking adherence to customs that relegate women to the spinning wheel and the needle.

Romance Epistolar / *Epistolary Ballad*

The Romance, a narrative Spanish poem corresponding to the English ballad, has an octosyllabic (eight-syllable) line. Alternate lines (second, fourth, etc.) rhyme assonantally. Like the ballad, the *romance* sprang from traditional popular origins and was put to literary use.

In the *romance* translated here, Sor Juana responds to mocking praise (so overstated as to be hostile) directed to her by a male poet. Energetic poetic interchanges were common in Spain and New Spain during the Baroque period: only the popular enthusiasm for sports and television in our own day compares to the lively interest that poetic challenges, debates, and contests aroused in Sor Juana's day. She entered and won prizes in such contests and answered several *romances* addressed to her.

In this ballad (poem 49), Sor Juana explores the unnamed "gentleman's" hyperbolic flattery. Domesticating the mythic-literary

---

[9]Méndez Plancarte (in vol. 2 of OC) presents, in addition, ten sets of *villancicos* he labels attributable to Sor Juana.

[10]Paz calls the poems to St. Catherine "aggressive," "defiant," and "strident," and he speculates that they were sung in the cathedral of Oaxaca – far from Mexico City and from Puebla – in order to avoid too much notice (*Sor Juana; or, The Traps of Faith,* p. 434).

metaphor of the phoenix,[11] she critiques the treatment of those women considered exceptional. We see a woman of immense achievement who is pleased to receive recognition, but who is highly ambivalent about the freakish status conferred upon her. Where the "gentleman's" poem ranges through classical references, Sor Juana's response situates herself concretely in the cloister as it weaves elements of convent life into her cheerful acceptance-rejection of the Phoenix epithet. The poem's jovial irreverence invents words; parodies flamboyant Baroque rhetoric; plays with popular idioms, interjections, and proverbs; derides the poet's craft; and punningly rejects women's work in the kitchen. Its deft handling of these diverse elements merits broader readership and study.

[11]The Greek historian Herodotus (fifth century B.C.) describes an Arabian bird like an eagle, with red and gold plumage; only one could live at any one time. Every five hundred years it set fire to itself and rose again, beautiful and young, from the ashes; therefore, it became a Christian symbol of the Resurrection (DCLL).

Sonetos

[Poema 145]

[Procura desmentir los elogios que a un retrato de la Poetisa inscribió la verdad, que llama pasión.]

Este, que ves, engaño colorido,
que del arte ostentando los primores,
con falsos silogismos de colores
es cauteloso engaño del sentido;
    éste, en quien la lisonja ha pretendido
excusar de los años los horrores,
y venciendo del tiempo los rigores
triunfar de la vejez y del olvido,
    es un vano artificio del cuidado,
es una flor al viento delicada,
es un resguardo inútil para el hado:
    es una necia diligencia errada,
es un afán caduco y, bien mirado,
es cadáver, es polvo, es sombra, es nada.

[Poema 149]

[Encarece de animosidad la elección de estado durable hasta la muerte.]

Si los riesgos del mar considerara,
ninguno se embarcara; si antes viera
bien su peligro, nadie se atreviera
ni al bravo toro osado provocara.
    Si del fogoso bruto ponderara
la furia desbocada en la carrera
el jinete prudente, nunca hubiera
quien con discreta mano lo enfrenara.
    Pero si hubiera alguno tan osado
que, no obstante el peligro, al mismo Apolo
quisiese gobernar con atrevida
    mano el rápido carro en luz bañado,
todo lo hiciera, y no tomara sólo
estado que ha de ser toda la vida.

All translations of these poems are by Amanda Powell.

Sonnets

[Poem 145]

[She endeavors to expose the praises recorded in a portrait of the Poetess by truth, which she calls passion.]

This object which you see – a painted snare
exhibiting the subtleties of art
with clever arguments of tone and hue –
is but a cunning trap to snare your sense;
   this object, in which flattery has tried
to overlook the horrors of the years
and, conquering the ravages of time,
to overcome oblivion and age:
   this is an empty artifice of care,
a flower, fragile, set out in the wind,
a letter of safe-conduct sent to Fate;
   it is a foolish, erring diligence,
a palsied will to please which, clearly seen,
is a corpse, is dust, is shadow, and is gone.

[Poem 149]

[She weighs the difficulties of electing a way of life that must last until death.]

With all the hazards of the sea in mind,
no one would set sail; if in advance
the dangers were foreseen, no one would dare
so much as taunt the mad bull in the ring.
   If the prudent rider were to weigh
the unleashed fury of a pounding beast
set free to race, we would not see
anyone set a skilled hand to the reins.
   But if one showed such brave audacity
as, despite the peril, to aspire
to take in hand the blazing chariot
   of the great god Apollo, drenched in light:
that one would do it all, not simply choose
a way of life that must endure till death.

Apollo refers to the myth of Apollo, Greek god of poetry, who drove the chariot of the sun across the sky each day; and to his half-mortal, overly daring son Phaethon, who set fire to the world when he lost control of his father's chariot (see Ovid, *Metamorphoses*).

[Poema 164]

[En que satisface un recelo con la retórica del llanto.]

Esta tarde, mi bien, cuando te hablaba,
como en tu rostro y tus acciones vía
que con palabras no te persuadía,
que el corazón me vieses deseaba;
    y Amor, que mis intentos ayudaba,
venció lo que imposible parecía:
pues entre el llanto, que el dolor vertía,
el corazón deshecho destilaba.
    Baste ya de rigores, mi bien, baste;
no te atormenten más celos tiranos,
ni el vil recelo tu quietud contraste
    con sombras necias, con indicios vanos,
pues ya en líquido humor viste y tocaste
mi corazón deshecho entre tus manos.

[Poema 174]

[Aunque en vano, quiere reducir a método racional el pesar
de un celoso.]

¿Qué es esto, Alcino? ¿Cómo tu cordura
se deja así vencer de un mal celoso,
haciendo con extremos de furioso
demostraciones más que de locura?
    ¿En qué te ofendió Celia, si se apura?
¿O por qué al Amor culpas de engañoso,
si no aseguró nunca poderoso
la eterna posesión de su hermosura?
    La posesión de cosas temporales,
temporal es, Alcino, y es abuso
el querer conservarlas siempre iguales.
    Con que tu error o tu ignorancia acuso,
pues Fortuna y Amor, de cosas tales
la propiedad no han dado, sino el uso.

[Poem 164]

[In which she answers a suspicion with the eloquence of tears.]

This afternoon, my darling, when we spoke,
and in your face and gestures I could see
that I was not persuading you with words,
I wished you might look straight into my heart;
    and Love, who was assisting my designs,
succeeded in what seemed impossible:
for in the stream of tears which anguish loosed
my heart itself, dissolved, dropped slowly down.
    Enough unkindness now, my love, enough;
don't let these tyrant jealousies torment you
nor base suspicions shatter your repose
    with foolish shadows, empty evidence:
in liquid humor you have seen and touched
my heart undone and passing through your hands.

[Poem 174]

[Although in vain, she wishes to convert the sufferings of a
jealous man to a rational process.]

What's this, Alcino? How could your good sense
allow its own defeat by jealousy,
and show the world, in wild extremes of rage,
this spectacle of one gone mad or worse?
    Now how has Celia hurt you, if she grieves?
Again, why do you blame Love of deceit
if he has never promised, for all his power,
lasting possession of such loveliness?
    Our possession of temporal things
is temporal, my friend; it is abuse
to wish to guard them always as they were.
    Your ignorance or your error I accuse,
because both Fate and Love, of things like these,
have given us not ownership, but use.

átira filosófica

Arguye de inconsecuentes el gusto y la censura de los hombres
que en las mujeres acusan lo que causan.]

Hombres necios que acusáis
a la mujer sin razón,
sin ver que sois la ocasión
de lo mismo que culpáis:

si con ansia sin igual
solicitáis su desdén,
¿por qué queréis que obren bien
si las incitáis al mal?

Combatís su resistencia
y luego, con gravedad,
decís que fue liviandad
lo que hizo la diligencia.

Parecer quiere el denuedo
de vuestro parecer loco,
al niño que pone el coco
y luego le tiene miedo.

Queréis, con presunción necia,
hallar a la que buscáis,
para pretendida, Thais,
y en la posesión, Lucrecia.

¿Qué humor puede ser más raro
que el que, falto de consejo,
él mismo empaña el espejo,
y siente que no esté claro?

Con el favor y el desdén
tenéis condición igual,
quejándoos, si os tratan mal,
burlándoos, si os quieren bien.

Opinión, ninguna gana;
pues la que más se recata,
si no os admite, es ingrata,
y si os admite, es liviana.

Siempre tan necios andáis
que, con desigual nivel,

156

Philosophical Satire

[Poem 92]

[The poet proves illogical both the whim and the censure of men
who accuse, in women, that which they cause.]

You foolish and unreasoning men
who cast all blame on women,
not seeing you yourselves are cause
of the same faults you accuse:

if, with eagerness unequaled,
you plead against women's disdain,
why require them to do well
when you inspire them to fall?

You combat their firm resistance,
and then solemnly pronounce
that what you've won through diligence
is proof of women's flightiness.

What do we see, when we see you
madly determined to see us so,
but the child who makes a monster appear
and then goes trembling with fear?

With ridiculous conceit
you insist that woman be
a sultry Thais while you woo her;
a true Lucretia once she's won.

Whose behavior could be odder
than that of a stubborn man
who himself breathes on the mirror,
and then laments it is not clear?

Women's good favor, women's scorn
you hold in equal disregard:
complaining, if they treat you badly;
mocking, if they love you well.

Not one can gain your good opinion,
for she who modestly withdraws
and fails to admit you is ungrateful;
yet if she admits you, too easily won.

So downright foolish are you all
that your injurious justice claims

a una culpáis por cruel
y a otra por fácil culpáis.

¿Pues cómo ha de estar templada
la que vuestro amor pretende,
si la que es ingrata, ofende,
y la que es fácil, enfada?

Mas, entre el enfado y pena
que vuestro gusto refiere,
bien haya la que no os quiere
y quejaos en hora buena.

Dan vuestras amantes penas
a sus libertades alas,
y después de hacerlas malas
las queréis hallar muy buenas.

¿Cuál mayor culpa ha tenido
en una pasión errada:
la que cae de rogada,
o el que ruega de caído?

¿O cuál es más de culpar,
aunque cualquiera mal haga:
la que peca por la paga, ⎫ PUN
o el que paga por pecar? ⎭

Pues ¿para qué os espantáis
de la culpa que tenéis?
Queredlas cual las hacéis ⎫ PUN
o hacedlas cual las buscáis. ⎭

Dejad de solicitar,
y después, con más razón,
acusaréis la afición
de la que os fuere a rogar.

Bien con muchas armas fundo
que lidia vuestra arrogancia,
pues en promesa e instancia
juntáis diablo, carne y mundo.

to blame one woman's cruelty
and fault the other's laxity.

How then can she be moderate
to whom your suit aspires,
if, ingrate, she makes you displeased,
or, easy, prompts your ire?

Between such ire and such anguish
—the tales your fancy tells—
lucky is she who does not love you;
complain then, as you will!

Your doting anguish feathers the wings
of liberties that women take,
and once you've caused them to be bad,
you want to find them as good as saints.

But who has carried greater blame
in a passion gone astray:
she who falls to constant pleading,
or he who pleads with her to fall?

Or which more greatly must be faulted,
though either may commit a wrong:
she who sins for need of payment,
or he who pays for his enjoyment?

Why then are you so alarmed
by the fault that is your own?
Wish women to be what you make them,
or make them what you wish they were.

Leave off soliciting her fall
and then indeed, more justified,
that eagerness you might accuse
of the woman who besieges you.

Thus I prove with all my forces
the ways your arrogance does battle:
for in your offers and your demands
we have devil, flesh, and world: a man.

Villancicos: a Santa Catarina de Alejandría
[Poema 317] Villancico VI

Estribillo
¡Víctor, víctor Catarina,
que con su ciencia divina
los sabios ha convencido,
y victoriosa ha salido
—con su ciencia soberana—
de la arrogancia profana
que a convencerla ha venido!
¡Víctor, víctor, víctor!

Coplas
De una Mujer se convencen
todos los Sabios de Egipto,
para prueba de que el sexo
no es esencia en lo entendido.
    ¡Víctor, víctor!

Prodigio fue, y aun milagro;
pero no estuvo el prodigio
en vencerlos, sino en que
ellos se den por vencidos.
    ¡Víctor, víctor!

¡Qué bien se ve que eran Sabios
en confesarse rendidos,
que es triunfo el obedecer
de la razón el dominio!
    ¡Víctor, víctor!

Las luces de la verdad
no se obscurecen con gritos;
que su eco sabe valiente
sobresalir del ruido.
    ¡Víctor, víctor!

No se avergüenzan los Sabios
de mirarse convencidos;
porque saben, como Sabios,
que su saber es finito.
    ¡Víctor, víctor!

Estudia, arguye y enseña,
y es de la Iglesia servicio,

Carols to Saint Catherine of Alexandria
[Poem 317] Carol VI

Refrain
Catherine bears the victory!
For with knowledge pure and holy
she's convinced the learned men
and has emerged victorious
—with her knowledge glorious—
from their arrogance profane,
which would convince and conquer her.
But Catherine is the victor!

Verses
The learned men of Egypt, by
a woman have been vanquished,
to demonstrate that sex is not
the essence of intelligence.
Victory! Victory!

A wonder it was, a miracle—
the wonder being not the fact
that she has triumphed over them,
but that they would admit defeat.
Victory! Victory!

How well we see that they were wise
in admitting they were beaten:
it is a triumph to concede
the supremacy of reason.
Victory! Victory!

All the clarity of truth
cannot be shouted down,
for its echo, brave and long,
surmounts the noisy crowd.
Victory! Victory!

The learned men think it no shame
that she has convinced them,
for they have learned, as learned men,
their learning has its limits.
Victory! Victory!

She studies, and disputes, and teaches,
and thus she serves her Faith;

que no la quiere ignorante
El que racional la hizo.
¡Víctor, víctor!

¡Oh qué soberbios vendrían,
al juntarlos Maximino!
Mas salieron admirados
los que entraron presumidos.
¡Víctor, víctor!

Vencidos, con ella todos
la vida dan al cuchillo:
¡oh cuánto bien se perdiera
si Docta no hubiera sido!
¡Víctor, víctor!

Nunca de varón ilustre
triunfo igual habemos visto;
y es que quiso Dios en ella
honrar el sexo femíneo.
¡Víctor, víctor!

Ocho y diez vueltas del Sol,
era el espacio florido
de su edad; mas de su ciencia
¿quién podrá contar los siglos?
¡Víctor, víctor!

Perdióse (¡oh dolor!) la forma
de sus doctos silogismos;
pero, los que no con tinta,
dejó con su sangre escritos.
¡Víctor, víctor!

Tutelar sacra Patrona,
es de las Letras Asilo;
porque siempre ilustre Sabios,
quien Santos de Sabios hizo.
¡Víctor, víctor!

for how could God, who gave her reason,
want her ignorant?
  Victory! Victory!

How haughtily they must have gathered
summoned there by Maximin!
But they exited with wonder,
who with such conceit went in.
  Victory! Victory!

Vanquished, then, with her the Sages
gave their lives up to the sword:
had she not been a learned woman,
we should have lost great good!
  Victory! Victory!

Never by a famous man
have we been shown such victory,
and this, because God wished through her
to honor womankind.
  Victory! Victory!

Just eighteen times round the Sun
was all the springtime space
of her few years; but of her learning
who can count the age?
  Victory! Victory!

Lost (alas!) are her wise words
of premise and conclusion;
but those she did not leave behind
in ink, in blood were written.
  Victory! Victory!

Sacred tutor, patroness,
she shelters all our learning;
that she who made of Sages, Saints,
new Sages may illumine.
  Victory! Victory!

Maximin (or Maxentius) was a fourth-century emperor in Egypt who persecuted Christians; according to legend, he convoked the "greatest philosophers" to convince Catherine to leave her faith, but she converted them by her learning. He had her beaten, imprisoned, and finally beheaded.

[Poema 320] Villancico IX: Para la Misa

—A la Epístola

Estribillo

1. —Catarina, siempre hermosa,
     es Alejandrina Rosa.
2. —Catarina, siempre bella,
     es Alejandrina Estrella.
1. —¿Cómo Estrella puede ser,
     vestida de rosicler?
2. —¿Cómo a ser Rosa se humilla,
     quien con tantas luces brilla?
1. —Rosa es la casta doncella.
2. —No es sino Estrella,
     que esparce luz amorosa.
1. —¡No es sino Rosa!
2. —No es sino Estrella.
1. —¡No, no, no es sino Rosa!
2. —¡No, no, no es sino Estrella!

Coplas

1. —Rosa es, cuyo casto velo,
     cuando el capillo rompió;
     el rocío aljofaró
     de los favores del Cielo,
     para aspirar sin recelo
     a ser de tal Lilio esposa
     la más bella.
2. —¡No es sino Estrella!
1. —¡No es sino Rosa!

2. —Si Catarina se llama,
     que Luna quiere decir,
     claro está que su lucir
     será de celeste llama,
     que al mundo en candor derrama
     la que el Sol imprimió en ella
     más fogosa.

1. —¡No es sino Rosa!
2. —¡No es sino Estrella!

[Poem 320] Carol IX: For the Mass

   —At the Epistle

Refrain
Voice 1. —Catherine's beauty ever grows;
            she is the Alexandrine rose.
Voice 2. —Catherine's loveliness shines fair;
            she is the Alexandrine star.
      1. —A Star? How ignorant can *you* be,
            when her dress is pink as rubies?
      2. —A Rose? How take herself so lightly,
            when her light shines forth so brightly?
      1. —She's a Rose, this damsel fair.
      2. —No indeed, she is a Star,
            and light she lovingly bestows.
      1. —No indeed, she is a Rose!
      2. —No indeed, she is a Star!
      1. —No, no, no, I say, a Rose!
      2. —No, no, no, I say, a Star!

Verses
      1. —She is a Rose, and when she flowered
            forth from a bud, the morning dew
            embroidered her chaste veil with pearls,
            granting her, by Heaven's favors,
            to aspire without misgiving
            to wed the holy, blessed Lily,
            blooming most fair.
      2. —No indeed, she is a Star!
      1. —No indeed, she is a Rose!

      2. —Knowing *Catherine* is her name,
            and that "Moon" is what it means,
            we see clearly that her beams
            must be a celestial flame
            which that Sun, majestic, gave
            so that on the world her candor
            ardently glows.
      1. —No indeed, she is a Rose!
      2. —No indeed, she is a Star!

   The "Holy, blessed Lily" refers to Christ, in the "mystic marriage" of St.
Catherine, a frequent subject in art since the fourteenth century.
   "Moon" has an uncertain etymology; Catherine may be from the Greek
katharos (pure).

165

1. – Rosa fue, que desplegó
      al viento su pompa ufana,
      teñida en la fina grana
      que en el tormento vertió,
      cuando grosero agostó
      Aquilón, cuanto su hermosa
      copa sella.
2. – ¡No es sino Estrella!
1. – ¡No es sino Rosa!

2. – Estrella es, sin que lo altere
      lo que en ella el rigor hace;
      pues a mejor mundo nace,
      cuando parece que muere:
      De esta propiedad se infiere,
      que vive la luz en ella
      más vistosa.
1. – ¡No es sino Rosa!
2. – ¡No es sino Estrella!

1.   — A Rose she was, when she unfolded
           to the air her brave display,
           crimson with the brilliant stain
           that spilled and fell when she was martyred
           in that cruel, parching harvest
           by which a stern North Wind blew closed
           this lovely flower.
2.   — No indeed, she is a Star!
1.   — No indeed, she is a Rose!

2.   — She is a Star, and steady shines
           unaltered by the chill or storm;
           to a better world she's daily born,
           when it seems to us she dies:
           it's clear, to the discerning eye,
           her living light even from afar
           most brilliant shows.
1.   — No indeed, she is a Rose!
2.   — No indeed, she is a Star!

[Poema 322] Villancico XI

       — Al "Ite Missa Est".

1.   — Un prodigio les canto.
2.   — ¿Qué, qué, qué, qué, qué?
1.   — Esperen, aguarden, que yo lo diré.
2.   — ¿Y cuál es? ¡Diga aprisa, que ya
rabio por saber!
1.   — Esperen, aguarden, que yo lo diré.

Coplas
     Erase una Niña,
como digo a usté,
cuyos años eran
ocho sobre diez.
Esperen, aguarden,
que yo lo diré.

     Esta (qué sé yo
cómo pudo ser),
dizque supo mucho,
aunque era mujer.
Esperen, aguarden,
que yo lo diré.

     Porque, como dizque
dice no sé quién,
ellas sólo saben
hilar y coser . . .
Esperen, aguarden,
que yo lo diré.

     Pues ésta, a hombres grandes
pudo convencer;
que a un chico, cualquiera
lo sabe envolver.
Esperen, aguarden,
que yo lo diré.

     Y aun una Santita
dizque era también,
sin que le estorbase
para ello el saber.
Esperen, aguarden,
que yo lo diré.

[Poem 322] Carol XI

> —At "The Mass is ended."

Voice 1. —A wondrous thing I'll sing to you.
Voice 2. —Oh what, what, what? Please say.
1. —Hush now, be patient, and I shall say.
2. —What is it? Tell me quickly now,
      for I am mad to know.
1. —Hush now, be patient, and I shall say.

Verses
Once upon a time this Girl,
as I say,
was a very young thing,
just eighteen.
Hush now, be patient,
and I'll explain.

   And they say (how should I know
if it's true)
she knew a lot, although she was
just a girl.
Hush now, be patient,
and I'll tell you.

   For, as we all know, they say
—*someone* says—
women can do nothing more
than spin and sew.
Hush now, be patient,
and you will know.

   So: her arguments convinced
mighty men!
(Any woman with a boy
easy wins.)
Hush now, be patient,
you'll hear it then.

   And a little Saint she was,
they say too,
nor did all her book-learning
hinder her.
Hush now, be patient,
we'll soon be through.

Pues como Patillas
no duerme, al saber
que era Santa y Docta,
se hizo un Lucifer.
Esperen, aguarden,
que yo lo diré.

Porque tiene el Diablo
esto de saber,
que hay mujer que sepa
más que supo él.
Esperen, aguarden,
que yo lo diré.

Pues con esto, ¿qué hace?
Viene, y tienta a un Rey,
que a ella la tentara
a dejar su Ley.
Esperen, aguarden,
que yo lo diré.

Tentóla de recio;
mas ella, pardiez,
se dejó morir
antes que vencer.
Esperen, aguarden,
que yo lo diré.

No pescuden más,
porque más no sé,
de que es Catarina,
para siempre. Amén.

But, as Satan never sleeps,
when he heard
she was Saint and Scholar both,
he went mad.
Hush now, be patient,
and you'll be told.

For he had to swallow
dreadful news,
that a lowly woman knows
more than he.
Hush now, be patient,
and you shall see.

What the devil does he do?
Tempts the King
to try and tempt her to betray
her belief.
Hush now, be patient,
and you shall hear.

Severely did he tempt her, but
by our Lord,
sooner than surrender, she
died by sword.
Hush now, be patient,
I'll say the word.

Ask me no more questions —
for more's beyond my ken
in this tale of Catherine
forevermore. Amen.

Romance Epistolar

[Poema 49]

[Romance que respondió nuestra Poetisa al Caballero recién llegado a Nueva España que le había escrito el Romance "Madre que
haces chiquitos . . ."]

¡Válgate Apolo por hombre!
No acabo de santiguarme
(más que vieja cuando Jove
dispara sus triquitraques)

de tan paradoja idea,
de tan remoto dictamen;
sin duda, que éste el autor
es de los *Extravagantes*.

Buscando dice que viene
a aquel Pájaro que nadie
(por más que lo alaben todos)
ha sabido a lo que sabe . . .

. . . .

En fin, hasta aquí, es nonada,
pues nunca falta quien cante:
Dáca el Fénix, toma el Fénix,
en cada esquina de calle.

Lo mejor es, que es a mí
a quien quiere encenizarme,
o enfenizarme, supuesto
que allá uno y otro se sale.

Dice que yo soy la Fénix
que, burlando las edades,
ya se vive, ya se muere,
ya se entierra, ya se nace:

la que hace de cuna y tumba
diptongo tan admirable,
que la mece renacida
la que la guardó cadáver;

Epistolary Ballad: Selections

[Poem 49]

[*Romance* with which our poet answered the gentleman recently arrived in New Spain, who had written to her the *romance* beginning "Mother who makes great men little . . ."]

Apollo help you, as you're a man!
It's the sign of the cross I'm making
(more than a little old lady, when Zeus
hurls down his firecrackers)

at an idea so paradoxical
and such an unlikely notion:
of those wandering tomes of Canon Law
this man must be the author.

He says that he has come to seek
the Bird that no one's tasted,
with flavor still unsavored, though
everyone sings its praises . . .

. . . .

But all this is nonsensical,
for someone croons or hollers,
"Your Phoenix here! Get your Phoenix!"
on every neighborhood corner.

What thrills me most is that it's I
whom he would thus be burning –
or, since the two are equivalent,
that is, whom he'd be *birding*.

He says I am the Phoenix, she
outwitting all the ages,
who brings herself to life, then death,
inters herself, and rises:

she who makes of womb and tomb
a unison so wondrous
that she is rocked, reborn just there
where her body was buried;

The **"wandering tomes of Canon Law"** are laws compiled by Pope Gregory XIII, in the late sixteenth century; these included *Extra-vagantes*, or laws previously uncompiled, thus "wandering" outside earlier collections.

The sought-after **"Bird that no one's tasted"** is the Phoenix. See note 11, above.

173

la que en fragantes incendios
de las gomas más suaves,
es parecer consumirse
volver a vivificarse;

la Mayorazga del Sol,
que cuando su pompa esparce,
le engasta Ceilán el pico,
le enriza Ofir el plumaje . . .

. . . .

Que es Arabia la feliz,
donde sucedió a mi Madre
mala noche y parir hija,
según dicen los refranes . . .

. . . .

en fin, donde le pasó
la rota de Roncesvalles,
aunque quien nació de nones
non debiera tener Pares.

Que yo soy la que andar suele
en símiles elegantes,
abultando los renglones
y engalando Romances.

El lo dice, y de manera
eficaz lo persüade,
que casi estoy por creerlo,
y de afirmarlo por casi.

¿Que fuera, que fuera yo,
y no la supiera antes?
¿Pues quién duda, que es el Fénix
el que menos de sí sabe?

Por Dios, yo lo quiero ser,
y pésele a quien pesare;
pues de que me queme yo,
no es razón que otro se abrase.

Yo no pensaba en tal cosa;
mas si él gusta de graduarme
de Fénix, ¿he de echar yo
aqueste honor en la calle?

who, nestling in the fragrant fires
of sweet gums and perfumes
reanimates herself just when
she seems to be consumed;

the first-born daughter of the Sun
who, when she shows her splendors
displays a beak worked in Ceylon,
and plumage curled in Ofir.

. . . .

Arabia is the blessed land
where it fell to my mother
"a bad night, and a girl-child's birth"
as we hear in the proverb . . .

. . . .

in sum, where she was made to bear
a rout like Charlemagne's;
though one who was so Oddly born
can't Even have peers or parents.

That I am she who is used to walk
among elegant similes,
loading the length and weight of the lines
and adorning rhymed *romances*.

He says this, in a manner so
effectively persuasive,
I'm almost ready to believe
and almost in agreement.

Could I—could I myself be she,
and not have known it sooner?
But who could doubt the Phoenix has
the very least self-knowledge?

Please God, I want to be that bird,
whomever it may bother;
for just because I'm to be burned,
no one else need get hotter.

I had thought of no such thing;
but if he would promote me
to Phoenix, shall I be the one
to shrug off such an honor?

. . . .

Quizá por eso nací
donde los rayos Solares
me mirasen de hito en hito,
no bizcos, como a otras partes.

Lo que me ha dado más gusto,
es ver que, de aquí adelante,
tengo solamente yo
de ser todo mi linaje.

¿Hay cosa como saber
que ya dependo de nadie,
que he de morirme y vivirme
cuando a mí se me antojare?

¿Que no soy término ya
de relaciones vulgares,
ni ha de cansarme el pariente
ni molestarme el compadre?

¿Que yo soy toda mi especie
y que a nadie he de inclinarme,
pues cualquiera debe sólo
amar a su semejante?

. . . .

¿Que mi tintero es la hoguera
donde tengo que quemarme,
supliendo los algodones
por Aromas Orientales?

¿Que las plumas con que escribo
son las que al viento se baten,
no menos para vivirme
que para resucitarme?

. . . .

Gracias a Dios, que ya no
he de moler Chocolate,
ni me ha de moler a mí
quien viniere a visitarme.

Ya, con estas buenas nuevas,
de hoy más, tengo de estimarme,
y de etiquetas de Fénix
no he de perder un instante . . .

. . . .

And this may be why I was born
here where the hot sun gazes
straight and directly down on me,
not cross-eyed as in other places.

It gives me greatest joy to see
that from this moment onward,
I and only I must be
my family and lineage.

Can anything compare with knowing
I depend on no one,
that I choose death, then birth myself
whenever I take the notion?

That I no longer play a part
in relationships low or common;
that I shan't be bored by family
nor annoyed by a companion?

That all my species is only I,
and I need incline toward none,
since any creature is only obliged
to love one of its own?

. . . .

That my inkwell is the simple pyre
where I set myself aflame,
using my cotton blotters in place
of unguents from the East?

That the very quills with which I write
are those that beat the wind,
as much to sustain me in this life
as to revive me again?

. . . .

Thanks be to God I need not grind
the Cocoa any longer,
nor will I have to be ground down
by the visit of friend or stranger.

Well this is happy news indeed;
henceforth I do myself honor,
nor will I tarry an instant more
in adopting the label of Phoenix!

. . . .

¡Qué dieran los saltimbancos
a poder, por agarrarme
y llevarme, como Monstruo,
por esos andurrïales

de Italia y Francia, que son
amigas de novedades
y que pagaran por ver
la Cabeza del Gigante,

diciendo: *Quien ver el Fénix*
quisiere, dos cuartos pague,
que lo muestra Maese Pedro
en la posada de Jaques!

¡Aquesto no! No os veréis
en ese Fénix, bergantes;
que por eso está encerrado
debajo de treinta llaves.

Y supuesto, Caballero,
que a costa de mil afanes,
en la Invención de la Cruz,
vos la del Fénix hallasteis,

por modo de privilegio
de inventor, quiero que nadie
pueda, sin vuestra licencia,
a otra cosa compararme.

. . . .

What would the mountebanks not give
to seize me and display me,
taking me round like a Monster, through
byroads and lonely places

in Italy and France, which are
so fond of novelties,
where the people pay to see
the Giant's head; and crying:

"If the Phoenix you would view,
step up and pay two farthings,
for the Mighty Pedro's showing the bird
here in Monsieur Jacques' tavern!"

Not that! Your fortune you'll not find
with that Phoenix, you merchants;
for this is why it is confined
behind thirty locks, in the convent.

And as we may suppose, good Sir,
that by trial and tribulation
on the Invention of the True Cross
you found this Phoenix-invention:

by way of the privilege that is shown
any esteemed inventor,
I want no one to compare me to anything else
without your express permission.

"The Invention [or Discovery] **of the True Cross"** refers to the fourth-century
finding of the cross on which Jesus was crucified; the event is celebrated on May
3. In this stanza and the next, there is wordplay on "invention, inventor."

Selected Bibliography

Works by Sor Juana Inés de la Cruz

Recent Editions

Antología. Prologue and selection by Margot Glantz. Caracas: Biblioteca Ayacucho, 1994.

"Carta de la Madre Juana Inés de la Cruz escrita al R.P.M. Antonio Núñez de la Compañía de Jesús." In Aureliano Tapia Méndez, *Carta de Sor Juana Inés de la Cruz a su confesor: Autodefensa espiritual,* pp. 14–25. Monterrey: Universidad de Nuevo León, 1981. The letter from Sor Juana to her confessor found in 1980.

Inundación castálida. Edited by Georgina Sabat de Rivers. Madrid: Editorial Castalia, 1983.

Obras completas. Vols. 1–4: *Lírica personal; Villancicos y letras sacras; Autos y loas; Comedias, sonetos y prosa* [1951–57]. Edited by Alfonso Méndez Plancarte (vols. 1–3) and Alberto G. Salceda (vol. 4). Reprint, Mexico: Fondo de Cultura Económica, 1976. Scholarly, annotated edition.

Obras completas. Prologue by Francisco Monterde. Mexico: Editorial Porrúa, 1985. This edition includes no notes.

Obras selectas. Edited by Georgina Sabat de Rivers and Elias L. Rivers. Barcelona: Editorial Noguer, 1976. Includes a useful introduction.

Early Editions

Early editions of Sor Juana's collected works were published in three volumes, as follows:

Inundación castálida de la única poetisa, musa décima, soror Juana Inés de la Cruz. Madrid: Juan García Infanzón, 1689, 1690; Barcelona: Joseph Llopis, 1691; Zaragoza: M. Román, 1692; Seville, 1692. After the 1689 edition, this volume was published under the title *Poemas de la única poetisa americana.*

Segundo volumen de las obras de soror Juana Inés de la Cruz. Seville: Tomás López de Haro, 1692; Barcelona: Joseph Llopis, 1693.

Fama y obras póstumas del fénix de México. Madrid: Manuel Ruiz de Murga, 1700; Barcelona: Rafael Figuero, 1701; Lisbon: Miguel Deslandes, 1701; Madrid: Gonçalez de Reyes, 1714. Includes the *Respuesta*. All three volumes were also republished together: Valencia: A. Bordazar, 1709; Madrid: J. Rodríguez de Escobar, 1714, 1715; Madrid: Angel Pasqual Rubio, 1725.

Translations

Barnstone, Aliki, and Willis Barnstone, eds. *A Book of Women Poets from Antiquity to Now*, pp. 262–68. New York: Schocken Books, 1980. Rev. ed. 1992.

Barnstone, Willis. *Six Masters of the Spanish Sonnet: Francisco de Quevedo, Sor Juana Inés de la Cruz, Antonio Machado, Federico García Lorca, Jorge Luis Borges, Miguel Hernández. Essays and Translations*, pp. 59–97. Carbondale: Southern Illinois University Press, 1993.

Campion, John, trans. *El Sueño*. Austin: Thorp Springs Press, 1983. Bilingual edition.

Cosman, Carol, Joan Keefe, and Kathleen Weaver, eds.; Joanna Bankier, Doris Earnshaw, and Deirdre Lashgari, consulting eds. *The Penguin Book of Women Poets*, pp. 137–39. New York: Penguin Books, 1979.

Dodge, Meredith D., and Rick Hendricks, trans. and eds. "The Poetry of Sor Juana Inés de la Cruz." In Gelvira de Toledo, Condesa de Galve, *Two Hearts, One Soul: The Correspondence of the Condesa de Galve, 1688–96*, pp. 163–78. Albuquerque: University of New Mexico Press, 1993. Contains the texts of poems dedicated to the Condesa de Galve.

Flores, Angel, and Kate Flores, eds. *The Defiant Muse: Hispanic Feminist Poems from the Middle Ages to the Present. A Bilingual Anthology*, pp. 20–27. New York: The Feminist Press, 1986.

Harss, Luis, trans. *Sor Juana's Dream*. New York: Lumen Books, 1986. Bilingual edition of the *Primero sueño*; introduction and commentary by Luis Harss.

Paz, Octavio, comp. *Anthology of Mexican Poetry*, pp. 78–92. Translated by Samuel Beckett. Bloomington: Indiana University Press, 1958. Works by Sor Juana are listed under the name Juana de Asbaje.

——, ed. "Letter from Sister Juana Inés de la Cruz Written to the R[everend] F[ather] M[aster] Antonio Núñez of the Society of Jesus." In Paz, *Sor Juana; or, The Traps of Faith*, Margaret Sayers Peden, trans., pp. 495–502. Cambridge: Harvard University Press, Belknap Press, 1988. Translation of the letter from Sor Juana to her confessor found in 1980.

Peden, Margaret Sayers, trans. *Sor Juana Inés de la Cruz: Poems*. Binghamton, N.Y.: Bilingual Press / Editorial Bilingüe, 1985. Bilingual anthology.

——, trans. *A Woman of Genius: The Intellectual Autobiography of Sor Juana Inés de la Cruz*. Salisbury, Conn.: Lime Rock Press, 1982. Translation of the *Respuesta*.

Rivers, Elias L., ed. *Renaissance and Baroque Poetry of Spain*, pp. 314–36. New York: Dell, 1966. English prose translation.

Thurman, Judith, ed. *I Became Alone: Five Women Poets. Sappho, Louise Labé, Anne Bradstreet, Juana Inés de la Cruz, Emily Dickinson,* pp. 86–106. New York: Atheneum, 1975.

Trueblood, Alan S., ed. and trans. *A Sor Juana Anthology.* Cambridge: Harvard University Press, 1988. A partially bilingual edition; the *First Dream,* the letter by Sor Filotea, and the *Respuesta* are presented in English only.

Warnke, Frank J., trans. *Three Women Poets: Renaissance and Baroque. Louise Labé, Gaspara Stampa, and Sor Juana Inés de la Cruz,* pp. 81–129. Lewisburg, Pa.: Bucknell University Press; London: Associated University Presses, 1987.

Works about Sor Juana Inés de la Cruz

Ackerman, Jane E. "Voice in *El Divino Narciso.*" *Bulletin of the Comediantes* 39, no. 1 (Summer 1987): 63–74.

Alatorre, Antonio. "Para leer la fama y obras póstumas de Sor Juana Inés de la Cruz." *Nueva Revista de Filología Hispánica* 29 (1980): 428–508.

Aldridge, A. Owen. "The Tenth Muse of America: Anne Bradstreet or Sor Juana Inés de la Cruz." In *Proceedings of the Xth Congress of the International Comparative Literature Association,* vol. 3, ed. Anna Balakian et al., pp. 177–88. New York: Garland, 1985.

Arenal, Electa. "The Convent as Catalyst for Autonomy: Two Hispanic Nuns of the Seventeenth Century." In *Women in Hispanic Literature: Icons and Fallen Idols,* ed. Beth Miller, pp. 147–83. Berkeley: University of California Press, 1983.

———. "Sor Juana Inés de la Cruz: Reclaiming the Mother Tongue." *Letras Femeninas* 10, nos. 1–2 (1985): 63–75.

———. "Where Woman is Creator of the Wor(l)d; or, Sor Juana's Discourses on Method." In *Feminist Perspectives on Sor Juana Inés de la Cruz,* ed. Stephanie Merrim, pp. 124–41.

Bénassy-Berling, Marie-Cécile. *Humanismo y religión en Sor Juana Inés de la Cruz.* Translated (from the French) by Laura López de Belair. Mexico: Universidad Nacional Autónoma de México, 1983.

Bergmann, Emilie. "Sor Juana Inés de la Cruz: Dreaming in a Double Voice." In *Women, Culture, and Politics in Latin America: Seminar on Feminism and Culture in Latin America,* pp. 151–72. Berkeley: University of California Press, 1990.

Cortest, Luis, ed. *Sor Juana Inés de la Cruz: Selected Studies.* Asunción: Centro de Estudios de Economía y Sociedad, 1989.

Franco, Jean. "Sor Juana Explores Space." In *Plotting Women: Gender and Representation in Mexico,* pp. 23–54. New York: Columbia University Press, 1989.

Friedman, Edward H. "Signs of Nature and the Nature of Signs in the Sonnets of Sor Juana Inés de la Cruz." *Romance Languages Annual* 1 (1989): 435–39.

Gimbernat de González, Ester. "Speaking through the Voices of Love: Interpretation as Emancipation." In *Feminist Perspectives on Sor Juana Inés de la Cruz*, ed. Stephanie Merrim, pp. 162–76.

Johnson, Julie Greer. "A Comical Lesson in Creativity from Sor Juana." *Hispania: A Journal Devoted to the Interests of the Teaching of Spanish and Portuguese* 71, no. 2 (May 1988): 442–44.

Kaminsky, Amy Katz. "Nearly New Clarions: Sor Juana Inés de la Cruz Pays Homage to a Swedish Poet." In *In the Feminine Mode: Essays on Hispanic Women Writers*, ed. Noel Valis and Carol Maier, pp. 31–53. Lewisburg, Pa.: Bucknell University Press, 1990; London: Associated University Presses, 1990.

Larisch, Sharon. "Sor Juana's *Apología.*" *Pacific Coast Philology* 21, nos. 1–2 (November 1986): 48–53.

Lee, Jill Brennan. "Love and Choice in Latin Love Poetry and the Poetry of Sor Juana Inés de la Cruz: An Essay in Feminist Literary Criticism." Ph.D. diss., University of Connecticut, 1990.

Leon, Tonia J. "Sor Juana Inés de la Cruz's *Primero sueño: A Lyric Expression of Seventeenth Century Scientific Thought.*" *Dissertation Abstracts International* 58, no. 9 (March 1990): 2916A. New York University.

Leonard, Irving A. *Baroque Times in Old Mexico: Seventeenth-Century Persons, Places, and Practices.* Ann Arbor: University of Michigan Press, 1959. See especially chapter 12, "A Baroque Poetess," pp. 172–92.

Long, Pamela H. "Sor Juana as Composer: A Reappraisal of the *Villancicos.*" In *Critical Essays on the Literatures of Spain and Spanish America*, ed. Luis T. González-del-Valle and Julio Baena, pp. 161–69. Boulder, Colo.: Society of Spanish and Spanish American Studies, 1991.

Luciani, Frederick. "Anamorphosis in a Sonnet by Sor Juana Inés de la Cruz." *Discurso Literario: Revista de Temas Hispánicos* 5, no. 2 (Spring 1988): 423–32.

———. "The Burlesque Sonnets of Sor Juana Inés de la Cruz." *Hispanic Journal* 8, no. 1 (Fall 1986): 85–95.

———. "Emblems of Praise in a Romance by Sor Juana Inés de la Cruz." *Romance Quarterly* 34, no. 2 (May 1987): 213–21.

———. "Sor Juana: Dressing the Part." In *Sor Juana Inés de la Cruz: Selected Studies*, ed. Luis Cortest, pp. 53–64.

Ludmer, Josefina. "Tricks of the Weak." In *Feminist Perspectives on Sor Juana Inés de la Cruz*, ed. Stephanie Merrim, pp. 86–93.

Malsch, Sara Ann. "Sor Juana Inés's *Respuesta a Sor Filotea* as Autobiography: The Prosopopeia of Voice and Name." M.A. Thesis, University of Massachusetts at Amherst, Sept. 1993.

Merrim, Stephanie. "Toward a Feminist Reading of Sor Juana Inés de la Cruz: Past, Present and Future Directions in Sor Juana Criticism" (chap. 1) and "*Mores Geometricae:* The 'Womanscript' in the Theater of Sor Juana Inés de la Cruz" (chap. 5). In *Feminist Perspectives on Sor Juana Inés de la Cruz*, pp. 11–37 and 94–123.

———, ed. *Feminist Perspectives on Sor Juana Inés de la Cruz.* Detroit: Wayne State University Press, 1991. See also essays, listed separately, by Arenal, Gimbernat de González, Ludmer, Sabat-Rivers, Schons, and the bibliography.

Montross, Constance M. *Virtue or Vice? Sor Juana's Use of Thomistic Thought.* Washington, D.C.: University Press of America, 1981.

Moraña, Mabel. "Orden dogmático y marginalidad en la *Carta de Monterrey* de Sor Juana Inés de la Cruz." *Hispanic Review* 58 (1990): 205-25.

Myers, Kathleen. "Sor Juana's *Respuesta:* Rewriting the Vitae." *Revista Canadiense de Estudios Hispánicos* 14, no. 3 (Spring 1990): 459-71.

Myles, Eileen. "Nun's Tale: The Selling of Sor Juana." *Village Voice Literary Supplement* 75 (June 1989): 30-31.

Nanfito, Jacqueline C. *"El sueño:* The Baroque Imagination and the Dreamscape." *Modern Language Notes* 106, no. 2 (March 1991): 423-31.

――――. *"El sueño:* The Spatialization of a Poetic Text." *Dissertation Abstracts International* 49, no. 2 (August 1988): 263A. University of California, Los Angeles.

Navarro Tomás, Tomás. "Los versos de Sor Juana." In Navarro Tomás, *Los poetas en sus versos: desde Jorge Manrique a García Lorca,* pp. 163-79. Barcelona: Ediciones Ariel, 1973.

Paz, Octavio. *Sor Juana; or, The Traps of Faith.* Translated by Margaret Sayers Peden. Cambridge: Harvard University Press, Belknap Press, 1988.

Peden, Margaret Sayers. "Building a Translation: The Reconstruction Business. Poem 145 of Sor Juana Inés de la Cruz." In *The Craft of Translation,* ed. John Biguenet and Rainer Schulte, pp. 13-27. Chicago: University of Chicago Press, 1989.

Perelmuter Pérez, Rosa. "La estructura retórica de la *Respuesta a Sor Filotea.*" *Hispanic Review* 51, no. 2 (Spring 1983): 147-58.

Powell, Amanda. "Women's Reasons: Feminism and Spirituality in Old and New Spain." *Studia Mystica* 15, nos. 2-3 (Summer-Fall 1992): 58-69.

Puccini, Dario. *Sor Juana Inés de la Cruz: Studio d'una personalitá del Barrocco messicano.* Rome: Edizione dell'Ateneo, 1967.

Sabat-Rivers, Georgina. "Biografías: Sor Juana vista por Dorothy Schons y Octavio Paz." *Revista Iberoamericana* 51, nos. 132-33 (July-December 1985): 927-37.

――――. *Estudios de literatura hispanoamericana: Sor Juana Inés de la Cruz y otros poetas barrocos de la colonia.* Barcelona: PPU, 1992.

――――. "A Feminist Rereading of Sor Juana's *Dream.*" In *Feminist Perspectives on Sor Juana Inés de la Cruz,* ed. Stephanie Merrim, pp. 142-61.

Schons, Dorothy. "The First Feminist in the New World." *Equal Rights,* October 31, 1925, pp. 11-12.

――――. "Some Obscure Points in the Life of Sor Juana." In *Feminist Perspectives on Sor Juana Inés de la Cruz,* ed. Stephanie Merrim, pp. 38-60.

Scott, Nina M. " 'If you are not pleased to favor me, put me out of your mind': Gender and Authority in Sor Juana Inés de la Cruz; and the Translation of Her Letter to the Reverend Father Maestro Antonio Núñez of the Society of Jesus." *Women's Studies International Forum* 11, no. 5 (1988): 429-38.

_____. " 'La gran turba de las que merecieron nombres': Sor Juana's Fore-mothers in *La Respuesta a Sor Filotea.*" In *Coded Encounters: Race, Gender, and Ethnicity in Colonial Latin America*, ed. Javier Cevallos-Candau. Amherst: University of Massachusetts Press, 1994.

_____. "Sor Juana Inés de la Cruz: 'Let Your Women Keep Silence in the Churches.' " *Women's Studies International Forum* 8, no. 5 (1985): 511–19.

Tavard, George H. *Juana Inés de la Cruz and the Theology of Beauty: The First Mexican Theology.* Notre Dame, Ind.: University of Notre Dame Press, 1991.

University of Dayton Review 16, no. 2 (Spring 1983). Features the proceedings of a bilingual symposium "Sor Juana Inés de la Cruz y la cultura virreinal / Sor Juana Inés de la Cruz and the Vice-royal Culture," held May 7, 1982, at the State University of New York at Stony Brook.

Other Works Consulted

Alford, John. "The Grammatical Metaphor: A Survey of Its Use in the Middle Ages." *Speculum* 57 (1982): 728–60.

Arenal, Electa, and Stacey Schlau. *Untold Sisters: Hispanic Nuns in their Own Works.* Translations by Amanda Powell. Albuquerque: University of New Mexico Press, 1989.

Barbeito Carneiro, María Isabel. "Escritoras madrileñas del siglo XVII: Estudio bibliográfico-crítico." 2 vols. Ph.D. diss., Universidad Complutense de Madrid, 1986.

Boccaccio, Giovanni. *Concerning Famous Women.* Translated by Guido A. Guarino. New Brunswick, N.J.: Rutgers University Press, 1963.

Bórresen, Kari Elisabeth, ed. *Image of God and Gender Models in Judaeo-Christian Tradition.* Oslo: Solum Forlag, and Atlantic Highlands, N.J.: Humanities Press, 1991.

Carmody, Denise Lardner. *Biblical Woman: Contemporary Reflections on Scriptural Texts.* New York: Crossroad, 1988.

Catholic Church. *Breviarium Romanum ex Decreto Sacrosancti Concili Tridentini Restitutum.* 4 vols. Malinas: H. Dessain; New York, etc.: Benziger Bros., 1914.

Christine de Pizan [Christine de Pisan]. *The Book of the City of Ladies.* Translated (from the French) by Earl Jeffrey Richards. New York: Persea Books, 1982.

Cohen, Thomas. "The Fire of Tongues: Antonio Vieira and the Christian Mission in Brazil." Ph.D. diss., Stanford University, 1990.

Del Río, Angel, and Amelia Agostini de del Río, eds. *Antología general de la literatura española.* 2 vols. New York: Holt, Rinehart & Winston, 1960. 3rd ed. 1982.

Dugaw, Dianne. *Warrior Women and Popular Balladry, 1650–1850.* Cambridge: Cambridge University Press, 1989.

Gracián, Baltasar. *The Art of Worldly Wisdom: A Pocket Oracle.* Translated by Christopher Maurer. New York: Doubleday, 1992.

_____. *Obras completas.* Edited by Arturo del Hoy. 3rd ed. Madrid: Aguilar, 1967.

Gutzwiller, Kathryn, and Ann Norris Michelini. "Women and Other Strangers: Feminist Perspectives in Classical Literature." In *(En)gendering Knowledge: Feminists in Academe,* ed. Joan E. Hartman and Ellen Messer-Davidow, pp. 66–84. Knoxville: University of Tennessee Press, 1991.

Jerome. *St. Jerome: Letters and Selected Works.* Translated by W. H. Freemantle. Vol. 6 of *A Select Library of the Nicene and Post-Nicene Fathers.* Grand Rapids, Mich.: William B. Eerdmans, 1892.

_____. *Select Letters of St. Jerome,* translated by F. A. Wright. New York: G. P. Putnam's Sons and London: William Heinemann, 1933.

Kelly, Joan. "Early Feminist Theory and the *Querelle des Femmes.*" In *Women, History, and Theory: The Essays of Joan Kelly,* ed. Catherine R. Stimson, pp. 65–109. Chicago: University of Chicago Press, 1984.

Martial (also Martialis, Marcus Valerius). Translated by Walter D. A. Ker. Cambridge, Mass.: Harvard University Press and London: William Heinemann, 1961.

Martín, Luis. *Daughters of the Conquistadores: Women of the Viceroyalty of Peru.* Albuquerque: University of New Mexico Press, 1983.

Nelson, Lowry, Jr. "Spanish." In *Versification: Modern Language Types,* ed. W. K. Wimsatt, pp. 165–76. New York: New York University Press, 1972.

Ovid. *The Metamorphoses.* Translated by Horace Gregory. New York: Mentor, 1960.

_____. *Tristia, Ex Ponto.* Translated by Arthur Leslie Wheeler. 2nd ed. London: William Heinemann, and Cambridge: Harvard University Press, 1988.

Pablo Maroto, Daniel de. "Meditaciones sobre los Cantares." In *Introducción a la lectura de santa Teresa,* ed. Alberto Barrientos, pp. 383–91. Madrid: Editorial de Espiritualidad, 1978.

Picón-Salas, Mariano. "The Baroque of the Indies." In Picón-Salas, *A Cultural History of Spanish America, from Conquest to Independence,* pp. 85–105. Translated by Irving A. Leonard. Berkeley: University of California Press, 1962. Originally published as *De la conquista a la independencia,* pp. 105–30. Mexico: Fondo de Cultura Económica, 1944.

Quintilian. *The Institutio Oratoria of Quintilian.* Translated by H. E. Butler. 4 vols. London: William Heinemann, 1953; Cambridge: Harvard University Press, 1953.

Schüssler Fiorenza, Elisabeth. *In Memory of Her: A Feminist Theological Reconstruction of Christian Origins.* New York: Crossroad, 1983.

Seneca, Lucius Annaeus. *De beneficiis.* In *Opera Quae Supersunt,* vol. 1, fasc. 2. Edited by C. Hosius. Leipzig: B. Teubner, 1900.

_____. *Seneca's Tragedies.* Translated by Frank Justus Miller. London: William Heinemann, and New York: Putnam, 1917.

Sheperd, Simon, ed. *The Women's Sharp Revenge: Five Women' Pamphlets from the Renaissance.* London: Fourth Estate, 1981.

Stolpe, Sven. *Christina of Sweden.* Edited by Sir Alec Randall. New York:

Macmillan, 1966. Translated from the abridged German version of the Swedish original, *Drottning Kristina.*

Suetonius. "Divus Julius." In *Opera,* vol. 1, *De Vita Cesarum.* Edited by Maximilian Ihm. Stuttgart: B. G. Teubner, 1964.

Teresa de Jesús [de Avila]. *Complete Works of Saint Teresa of Jesus.* 3 vols. Translated and edited by E. Allison Peers. London: Sheed & Ward, 1946.

_____. *Escritos de Santa Teresa.* Edited by Vicente de la Fuente. Madrid: M. Rivadeneyra, 1861.

_____. *Libro de la vida.* Edited by Otger Steggink. Madrid: Editorial Castalia, 1986.

Weber, Alison. *Teresa of Avila and the Rhetoric of Femininity.* Princeton, N.J.: Princeton University Press, 1990.

Wollstonecraft, Mary. *A Vindication of the Rights of Woman* [1792]. Edited by Charles Hagelman, Jr. New York: Norton, 1967.

Reference Tools

Bover, Rvdo. P. José María, S.I., and Francisco Cantera Burgos, eds. *Sagrada Biblia: Versión crítica sobre los textos hebreo y griego,* Biblioteca de Autores Cristianos. Madrid: La Editorial Católica, 1957.

Catholic University of America. *New Catholic Encyclopedia.* 18 vols. New York: McGraw-Hill, 1967–89.

Delaney, John J. *Dictionary of Saints.* Garden City, N.Y.: Doubleday, 1980.

Guterman, Norbert, trans. and comp. *A Book of Latin Quotations.* Garden City, N.Y.: Anchor Books, 1966.

The Holy Bible, Translated from the Latin Vulgate. Douay-Rheims English Version (1609). Rockford, Ill.: Tan Books, 1991. Photographic reproductions of 1899 Baltimore edition.

Holy Bible and Apocrypha. Revised Standard Version. New York: Thomas Nelson & Sons, 1952.

Lefkowitz, Mary R. *Women in Greek Myth.* Baltimore: The Johns Hopkins University Press, 1986.

Lefkowitz, Mary R., and Maureen B. Fant, comps. *Women in Greece and Rome: A Source Book in Translation,* 2nd ed. Baltimore: The Johns Hopkins University Press, 1992.

Lempriere, John. *Lempriere's Classical Dictionary.* London: Bracken Books, 1984.

Levey, Judith S., and Agnes Greenhall with the staff of the Columbia Encyclopedia, eds. *The Concise Columbia Encyclopedia.* New York: Columbia University Press, 1983.

Metford, J.C.J. *Dictionary of Christian Lore and Legend.* New York: Thames & Hudson, 1983.

Smith, William, ed. *Dictionary of Greek and Roman Biography and Mythology.* 3 vols. Boston: Little, Brown & Co., 1967.

Smith, William, and Henry Wace, eds. *A Dictionary of Christian Biography: Literature, Sects and Doctrines.* 4 vols. London: J. Murray, 1877–87; reprint, New York: AMS Press, 1967.

Snyder, Jane McIntosh. *The Woman and the Lyre: Women Writers in Classical Greece and Rome.* Carbondale, Ill.: Southern Illinois University Press, 1989.

Tuñón de Lara, Manuel, ed. *Historia de España.* Vols. 5 and 6. Barcelona: Editorial Labor, 1984.

Vogt, Kari. "The Hierophant of Philosophy: Hypatia of Alexandria." In Kari Elisabeth Børresen and Kari Vogt, *Women's Studies of the Christian and Islamic Traditions: Ancient, Medieval, and Renaissance Foremothers,* pp. 155–75. Dordrecht, Boston and London: Kluwer Academic Press, 1993.

Walker, Barbara G. *The Woman's Dictionary of Symbols and Sacred Objects.* San Francisco: Harper & Row, 1988.

_____. *The Woman's Encyclopedia of Myths and Secrets.* San Francisco: Harper & Row, 1983.

Index